KNIGHTHOOD
OF
CHRISTIAN WARRIORS

Equipping God's Warriors for the End-Time Tribulation

BY

DR. DONALD BELL

This book is dedicated to the memory of Russell John Berg, who possessed a passionate heart for justice, righteousness, honor, and integrity and spent much of his time walking moment-by-moment alone with God. He was my very first mentor in the ways of the Lord. Russ was a man gifted with strong, spiritual discernment who saw the lateness of the hour and who initially encouraged me in the study of eschatology. His warrior spirit is reflected in the following poem that he wrote in 1982.

Dare to be the man –
    Who will look inside!
    Who will bow to his pride!
    Who will seek the truth!
    Who will bow before God!

Dare to be the man –
    Who will suffer reproach!
    Who is called a fool!
    Who has lost his friends for Christ!
    Who will bow before God!

Dare to be the man –
    Who resists temptation!
    Who makes time for prayer!
    Who will sacrifice!
    Who will bow before God!

Dare to be the man –
    Who will speak the truth!
    Who will not retreat!
    Who is lowly and meek!
    Who will bow before God!

Dare to be the man –
    Who will suffer trials!
    Who in weakness is strong!
    Who gains strength in tribulation!
    Who will bow before God!

Dare to be the man –
    Who will yield to God's call!
    Who gives all for all!
    Who will give his life!
    Who will be a living sacrifice!

—Russell John Berg

Acknowledgments

I am very grateful to my wife, Gery, my sons, Jeff and Bucky, and their wives, Colleen and Bree, and my daughter, Christian, and her husband, Robert, for their steadfast support in the writing of this book. I am also indebted to those close friends who provided valuable insights concerning the editing, designing and marketing of the book: Cleveland Futch, Mike Stoltenberg, David Gorospe, Ty Belknap, Jeff Hochstrasser, and Jarl Waggoner. Last, but certainly not least, I want to thank a host of encouragers throughout this writing endeavor: Jim Ray, Rod Graciano, Lynn Henry, Greg Austin, Tim Taylor, Bill Sparks, Catherine Armacost, Stan Berman, Helen Dent, Dick Nichols, Rob Nelson, Eric Hancock, William Bartley, Steve Hjelmstad, Terry Posey, Jesse Hjelmstad, Jacqueline deLeon, Mark deMers, Neil deLeon, Darren Lawrence, Gary Waldron, Jay Diller, Kevin Hearon, Tyrone Harris, Scott Browning, Buddy Moegling, Daryl and Karen Moegling, Mike and Brenda Keith, all the staff at the Bell & Futch firm, and the entire Bell, Gorospe, Ereth, Evans, deLeon, Roberts, Robinson, and Chuck Wilson families. This is my family.

It is also fitting to express my gratitude to my close friend Chris Berg for directing me toward the Lord at a very critical time in my life and then introducing me to his father, my early mentor. Additionally, I wish to acknowledge the impact that Western Reformed, Westminster West, and Faith Evangelical Seminaries have had on my life. Finally, my thanks to Dr. Michael Adams, president of Faith Evangelical Seminary; who encouraged me to complete my Doctor of Ministry degree and write a dissertation that later formed the foundation for this book.

TABLE OF CONTENTS

INTRODUCTION

MISSIONAL ASSIGNMENT: CALLING OUT TO CHRISTIAN WARRIORS

The primary mission of this book is to provide warrior-spirited Christians with insight into extremely important events recorded in the book of Revelation. These are end-time events that are quite mystifying but extremely critical for the twenty-first-century Christian to understand. Hopefully, this book will encourage many Christians who are discerning that troubling times are about to descend upon the United States, as well as the entire world, to begin preparing now. Those who have seriously prepared will be among the Christian leaders who will stand strong when these catastrophic events come.

I realize that the contents of this book will not be appreciated by many in the churches of today. Yet, there are also those within these churches who are searching for an understanding of their role in the Army of God during the time of coming tribulations. These are men and women who deeply desire to make an impact within the kingdom of God during their short life span upon this earth. By making an impact, I mean playing a visible role in the strengthening and growth of God's kingdom during a time when the attack upon His people will greatly intensify. These are Christian warriors who deeply desire to be a strong light in the darkest of times, who deeply desire to make a positive impact in the lives of both believers and unbelievers in the midst of chaos, and who deeply desire to hear our Lord Jesus Christ say, "Well done, good and faithful servant" when they enter into His presence. When that occurs, these Christian warriors will know that their calling in this life has been completely fulfilled. Well done!

A PACIFIST CHURCH IS UNPREPARED FOR WARFARE

The great majority of the twenty-first-century American church is not preparing for the challenging events that the Lord Jesus Christ warned us about—events that precede His second coming to physically establish the kingdom of God on this earth. Most leaders within today's churches acknowledge the truth of the future return of the Son of God, yet they continually ignore the multiple warnings concerning the tremendous warfare the church will face in both the natural and spiritual realms preceding His coming. Although the church may admit to the reality of warfare between the kingdom of God and the world, it continues to function as if it is only passively involved. Most allusions to spiritual warfare simply emphasize the assurance of complete victory at the second coming of Christ and avoid speaking of our lifelong participation in this spiritual war. Thus, the church busies itself with the more tangible and visible aspects of religion, preferring to believe that Christ already has achieved total victory over these evil forces and that there is nothing more to do except attend church regularly and await that time when we will be united with Him in heaven.

Compounding the problem, these same church bodies are impervious to their lack of spiritual strength, thinking themselves strong because of the vastness of their resources or the correctness of their doctrine. No matter what is said from the pulpit, more often than not, the normal vision and programs of churches are primarily focused upon internal growth rather than the transformation of people and cities outside of their walls. Thus, many in the body of Christ are living as if there is no ongoing warfare or that we are already in possession of the ultimate victory. This mind-set is certainly similar to that found in the parable of the five foolish virgins who failed to maintain oil in their lamps and when the night came, they found themselves locked out from the presence of the Lord.[1] In truth, a tremendously violent war is accelerating, and individual Christians must either fight the good fight of faith as soldiers of the kingdom or they will become spiritual casualties in the days that lie shortly before us.

An additional problem that has significantly weakened the combat readiness of the church body is that only 39 percent of churchgoers are men.[2] There is a growing recognition of this problem within the Christian community, as more and more books that address the ineffectiveness of the traditional American church within the emerging American culture are surfacing. During his ongoing research, George Barna discovered that today's churches are led by wonderful, caring people who are not gifted in the area of leadership. He states that most paid ministers in America's churches today are exceptionally gifted teachers or musicians who may never have been trained in leadership. In other words, many traditional church pastors tend to have caring, yet passive and inoffensive personalities that will drive away warrior-spirited men who are seeking strong direction for their lives.[3] This certainly creates a significant pastoral communication problem with regard to men. It is not that pastors are unwilling to communicate with men, but men are unwilling to open themselves up before pastors. During my years in the military and in the workplace, as well as in the church, I have observed that many spiritually hungry men are not moved by the traditional church services. There's a warrior spirit in men, and entertaining messages and easy believism in many of our churches today certainly do not address it. Men deeply hunger for strong Christian leadership with whom they can identify, but unfortunately most of these types of leaders are to be found in the military and business world, not in the traditional church system.

PACIFISTS ARE TEACHING ESCHATOLOGY

Throughout most of the twentieth century, the subject of eschatology (end-times teachings) certainly has been a key factor in contributing to the disunity among Protestant churches. Theologians have been debating controversial issues of eschatology for centuries; yet advocates of each of the different viewpoints state that their respective views are all clearly supported by Scripture, and they all attempt to provide the interpretations that support their personal viewpoints. Most recent books on biblical prophecy are, as a rule, simply restatements of what has been previously published. Yet, there is common ground on one issue among most of the differing views of eschatology, and that is that Christians need not be concerned about preparing themselves for times of tribulation. Instead, they teach that the church will be raptured prior to tribulation, or that the tribulation is what has been experienced throughout the Christian age, or that it already occurred in AD 70 with the destruction of Jerusalem. These are all warm and fuzzy teachings that put the church to sleep and fail to challenge Christians to prepare for the reality of the coming tribulations preceding the second coming of our Lord. There has been much written about the end times and the book of Revelation over the centuries, with view after view contending against one another, and yet little is happening within the church as a result of all this writing. The Lord's people are not being prepared by the church for the Day of the Lord as commanded by our Commander in Chief.[4]

JESUS' TEACHINGS – "MAKE WAR, BECAUSE WE LOVE!"

The messages of most gospel teachings in our generation are quite similar to those pacifists, hippie protestors who opposed our involvement in the Vietnam War. Their slogan was "make love, not war!" Surely this is not the time for God's people to withdraw into passivity—to refuse to look at the reality of a rapidly decaying society that affects all of us and our loved ones. We are in Christ and He is in us, and that means that His aggression against Satan must be expressed through us. We are not free to play the role of civilians, living as if there were no war. Our military role is pictured to us throughout the Bible—for the history of Christianity in every age is one of conflict. The pathway the disciple treads as he follows the Lord is one of intense and challenging warfare. The "Knighthood of Christian Warriors" is the author's description of those disciples who will be called by Jesus Christ to minister in the midst of the end-times tribulation with an anointing of unprecedented power.

Satan knows that his time is running short, and he is accelerating his efforts in a desperate last-ditch attempt to defeat the redemptive purposes of God. Although our spiritual weapons are as powerful today as they were in the early church, our strategies have to be reevaluated in the light of contemporary times, for the technologies of today are mighty weapons being used in the strategies of Satan against the kingdom of God. Therefore, we must have a deeper understanding of today's spiritual warfare if we are to properly prepare for His coming—for we have been commanded to stay ready and alert by the Commander-in-Chief Himself.

TARGET AUDIENCE – WARRIOR-SPIRITED CHRISTIANS

The target audience for this book is a group of leaders, or potential leaders, who, like the sons of Issachar, are a remnant of the people of God who have an understanding of the times during a very challenging period of history.[5] We are right on the verge of devastating events that will create great fear and chaos throughout the world and especially in our comfort-seeking nation. Many Christians are aware that over the last few years world events have been rapidly accelerating downhill toward what many recognize as a time of tribulation like the world has never before experienced.[6] These are men and women who understand that a tremendous crisis is rapidly approaching, and yet they are not certain of their role. This book is intended to provide direction, preparation, and encouragement that you are not alone, for our Lord is raising up many others who, like you, are to be a light within your community.[7] This is truly an exciting time for this generation; a time of opportunity to stand and fight for the kingdom of God against an enemy that will soon launch the most powerful offensive attack against the church since the beginning of time. But first, we must learn to walk through the valley of the shadow of death without fear, knowing that our Lord walks right alongside of us.[8]

We are under attack, and the battle is rapidly intensifying, and Christians need to understand what enlistment as warriors in the Army of God truly entails. The focus of this presentation is to reach out to those who sigh and groan over the abominations that are committed in this country, with the hope of raising up strong, strategic leaders among these Christians who will lead many to prepare for those terrifying events that precede the second coming of our Lord.[9]

KNIGHTHOOD OF CHRISTIAN WARRIORS

The title of this book, "Knighthood of Christian Warriors" is meant to convey that deep, passionate heart commitment for the Lord within a remnant of Christianity. Knights are acknowledged as mighty warriors who are determined to do battle for their beloved King and their kingdom. They are prepared soldiers who will fight to the last breath for the mission that has been assigned them. Although there are different levels of commitment among soldiers comprising an army, as there are within the Christian church, the author uses the term "warriors" as representative of those Christian soldiers who will run to the frontlines of the battlefield without regard for personal consequences. The terms "knights, warriors, and warrior-spirited soldiers in the Army of God" are all used synonymously within this book to convey a similar heart that is totally sold out to the Lord —hearts that will never compromise their faith in Jesus Christ even if it leads to martyrdom. They possess the attributes of the true leaders within the world of Christianity.

Additionally, in this book, the term "knighthood" is representative of a select Christian remnant known as the 144,000 who will be anointed (sealed) as disciples of Jesus Christ for ministry in the midst of Great Tribulation. This is discussed in greater detail in chapter six.

GENERAL OUTLINE AND PURPOSE OF THIS BOOK

Numerous fine books have been written on the subjects of Christian leadership, the kingdom of God, and the state of the church, along with the more popular books concerning eschatological events. This book presents an overview of all of these subjects but combines them in such a way that allows the readers to more clearly relate these subjects to our present circumstances. The first two chapters of this book provide foundational insights into spiritual warfare, the problem of evil, the mystery of the kingdom, and a calling for Christian soldiers to rise up and join our Commander-in-Chief on the battlefield. After establishing these foundational teachings, the next twelve chapters move through the book of Revelation, attempting to provide understanding of what Christian warriors in this generation will soon face and how to answer the call to battle. A final chapter will teach how to lead and prepare other American Christians to stand strong in the midst of the Great Tribulation. Although I have borrowed from many Christian writers, whose works are listed in the bibliography, they are in no way responsible for what I have made of their works. All Scripture references are from the English Standard Version (ESV) of the Bible unless otherwise noted. Also note that it is important to read the associated Bible passages in the book of Revelation together with the related chapters in this book.

I certainly understand that none of us has all the answers, and I know that the various scenarios that are presented in this book certainly will not be 100 percent correct. However, I am convinced that the challenges the church will soon face will be just as difficult, if not worse, than the chaotic events described in this book. Although I don't pretend to know the exact nature of the coming tribulation events, I am absolutely certain of the following two truths:

- Judgment will first come to the household of God before coming to those in the world.[10]

- We may not know the exact times of these approaching events, but our Lord assures us that those of His people who walk in His light will know when the time is dawning. And today, there are many worldwide who are hearing His call to "prepare."[11]

This book is not intended to be an apologetic for theological discussion; it is meant to feed the hungering, warrior spirit within that Christian remnant who are aware of the tremendous challenges that lie before us and are seeking guidance as to what we are about to confront and how to prepare for it. It is intended for those who discern the times and hear the call to prepare for a leadership role in the Army of God during the time of coming tribulations. Thus, this book will not effectively speak to the entire body of Christ, nor will it be welcomed by many.

My approach to addressing these end-time events is from a military perspective since much of who I am today is the result of my twenty years in the Marine Corps. The Lord has put a deep burden in my heart, and that is to arouse a remnant of Christian warriors to visualize their heritage and purpose in life. The common purpose for all volunteers in the Army of God is to prepare in the bootcamp of life in order to allow the light and glory of our Commander in Chief, Jesus Christ, to be clearly manifested on the battlefield that lies in the midst of this world.

**"Christian warriors, we are called to fight,
not run from the battle."**

CHAPTER 1

WARRIOR LEADERSHIP IN THE ARMY OF GOD

THE OPPORTUNITY FOR CHRISTIAN WARRIORS

The Lord is calling many among His people to champion His kingdom purposes, both on the spiritual and earthly battlefields. This book is intended for those Christians who possess a warrior spirit deep inside and are searching for their individual mission within the Army of God. Men and women who really want to stand strong for the Lord in the face of a world that is becoming increasingly darker year by year. These are Christians who will not shy away from being counted among those in His army who can identify with the following passage.

> *"If the world hates you, know that it has hated me before it hated you. If you were of the world, the world would love you as its own; but because you are not of the world, but I chose you out of the world, therefore the world hates you. Remember the word that I said to you: 'A servant is not greater than his master.' If they persecuted me, they will also persecute you. If they kept my word, they will also keep yours." (John 15:18-20)*

This chapter is intended to speak to these Christians about becoming a true champion leader equipped with a warrior spirit—not a Michael Jordan or a Tiger Woods type of champion but something so much greater and more challenging than a famous sports celebrity. Such Christian warriors will not be idolized but will compete on a battlefield where one's age, gender, or physical handicap is not an issue; he or she will be a champion leader in the Army of God. The opportunity to become that champion leader that our Commander in Chief is looking for is available to all, but history and experience shows that very few have the desire to step onto this battlefield. Yet for those who want to make a deep impact for the kingdom of God in their lifetime, the world is on the verge of an age that will require warrior-spirited leadership in the body of Christ. The purpose of this chapter is to inspire and provide additional understanding for those whose primary desire in this life is to "love our Lord with all of our heart, soul, mind, and strength." The focus here is on "strength" because of the huge sacrifice that this level of warrior-spirited leadership must undergo in order to finish the race of their respective callings.

First of all, Christian warriors must recognize that they are up against an enemy who is incredibly powerful—one whom the great majority of the world's population ignorantly embraces. Since the days of mankind's fall in the Garden of Eden, there has been ongoing warfare between Satan and his vast and powerful army of darkness and the eternal purposes of our Lord. Over and over, the Scriptures reveal that there is a violent, ongoing war occurring in the spiritual realm in which the people of God on earth must actively participate. The New Testament Christian, like the Old Testament Israelite, continues to be engaged in a battle, and it is a battle:

> ....*not directed against flesh and blood, but against the rulers, against the authorities, against the powers of this dark world, and against the spiritual forces of evil in the heavenly realms. (**Ephesians 6:12**)*

GOOD VERSUS GREAT LEADERSHIP

There are many good leaders in the contemporary church, and certainly good leaders get things done. In normal times we can generally get by with good leadership. But, as many in today's church recognize, we are no longer living in normal times, and we need great leaders who will display both courage and wisdom in the face of unprecedented challenges that lie ahead. The church needs good leaders, but it is desperate for great leaders.[12]

A MILITARY PERSPECTIVE OF A GREAT LEADER

A leader does not abide in his tent while his men bleed and die upon the battlefield. A leader does not dine while his men go hungry or sleep when they stand at watch upon the wall. A leader does not command his men's loyalty through fear or purchase it with gold; he earns their love by the sweat of his own back and the pains he endures for their sake. That which comprises the harshest burden, a leader lifts first and sets down last. A leader does not require service of those he leads; he provides it to them. He serves them, not they him.[13] These certainly are the leadership traits inherent within the greatest Leader that ever walked on this earth and who currently serves as the Commander in Chief over the Army of God.

Many within God's kingdom recognize that a tremendously violent war is increasing in intensity, that the world is rapidly becoming darker than ever before, and that believers have been called to fight battles against the enemies of our Lord. Yet these Christian warriors, like the sons of Issachar, who understood their times, are deeply concerned that the traditional Western church is asleep during one of the most critical times since the creation of the world.

DEAFNESS AMONG THE MULTITUDES

The Lord has been calling His people to champion His truths during their day-to-day lives on the worldly battlefields, and yet it appears that the voice of the enemy is becoming more and more influential throughout America. What is causing this deafness to His calling? Are believers not hearing the call because of their day-to-day busyness with worldly issues and their continuing pursuit of worldly pleasures? Is the church not listening because they do not want to hear that difficult times may be approaching? There certainly appears to be a strong tendency on behalf of believers to stick their heads in the sand and simply enjoy the social aspect of church life. Could it be that a lack of understanding of individual missions within God's kingdom causes deafness?

Perhaps the popular, modern-day teaching of the pretribulation rapture provides many with an excuse not to listen to His call. It is certainly pleasing to believe that when things get rough, those in the Western church will be gone from the earth. But I often wonder if the advocates of this teaching are absolutely certain that believers will escape all the difficulties that precede the coming of the Lord Jesus?

Perhaps, a significant roadblock causing deafness among many in the church can be attributed to the following mind-set among many in church leadership:

- Why has Christ's church been called into an offensive role in spiritual warfare when we serve a sovereign God who doesn't need our help to ensure victory? Doesn't the Word of God teach that God is omnipotent? Therefore, there is no reason to believe that He needs us to fight any battle.

Also, there is another extremely critical issue that causes Christians to back away from the battlefield, and that is a lack of understanding of what is commonly described as the "problem of evil:"

- If God is so loving and all-powerful, then why is there so much evil and suffering in the world?

This is a centuries-old issue that worldly philosophers continually use to confront the church in order to support their own unbelief.

Believers need to understand that the problem is not evil itself; the problem is the failure to confront evil in our individual lives. This chapter is meant to examine some of these issues that continually hinder Christians from taking their combat role seriously. Hopefully, with insight into these historically perplexing questions, warrior leadership will be better equipped to hear the trumpet of God summoning His people to the battlefield.

Now, in order to assist our endeavor to gain deeper insight into this invisible realm of spiritual warfare, let's begin by examining three separate, historical eras where Satan and his demonic allies attempted to usurp the purposes of almighty God.

- Before the foundation of the world.
- In the Garden of Eden
- The tribulation of Job

BEFORE THE FOUNDATION OF THE WORLD

What is evil, and where did it come from? This is a great and important question from the standpoint of our belief in God. Many people say they don't believe in God mainly because evil and its origin perplex them. People certainly cannot understand the course of biblical history or grasp their individual role in mankind's story without having insight into the origin of evil. Let's begin with the Word Himself, who teaches that He is the beginning of all things.

<u>In the beginning was the Word, and the Word was with God, and the Word was God.</u> He was in the beginning with God. All things were made through him, and without Him was not anything made that was made. . . . <u>And the Word became flesh and dwelt among us</u>, and we have seen his glory, glory

as of the only <u>Son from the Father</u>, full of grace and truth.
(*John 1:1-3; 1:14*)

However, sometime prior to the creation of the world as we know it, God created the heavens and its angelic inhabitants. God created all, and thus all things were created in perfection and evil did not exist. So, there was a time when evil did not exist—when the heavenly principalities and powers were all perfect, all glorious, and all worshipping and serving their Creator. However, in the course of time, a rebellion occurred in the heavens that brought about the advent of evil into the creation. This rebellion was led by Lucifer, who was perhaps the highest ranking being among the angelic world.

Who was this Lucifer (Satan), who would lead a rebellion against God? It is inconceivable that God would have created something other than a universe endowed with a perfect harmony of righteousness, joy, peace, and love—and He didn't. Scripture appears to indicate that Satan was the most beautiful and powerful angelic being in the creation. Listen to an abbreviated description of Satan as spoken by the Lord before the rebellion:

> *"You had the seal of perfection, full of wisdom and perfect in beauty and you were covered with every precious stone. You were an anointed guardian cherub and you were on the holy mountain of God where you walked in the midst of the stones of fire. <u>You were blameless in your ways from the day you were created, until unrighteousness was found in you.</u>"(Ezekiel 28:11-15)*

So, what occurred in Satan's life to cause him to rebel against his Creator? The Lord goes on to say to Satan,

> *<u>"Your heart was lifted up because of your beauty</u> and thus, you corrupted your wisdom by reason of your splendor. You were filled with violence and you sinned so I cast you as a profane thing from the mountain of God. . . . <u>How you have fallen O Day Star, son of Dawn!</u>"(Ezekiel 28:16; Isaiah 14:12)*

What did Satan desire that he did not already have?

But you said in your heart, "I will ascend to heaven—I will raise my throne above the stars of God—I will ascend above the heights of the clouds—<u>I will make myself like the Most High.</u>" (Isaiah 14:13-14)

Prior to his rebellion, Satan appears to have been the most powerful of all the angelic beings created by God, having the greatest anointing. However, as time passed, Satan became more and more dissatisfied with his position. He came to believe that greater personal fulfillment was available only if he could be free to pursue it. Thus, he conspired against his Creator God and began to recruit allies among his angelic friends. He built an army designed to overthrow the Lord and assert his contention that he was the one most qualified to rule the universe.

How did Satan proceed with his desire to take the throne of God? One can only speculate, but it certainly is reasonable to assume that Satan raised support for his cause by convincing other angelic beings that their Creator was not allowing them to reach their fullest potential. Thus, if they were to achieve their desired destiny, they would need to take matters into their own hands. In other words, Satan said, "God doesn't care about us. We need to stand up against Him and do what is right in our own eyes." Sound familiar? Satan challenged God's authority to the heavenly throne by claiming that he had just as much right to rule over the creation, and he convinced a multitude of his angelic friends to join him in his rebellion against their Creator.

So how did the Lord handle this rebellion? Listen to a summarization of His words as spoken to Satan:

"How you have fallen from heaven O star of the morning, son of the dawn. . . . <u>You said in your heart that you would make yourself like the most High</u>. Nevertheless you will be thrust down to hell. I have brought fire from the midst of you and it has consumed you—and you will be no more. You have

come to a dreadful end and will be no more forever." (Isaiah 14:9-11; Ezekiel 28:18-19)

But Satan's end has not yet come, for God still has a purpose for Satan within His eternal plan for the creation.

THE REBELLION OF SATAN CONTINUES! WHY?

Now here is an important question before us that we need to consider in order to get a deeper understanding of our role in today's spiritual warfare:

- Why didn't God cast Satan and the other usurpers into the lake of fire immediately after their heavenly rebellion and protect mankind from his deception?

The great principle that we must lay hold of here is that God, in His wisdom, allowed this to happen. Think about this:

- If God had destroyed Satan and his angelic allies at the moment of their rebellion, would He have proved Himself as being the Righteous One in this conflict having the sovereign right to rule over all creation?

Certainly, He would have proved His power over this rebellious army of angels, but would the unleashing of this power have created questions in the hearts of the remaining angelic populace? Might some of these remaining angels have doubted the love of God toward them and His creation? Would they have secretly believed that their destroyed kin had some legitimate points in their claim against God? Perhaps they too needed to be confirmed in righteousness. If so, then the immediate crushing of the rebellion would not change the scenario that caused the initial uprising. Therefore, the possibility of subsequent angelic rebellions must be considered.

The inescapable truth is that it was our sovereign Lord's eternal plan to allow evil to enter the creation, but because we know of His tremendous hatred of sin, we can conclude that the continuing presence of sin is serving a greater purpose within His plan. Now, with these foundational insights let's examine the confrontation that took place in the Garden of Eden.

IN THE GARDEN OF EDEN

In the biblical story of the creation of our world, we learn that man was created in the image of his God—a creature of perfection who walked with God daily in the garden and enjoyed close communion and fellowship with his Creator. Thus, in the beginning, there was a deep, loving relationship between Adam and the Lord. Subsequently, God, the Creator of the entire cosmos, gave man dominion over all of His earthly creation. Then one day Satan suddenly appears before Adam and Eve and alleges that God has deceived them and is withholding greatness from them. Satan then promises that if they would listen to him, they too could become like gods.

It is certainly feasible to believe that both Adam and Eve began to think, "I will make myself like the Most High!" Subsequently, they both rebelled against their Creator by believing the words of Satan. Their action alleges God to be a lying deceiver and Satan to be their real friend who wants them to have more greatness. The consequence of this choice meant that they now assumed the image of Satan and his sinful nature and established him as their lord. Thus, Satan becomes the prince of this world, and all human offspring inherit this sinful nature, which results in separation from their Creator and introduces death into the creation.

What did God do about this sudden turn of events? After cursing the serpent, Satan, and condemning our first parents for their rebellion, He then promised that mankind would be redeemed from this sinful nature and would again be restored to a close relationship with the Lord. This would be accomplished when a mighty Warrior Leader from God would be born from the seed of the woman—a Warrior who would perfectly reflect the true image of God throughout His life and thus, with His sacrifice for mankind, crush the head of

Satan and gain a complete victory over sin and death.[14] As a result, mankind had an opportunity to be restored to their relationship with almighty God, and Satan would be defeated and eventually thrust into the lake of fire.

QUESTIONS TO CONSIDER FOR THE ARMY OF GOD

In light of this rebellion in the garden, there are some key questions to consider if warrior leadership is going to gain deeper insight into the mission of the Army of God:

- Even if God did not throw Satan and his legions into the lake of fire following their initial rebellion, why did He allow Satan to enter into the Garden of Eden and entice mankind into sin?
- Didn't our Lord know that Satan would deceive mankind into sin? Wouldn't mankind have benefited if Satan had been cast into the lake of fire prior to God's creation of the earth and mankind?
- Why would a Tree of the Knowledge of Good and Evil even be placed in the Garden?
- Was it the eternal plan of our Lord that mankind would fall into sin at the beginning?

These questions must be prayerfully contemplated in light of the Scripture that reveals that the redemption of mankind from sin was in view even before man was created.

> *He chose us in him **before** the foundation of the world, that we should be holy and blameless before him. In love he predestined us for adoption through Jesus Christ, according to the purpose of his will. (**Ephesians 1:4-5**)*

In light of the above, did Adam pass or fail the "test" when he ate the fruit of the tree? Perhaps the answer is not as simple as it appears on the surface. He certainly failed if viewed from the perspective of disobedience to the Lord's command, but perhaps he passed when viewed by the bigger picture that we will continue to explore.

Obviously, one's perceptions of all these questions affect what one thinks about God. For example, those who would argue against the sovereignty of God would claim that either He was not able to put down the rebellion at its origin, or that He is not concerned with the resultant death and suffering that sin has ushered in, or that He was simply outsmarted by Satan. Even many faithful believers in God wrestle with this problem of evil but believe that it is not for them to understand. Some may even call this attitude being faithful. Christians need to stop hiding behind the excuse that "it's not for us to know;" for it is for us to know. It is my firm belief that these questions are for us to understand and the understanding of them helps to build warrior leaders in the kingdom of God.

Now let's continue further into a biblical period that might aid our understanding of the ongoing conflict between almighty God and Satan and the believers' part in it. Insight into the conflict in the life of Job, where we see behind the spiritual veil, can shed much light upon the ongoing spiritual conflict and the purpose behind it.

JOB—A MIGHTY WARRIOR OF GOD

A brief overview of the background of Job reveals that he was a man who received a loving and powerful testimony from God for being "blameless, upright, fearing God, and turning away from evil." Additionally, Job was an extremely wealthy man who was known to be the "greatest of all the men of the east"; and he was the head of a large family consisting of seven sons and three daughters, for whom he continually interceded before God. Thus, Job was a loving, righteous man in the eyes of God, as well as within his family and circle of friends.[15]

However, grievous tribulation was about to erupt in the life of Job and his family that is probably unparalleled in the life of any family. Our Lord, who dearly loved His servant Job, gives permission for Satan to slaughter his family and destroy all of his possessions. Shortly after this devastation, Satan, with God's permission, attacks Job's physical body with innumerable painful boils.

Now how could a loving God allow such a thing to happen to one of the most righteous men of that age? When confronted with this question, many Christians would respond that God doesn't really care what we have to go through in this life, for only eternal salvation is His focus and it should be ours. This mind-set is simply a form of religious deism—the belief that God does not interact within our earthly lives. Obviously, there is so much to learn here concerning the Christian role in spiritual warfare that it is vitally important for warrior leadership to look closer at this devastating and largely misunderstood event in the life of Job by examining what is simultaneously taking place in the heavenly realm.

The first chapter in the book of Job reveals that the court of heaven, where our Lord has His throne, was the operations center where all decisions were made involving the warfare that took place in the life of Job and his family. It began on a day when all the sons of God came and presented themselves before the Lord. Satan was also among them, and as he was questioned by God concerning where he had been, Satan responded that he had been walking back and forth across the earth. Then the Lord said to Satan,[16]

"Have you considered my servant Job, that there is none like him on the earth, a blameless and upright man, who fears God and turns away from evil?" (**Job 1:8**)

Obviously it is not possible for servants of Satan to be blameless before God, and therefore this statement implies that the Lord is in the process of reconciling to Himself a new mankind by delivering man from his covenant of death with Satan. God is on the offensive in this spiritual battle, and Satan is challenged to confess that God can redeem mankind from under his power or prove otherwise. Thus, Satan is backed into a corner, although he doesn't know it. It is important to understand that by making this statement, the Lord is the one who initiates all that is to follow in the saga of Job. This scenario is very similar to the confrontation with Adam and Eve, where God sets the stage and allows man to be put to the test.

However, the purpose here is not to test Job's allegiance to God but to allow him the opportunity to honor his Lord before all the hosts of heaven.

Satan then responds by questioning the genuineness of Job's allegiance to God for he answers the Lord, saying,

> *"Does Job fear God for no reason? Have you not put a hedge around him and his house and all that he has, on every side? You have blessed the work of his hands, and his possessions have increased in the land." (Job 1:9-10)*

Here Satan is saying that the Lord is simply creating the appearance of righteousness by blessing Job so abundantly—thus Satan is intent on accusing the Lord of being a deceiver rather than a God of truth.

Satan then proposes a challenge to God:

> *"But stretch out your hand and touch all that he has, and he will curse you to your face." (Job 1:11)*

This challenge was intended to expose the Lord before all the heavenly hosts as a deceiver who's Word cannot be trusted. In effect, Satan is saying that what he did to Adam, he will also do to Job. He is out to prove that he can thwart the purposes of God in creation. The Lord accepts this challenge and grants permission for Satan to proceed against all of Job's family and wealth, with the exception that Satan is not allowed to take Job's life.[17]

Thus, the battle in the life of Job begins. This challenge by God and acceptance by Satan was to be settled by a spiritual battle designed to demonstrate whose power actually prevailed in the life of Job. Also, this battle is being fought before the entire heavenly host; they are all witnesses to this event. What will determine the outcome of this battle? Answer: it will be determined by whether Job will curse God in the midst of his grievous suffering or remain faithful even though he has lost everything in life.

It is extremely important to understand what is at stake here. The Lord's Word says that His servant Job is a blameless and upright man, a man who loves God with all of his heart, soul, mind, and strength. Satan's word says, "Not true, and I can prove otherwise." The Word of God is at stake, and amazingly our Lord has chosen a common man who is about to endure tremendous suffering to demonstrate the truth and righteousness of the Word of God. On the other hand, Satan's mission is to make void the Word of God. If he is victorious, the curse pronounced against him in the garden becomes questionable, for then the Word of God cannot be relied upon. Therefore, Satan's attack is primarily against God, not Job. The only way Satan can be proved false is through Job maintaining a positive response during a prolonged, painful trial. Whose word will prevail—the Lord's or Satan's? This is what spiritual warfare is about.

The Lord God had entrusted the honor of His holy name to a man. Job was selected to champion the truth of God, and he doesn't even know it. The battle was about to reveal that Job's devotion to his Lord was genuine and was not prompted by temporal benefits. He was in a condition of tremendous misery, both physical and emotional, without any hint of improving his circumstance; but in the face of continuing temptations, he remained faithful in his love for God.

It is important for Christian warriors to remember this lesson: They serve a God who not only gives His Word but also allows it to be tested under the most difficult of conditions. Now, having received these insights into the spiritual battle, let's return to the Garden of Eden with this renewed perspective.

RETURNING TO THE CONFRONTATION IN THE GARDEN OF EDEN

What if Adam and Eve had remained obedient to God and rebuked Satan as the deceiver—would it have proved that they loved God with all their heart, mind, soul, and strength?[18] Would it have proved they did so from a heart of free will? Could not Satan have made the following statement to God?

"Have you not put a hedge around him and his house and all that he has, on every side? You have blessed the work of his hands, and his possessions have increased in the land." **(Job 1:10)**

Satan could have accused the Lord of practicing deception by denying the freewill aspect of mankind by claiming that God had created obedience. Adam was not God's intended champion! Champions are warriors in the Army of God who fight the battle using the Lord's strength.[19] Adam was a good man, and he possessed the authority to deal with Satan, but he was not trusting in God for the victory. Adam stood by his own strength, but Job stood by God's strength.

Additionally, God did not place the Tree of the Knowledge of Good and Evil in the garden for the primary purpose of testing man. It was more an invitation to Satan to engage in warfare for the dominion of creation. This becomes even clearer when we consider the pre-creation covenant between God the Father and His Son, Jesus Christ.

A PRE-CREATION COVENANT BETWEEN FATHER AND SON

It certainly appears that the Lord, in His absolute sovereignty, already had ordained the fall of mankind in the garden long before it actually occurred. His Word tells us that the sacrifice of the Son of God was foreknown before the foundation of the world and that the names of those who have been chosen for eternal salvation were written in the Book of Life prior to the creation.[20]

The provision for grace that God made for His people before the foundation of the world involved His own Son and His assumption of human nature, the offering of Himself as a sacrifice for sin, His resurrection, and His supremacy over all the church.[21] Clearly, these were matters of arrangement between God the Father and His Son prior to the creation. The first pronouncement of this redemptive plan was to Satan himself immediately after the fall of mankind when God told him,

> *"I will put enmity between you and the woman, and between your offspring and her offspring; he shall bruise your head, and you shall bruise his heel."* (**Genesis 3:15**)

Since we recognize the scenario that the Lord placed the Tree of the Knowledge of Good and Evil in the garden and also allowed Satan access to mankind, we may now ask, "Was it the Lord's eternal plan that Adam fall into sin?" Answer: "Yes, it certainly was." But, because we know of the Lord's tremendous hatred of sin, we can easily conclude that a higher purpose is being served by the allowed presence of sin into His creation.[22] Now with this background in mind, let's examine some glorious truths that may provide a clearer understanding of the problem of evil.

SEVEN WONDROUS TRUTHS UNVEILED BY ADAM'S FALL

First Truth Unveiled: A Heart of True Love

Adam's fall revealed that mankind did not yet have a heart of love for God. *God cannot create a heart of true love,* and thus the weakness of the heart of mankind would not have been revealed without the fall. It is through periods of tribulation that we grow nearer to our Lord, for it is mostly during these hard times when His people cry out to Him and discover that He hears and acts on their behalf. Thus, that love which is not a created thing grows within us as we see Him deliver us from evil and bless us. Yes, the problem of evil causes much suffering, but it's not only mankind that suffers; the Lord has suffered alongside of us.

Second Truth Unveiled: God's Attributes

The fullness of our Lord's attributes would not have been seen and understood without the fall and thus, we would not have known Him as He desired.

Who is like you, O Lord, among the gods? Who is like you, majestic in holiness, awesome in glorious deeds, doing wonders? (Exodus 15:11)

We learn that He is righteous in all of His ways and He will never violate His laws; yet, He is overwhelming in His love for His people. How could believers know about the patience and long-suffering of our Lord without it being demonstrated toward His people as they rebelled against Him century after century? Or how could they know the depths of His love apart from His continually reconciling mankind to Himself and casting their past sins as far from Him as the east is from the west, even after years of rebellion? His love ultimately was demonstrated at the cross of Calvary, when He willingly sacrificed Himself in order to free His people from the bondage of Satan.

Third Truth Unveiled: Man's Dependency

The fall of mankind demonstrates the dependency upon God that is needed to sustain life. Even the perfect creature is fully dependent upon his Creator for continued perfection. This is a truth that would never have been known if the rebellion had been squashed at its source. The sin of Satan was that, in his perfection, he saw no need for God. If evil had not been present in the Garden of Eden, perhaps it was only a matter of time before Adam, in all of his splendor, or one of Adam's posterity would have committed the same sin as Satan.

Fourth Truth Unveiled: Knowledge of Good and Evil

Knowledge of good and evil is necessary in order to truly understand and fully appreciate the perfect world in which believers will eternally live. How can perfection be known unless it is contrasted in some way with its diametric opposite? For example, can one know righteousness unless he is familiar with unrighteousness? In the same way, can love, joy, and peace be known and appreciated without knowledge of hatred, sorrow, and war?

Fifth Truth Unveiled: Kingdom Warriors

The fall provided the opportunity to bring forth kingdom warriors empowered by God for battle. Like Adam, each of us is provided with the same opportunity to choose whom to follow—God or Satan. We have an opportunity during our short life on earth to join the Army of God against this ancient archenemy. Additionally, like Job, we need to understand that it is during times of tribulation when believers truly can have a strong impact in the heavenlies, for it is during these times that the following words of the enemy come into our hearts: "If God is real and loves you, why does He allow these things to happen to you?" Christians must recognize that the spiritual battle is upon us and how we respond to these difficult times determines whether or not we are standing alongside our Lord on the battlefield.

Sixth Truth Unveiled: A Mighty Savior

Jesus Christ, not Adam, is our Savior. We would not have come to know Him without the fall. The fall provided the opportunity to bring forth a perfect Warrior from the seed of Adam who would demonstrate an incomprehensible love of God for His redeemed ones. It was an opportunity for our heavenly Father to introduce His Son, who would reflect God's character in a way that mankind can understand. This Warrior would have to come from the seed of Adam, but also be the eternal Son of God. In other words, He must be fully Man to fairly defeat Satan, but He also must be fully

God—for He must be free of the sin nature in order to destroy the Adversary, whose servants are slaves to sin. There were other victories as warriors were brought forth in redemptive history, but the essence of sin in man thwarted any opportunity of obtaining perfect victory over the Adversary. The nature of the battle to be fought between Jesus Christ and Satan was that man was to exhibit the full image of God throughout his lifetime and in the face of constant assault.

Seventh Truth Unveiled: A New Relationship

Those who are born again by the blood of Christ have a new relationship with God that was not available to Adam in his original state. This is a relationship of family purchased by the blood of God Himself. The blood of the Lord Jesus, which provides redemption, has given birth to sons and daughters of God who are in such an intimate relationship with Him that they are called the body of Christ. Mankind no longer appears simply in the image of God, as Adam was before the fall; we have been born again, and our identity is now sons and daughters of God. God walked with Adam in the garden. In the new creation, God lives within His people. A former friend now becomes a son.

Thus, soldiers in the Army of God can say,

Thank you, Father, for allowing the fall to occur, for it has provided us with the opportunity to grow more and more into the likeness of Your glorious Son through our growing understanding of good and evil; and thank You for allowing us to stand against the darkness of evil as we allow the light of Christ to shine through us.

This provides some answers to the previous questions regarding the problem of evil if believers truly understand and accept the fact that their righteous and omnipotent Lord frequently chooses to tie His hands while waiting for His army of warriors to come forth onto the battlefield.

TRIAL BY ORDEAL—A HISTORICAL PERSPECTIVE

Ancient pagan kingdoms frequently elected to have judicial disputes resolved by an appeal to their respective gods. The idea was that divine intervention would take place and the party in the right would be vindicated.

A common method used to call their pagan gods into a dispute was to engage in a trial by ordeal, whereby the dispute was settled by combat. The kings involved in the dispute would select their individual champions, who would physically fight until a winner was proclaimed—usually this was a fight to the death. Although the champions were pitted against each other, it was believed that the divine power of their respective gods was what determined the outcome.[23]

History appears to reveal that our Lord also condescends to handle disputes arising from the lips of His accuser by such ordeals.

BIBLICAL EXAMPLES OF ORDEALS BY COMBAT

God's Champion	versus	Satan's Champion(s)
David	versus	Goliath
Moses	versus	Pharaoh
Elijah on Mount Carmel	versus	450 Prophets of Baal

These singular events certainly stand out, but we need to remember that life is a battlefield on which God's people are confronted again and again by Satan's chosen vessels. Other examples include Joseph versus Joseph's brothers and the wife of Potiphar; Jacob versus Esau, Laban, and his kidnapping sons; and the trials of Jonathan, Joshua, Gideon, Abraham, Hannah, Ruth, Esther, the prophets, the apostles, Irenaeus, Eusebius, Polycarp, the martyrs, Luther, Calvin, George Whitfield, Jonathan Edwards, Watchman Nee, David Wilkerson, etc.

The whole history of the church is the arena of God versus Satan in trials by ordeal. It hasn't changed; running the twenty-first-century race of champions is likewise a trial by ordeal. Satan's champions will always visibly appear to be greater and more powerful than God's champions, and fear is a tremendous power utilized against Christians. The only way leaders will develop a champion mentality is by spending our time in God's presence. That brings us to the second ordeal.

A SECOND ORDEAL

God's potential champions first must prevail with the Lord Himself. We see this important truth demonstrated in the life of Job. The primary ordeal between God and Satan is to be decided by God's ordeal with Job; for in order to subdue Satan by the hand of Job, God must first subdue Job. Job can prevail with God only as he is brought to his knees in submission before Him. Listen to Job's confession at the end of his terrible ordeal:

"I had heard of you by the hearing of the ear, but now my eye sees you; therefore I despise myself, and repent in dust and ashes." (Job 42:5-6)

It is God, not Job, who is the real conqueror of Satan, but Job will be eternally honored as the type of overcoming champion our Commander in Chief is searching for among His people.

CONTINUING WARFARE UPON THE CHURCH

The armies of Satan continually fight to thwart God's purposes and to prevent the return of Jesus Christ in victory. Satan's very survival depends upon it. As always, this battle is directed against those whom God has declared righteous through the blood of Christ. Therefore, Christians continue to be called upon to wage war against their spiritual adversaries and the worldly kingdom that is committed to the defeat of Christianity.

Christians have been brought into the story of life at this time in the history of the world in order to enlist in the Army of God. Believers need to put on the armor of God and allow His light to shine through them in the workplace, their neighborhoods, and their families. These places are the true front lines of the battlefield.

You are the light of the world. A city set on a hill cannot be hidden. Nor do people light a lamp and put it under a basket, but on a stand, and it gives light to all in the house. In the same way, let your light shine before others, so that they may see your good works and give glory to your Father who is in heaven. (**Matthew 5:14-16**)

Participants need to remember that this is a Holy War and that the required power for victory is not found among its human participants but in the power of God. Thus, believers need to understand the power of prayer, which may be likened to the wrestling that took place between God and Job. This is the "second ordeal" that should be taking place within each member of the body of Christ. Believers must prevail with God before Satan can be subdued in their lives. Believers will never prevail by battling in the flesh. The victory is to be the Lord's, and Christians can prevail only if they humble themselves before Him in true heart repentance. Prayerlessness is proof that our life is still under the power of the flesh. It proves that the life of God in the soul is mortally sick and weak. The sin of prayerlessness is the cause of a powerless spiritual life.[24]

For God to subdue Satan through the hand of His people, God must first subdue His people. But just as Job wrestled long with God, the Christian may, at times, have to wrestle long in prayer. However, the victory is certain if believers will exercise the patient, long-suffering faith that brought Job through the battlefield. The testing in our lives is a daily one. Certainly it is not to the depth that we read about in Job, but all that happened to Job happens to many of us over a period of time. Yet, since it happened to Job all at once and with much greater severity, his reaction as a warrior of God should influence all believers.

It is important to remember that Adam did not rely upon God in the battle, and he lost. All of God's champions lose some battles now and then, but they continue to be strengthened by their experiences and do not succumb to self-pity. That warrior spirit may be knocked down on occasion, but it will always seek the strength of the Lord in order to get back up and again run to the battle. These are the Christian warriors who will never quit.

REMEMBER THIS WELL

God may choose to tie His hands since He is fighting the battle through His warrior army. Otherwise the Accuser can cry out before God,

> *"Have you not put a hedge around him and his house and all that he has, on every side? You have blessed the work of his hands, and his possessions have increased in the land."* (***Job 1:10***)

Soldiers in the Army of God should not allow the Accuser to say that they are not truly righteous but profess Christ merely because of their earthly prosperity or their desire to achieve earthly prosperity. They must stand as warriors in the midst of prosperity and adversity; for both will be faced in life.

WALKING AS GOD'S WARRIORS DAY TO DAY

Redeeming the time may be extremely difficult, but it is also one of the most important areas of daily life that champion leaders must master. Stay on the offensive; take the sword of the Spirit, which is the Word of God, and know it, memorize it, and take it up daily. Stand firm; when under daily fire, remember Job. Intercessory prayer must become heart driven, for this is where your one-on-one relationship with the Lord truly grows powerful. Let your faith shine within your environment; remove the basket, and be the light that you are called to be in the world. Anticipate the battle, and allow it to cause growth in strength and intimacy with the Lord.

This is our call, though perhaps it is not for everyone. But for those who hear this call to be warriors and overcomers, this is an opportunity that was offered to warriors like Paul, David, and Elijah, and it is offered to each of us in our lives. We only have one life and thus, one opportunity to stand for our Lord on the front lines of the battlefield and fight against His enemies. The rewards that are promised in the afterlife are predicated upon our kingdom work during this lifetime. Some will rule ten cities, some five, and some one, but most will be citizens, not leaders. All will receive rewards, but there is a difference—His warriors will be called to eternal leadership in the eternal kingdom. Let us not go to the grave wishing that we had answered this call. Now is the time, not tomorrow or next week; the call is now to "those who hear."

CONCLUDING THOUGHTS

Regarding the Problem of Evil

Hopefully, this chapter provides some answers to the problem of evil as we see our righteous and omnipotent Lord tying His own hands while waiting for His champions to come forth into the battle.

Regarding the Importance of Intercessory Prayer

Even though God knows our needs, there may not be an unleashing of divine blessing to meet these needs until we demonstrate a meaningful relationship that continues to seek and obey our heavenly Father in our day-to-day activities. Otherwise, Satan can cry, "Foul!"

Regarding Encouraging Us to the Battle

The idea that we are called as individuals to be warriors for the Lord in this life where His truth and righteousness are being called into question should encourage us to the battle. A Christian believer's strength and determination during times of hardship has a profound impact upon the world. Many have come to acknowledge God as they witness the attitude of God's warriors during periods of tribulation.

EMBRACE THIS TRUTH: "LIFE IS MEANT TO BE CHALLENGING"

The "easy believism" gospel message that is so popular today is not true. This is the belief that we can have spiritual power and prosperity and be pleasing to God in this life without sacrifice and suffering. Those who embrace this popular message will live a life of whining and self-pity and will not really grow in their understanding of God and His ways. It's a self-focused gospel message, and its teaching will cause many to "fall away" during the times of deep tribulation.

In the wilderness, Israel lived a wandering lifestyle that God had led them into for a season of time. They were on their way to being restored, but they continually responded in a negative way. They developed a victim mentality and constantly grumbled about their state of discomfort. They had sunk into a maintenance mentality, trying to stay alive, rather than a victory mentality of ruling and reigning with God. They seemed to believe that when they entered the Promised Land that all fighting would cease and their worries would disappear. They had no idea that they were the weapon in God's hands that would establish the rule of God on earth. This sounds like much of the contemporary church.[25]

Believers have not been put on this earth simply to be saved and then to sit around living life as usual. We are being presented with the opportunity that Jesus offered His disciples: making an eternal impact for the kingdom of God and becoming a warrior-spirited soldier in His army. If believers decide for greatness, it will cost everything they have and are, for they may even have to give up their very lives. The choice is momentous, but amazingly, it is for every believer to make.[26]

CHAPTER 2

ONE WORLD - TWO KINGDOMS

THE KINGDOM OF GOD

The kingdom of God was one of the most prominent teachings of Jesus during His time upon earth, and yet it is a biblical teaching that is largely overlooked by the contemporary church. Perhaps this is understandable, for Jesus Himself refers to the kingdom of God as a mystery; yet it is a mystery that He expects His people to understand.[27] Our Lord continually admonishes us, as Christians, to be awake and prepared for the coming kingdom of God, a time when all things in heaven and earth will be united in Jesus Christ, the Son of our living God.[28] An insightful understanding of our Lord's kingdom is more important today than at any other time in the history of the church, for it appears that we are rapidly approaching the days preceding His second coming. Therefore, in order to have a clearer understanding of the events that usher in this soon coming of the King of Kings, Christians need to have a clearer understanding of the meaning and purpose of the kingdom of God.

THE MYSTERY OF THE KINGDOM

The Jews of antiquity expected the coming of God's kingdom, which their Messiah would usher in, to bring a mighty manifestation of divine power that would break apart the godless nations of the earth. They expected God's power to overthrow Rome, sweep away the godless Gentiles, purge the earth of unrighteousness, and exalt God's people, Israel, in their own land over all the nations of the earth. However, the reality is that the kingdom of God came in fulfillment of the Old Testament promises but in different terms than was anticipated by the religious leaders of Israel. The kingdom of God had arrived but as a mystery that they failed to comprehend.

This mystery of the kingdom of God may be summarized as follows: During the era between the first and the second comings of Jesus Christ, the promised Messiah, the glory of His kingdom will enter into His people and launch a powerful offensive against the kingdom of darkness—which will deliver many out of the world and into the blessings of the reign of Jesus Christ. This has been happening for two thousand years, as millions of people have responded to the gospel of the kingdom.

However, it is important to note that the kingdom of God is with us only in part and not yet in fullness, although its numbers have greatly increased over the past two thousand years. It is necessary to understand that this kingdom can be comprehended only by the Spirit of God residing within us. It requires our individual response in order to be intelligible. That is, even though the activity of this kingdom is an objective fact, its recognition by mankind requires individual personal participation. In other words, one must be born again as a child of God in order to enter into the eternal kingdom of God.[29] He calls each one of us individually, and we must respond individually—not through a third-party intermediary such as a priest or a church. We must respond directly to the person of Jesus Christ, for He is our one and only intermediary before His Father, almighty God.[30]

OUR KING PROVIDES INSIGHT INTO THE MYSTERY OF HIS KINGDOM

The parable of the "four soils" in Matthew 13:3-23 describes how the kingdom of God currently operates in today's world.[31] Here

Jesus taught that this transitional period between His first and second comings is a period of seed sowing in which different "soils" will respond differently to the message of the kingdom.

This teaching informs us that there are four ways for hearers to receive the gospel message, but three of these ways will not result in a true heart response.

- The first is the heart that hears the word but doesn't understand it. The Evil One then comes and quickly snatches away whatever was temporarily sown in the heart. This is the seed that is sown but quickly devoured by birds.
- The second is the heart that initially receives the gospel message with great excitement. But this is only a superficial emotional experience, for when challenges arise in the lives of such people they will fall away. These are people who gravitate to the attractional-style churches, but they continue to live like the world. This is the seed sown on rocky ground and thus has no root in itself.
- The third is the heart that receives the gospel message, but the cares and riches of this world continue to dominate these people's lives and choke out the word. Such people may be regular churchgoers—many may currently be pastors, elders, and deacons who take a businesslike approach to building their individual churches. This is the seed sown in thorny areas of the ground, and when the thorns rise up, they choke the truth of God's Word out of people's hearts.
- The fourth is a heart that receives and turns from the cares of this world, and through its allegiance to Jesus Christ, the kingdom expands throughout the world. This is the true "born again" believer, who certainly spends time in church but considerably more time in the prayer closet growing in intimacy with the Lord. This is the seed sown on fertile ground, which the Evil One cannot uproot.

Thus, the kingdom of God is present among us in a stage of seed sowing as people are extended an offer to enter the kingdom and be fruit bearers. Three kinds of people are "pretenders" and will not come in, but one kind will; and they will manifest the gospel throughout their remaining lives, greatly strengthening the kingdom of God both in size and power among the nations of the world.

EVIL SEED SOWN IN FERTILE SOIL

The kingdom of God indeed has come among men but not for the immediate purpose of shattering evil in the world. It is like a farmer sowing seed, for it is working quietly and secretly among people. It does not force itself upon them, for it must be willingly received. Eventually, both a harvest of wrath and a harvest of salvation will take place at the end of the age. However, until then, the Evil One is intent upon weakening and rendering impotent the good seed of God's kingdom by sowing bad seeds in its midst. Warrior leadership must recognize that an evil remnant continues to exist in the midst of God's people. Shortly, however, a great tribulation that is coming will cause a visible separation between those who are truly people of God and those who are "wannabees" but are not willing to submit in total repentance.[32]

HANDLING SUFFERING IN GOD'S KINGDOM

Christian soldiers need to get over the tendency to view evil and suffering solely from an individual perspective, focusing on when they or their family suffers. We may ask why babies are starving, women are raped, and innocents are slaughtered while wicked and greedy people continue to live in luxury; but when we are able to see the broad picture, it is easier to make sense of suffering. Everything depends on where we start. If we begin by envying the prosperity of the wicked, we will charge God with unfairness. But if we begin by delighting in God, we are far from being a victim of injustice; we trust that justice will prevail in God's timing. The point is that God is entirely just and therefore a time is coming when all of mankind will appear before the throne of God, and His judgment and sentencing will determine the eternal destiny of every human being that has ever been born. Since this entails awaiting the end, it involves walking by faith. Christians need to develop a kind of "homesickness" for heaven.[33]

A scene from the popular movie The Lord of the Rings: *The Fellowship of the Ring* also provides some insights into the mystery of suffering and injustice. There we see Gandalf counseling Frodo as they are confronting dark forces within the caves of Moria. Gandalf says, "Many that are living deserve to die, and some that died deserved to live. So do not be too eager to deal out death and judgment, for even the very wisest of men cannot see all the ends." Frodo then says, "I wished none of this had happened." Gandalf replies, "So do all that live to see such times, but it's not for us to decide. All that we have to decide is what to do with the time that is given to us. There are other forces at work in this world besides the forces of evil."

THE KINGDOM OF GOD IS COSMOLOGICAL

Finally, we need to be aware that the establishment of God's kingdom encompasses more than just the redemption of His people; this redemption process includes the entire creation "which labors and groans awaiting the revealing of the sons of God."[34] All of creation requires cleansing from the effects of sin. This cosmological view of salvation helps us to better understand the coming massive destruction, which occurs in the heavenlies as well as upon this world prior to the second coming of our Lord.

The contemporary American church is accustomed to focusing only upon our individual salvation. Simply put, we must be born again, sanctified, and delivered from sin, and then we will go to heaven. End of story. In brief, this is the entire story of our salvation lodged in the minds of many. Of course, all of this is important and perfectly true as far as it goes. Nevertheless, it is only part of the truth, not the whole of it. Instead, believers must realize the biblical truth that all the world, the entire kingdom, including the earthly environment and the animal kingdom, which God originally created and which fell under the power of sin and the devil, will again be restored and even raised to a higher glory than it originally possessed, even as we shall be.

THE KINGDOM OF THIS WORLD

An overview of some significant differences that separate the kingdom of this world from the kingdom of our Lord will help in understanding those events that will confront the church before the second coming of our Lord.

To begin, there are not two worlds; there is only one. There is but one world; and from the fall of Adam to this day, there are two powers that fight for dominion over that one world. On the one hand, there is the dominion of Satan, who apparently gained the victory in the Garden of Eden. On the other hand, there is the dominion of Christ, who is called to restore the kingdom to the Father. Now the kingdom of God in the Christian era reaches beyond the bounds of Israel's national existence and is international. Christ now gathers His subjects from all parts of the world and out of every nation and tongue and tribe, for it is no more a battle between nations as in the Old Testament era.

Both kingdoms reside in the same world and outwardly enjoy the same benefits. They enjoy the same rain and sunshine, and it is here that our view often becomes obscured and needs to be clarified. Understand that because the kingdom of God lies within the hearts of His people and not within geographical boundaries, as does the kingdom of Satan, yet both powers make use of all outward institutions that God has set up in the world. In this world, where both the principles of sin and grace operate simultaneously, God created various institutions designed to maintain the possibility of an orderly life that would allow the human race to develop as far as possible in spite of the inherent presence of sin.[35] These institutions are summarized as follows:

- *The institution of various forms of government* were established by God and equipped with the sword to maintain order in society and to punish the evildoer so that the kingdom of

God might have a place to develop. Without this restraint upon the development of sin, the principle of evil would develop prematurely, and life on earth would soon prove impossible, as it did in the pre-flood era.

- *The institution of the church* has been established in the world for the upbringing and edification of the sons and daughters of God and for the extension of God's Kingdom throughout the world.
- *The institution of society in general—the home, the school, and the workplace*—were all established to bring order and progress in society.

The two powers fight for nothing less than possession of the whole world, and in this fight they both make use of all the institutions that God has established. Therefore, we see that the battle against the forces of darkness rages along a huge front.

INSTITUTIONS IN THE KINGDOM OF THE WORLD

The anti-Christian world also has established a kingdom using the institutions that God has established. However, theirs is a kingdom without Christ and without His atoning sacrifice. Instead of God, man is the absolute sovereign within this kingdom. Progress in business, industry, and commerce, as well as in the arts and sciences, is characteristic of this kingdom, all without God and without His Son. Moreover, citizens of this kingdom will speak of righteousness and brotherly love and strive to realize the universal brotherhood of man. They want to abolish the effects of sin and usher in a universal, blissful state. Thus, they essentially strive for the consummation of what they call the kingdom of mankind in the world.

In order to accomplish their purposes for a perfect world, these children of darkness manipulate the institutions that God has set up in the world.

Institution of the State

A worldly view of the institution of the state encourages govern-ments to emphasize the rights of humans even at the expense of justice. The acceptable philosophy is that all mankind is basically good and any committed acts of evil are the result of living in a poor environment. Accepted and encouraged within this worldview are individual rights, which approve of abortions, same-sex marriages, releasing of criminals on legal technicalities, and so on. Their belief is that a caring society along with psychiatric counseling is what is needed to properly reduce acts of evil within the world.

Institution of the Church

A worldly view of the institution of the church invites the church to cooperate in the establishment of this worldly kingdom. However, the acceptable gospel of the church is a social gospel. That old message of sin and guilt and total depravity and that one can be cleansed only by the blood of Jesus Christ has become antiquated and will not satisfy the needs of the modern generation. Thus, a new gospel has come to the forefront, a gospel of love and peace for all people—without the deeming blood of Christ. Here mankind is not spiritually impotent, but is divine. He is not by nature a sinner, but is naturally righteous as a child of God.

In order to function in this kingdom mind-set, the church must allow itself to become a powerful agency for the establishment of this universal kingdom of peace and righteousness. Today, the vast majority of churches and seminaries do not accept the truth of the inerrancy of Scripture. Non-evangelicals maintain that Scripture is of human origin, though it could *possibly* communicate a divine message and thus it could be profitable even though it contains many errors. As pertains to eternal salvation, they maintain that either all are saved (universalism) or that the saved ones are those who work for the welfare of others in various social programs. They may even encourage imitating Christ as an example of a good man who performs good works for society. Finally, the liberal churches believe Jesus was a good man who was aligned with God in nebulous ways. However, actual miracles and a resurrection are not really necessary but can be viewed as symbolic of a higher reality. What they believe is truly important is the example Jesus portrayed in His love toward people. They love the hymn, "Peace on Earth, Goodwill toward Men."

Institution of the Home, the School, and the Workplace

A worldly view of the institution of society in general, as characterized by the home, the school, and the workplace, is summarized as follows: If family life would obstruct the development of their ideal worldview, it must be transformed. If free love, homosexual marriages, and the murder of unborn children are advantageous to the establishment of this kingdom, their practice must be encouraged. Child discipline is viewed as archaic and criminal. Divorce is acceptable in this society, and adultery is certainly not frowned upon. Schools are required to adhere to and teach this worldview. They may not teach a definite religion or allow prayer, for that would not be in harmony with a universal brotherhood. Differences must be removed and competition must cease, and an acceptable socialistic state of things must be established and taught. Academic scholarship is encouraged but is secondary to one's social standing or athletic ability when it comes to applying for acceptance to a university. Business is largely motivated by the desire to acquire rather than to serve the consumer as well as its employees. Who gets hurt in the process of commercialism is not all that important, for what is important is the financial power that can be achieved.

In summary, the great aim of this worldview is to establish a kingdom that is in outward form like the kingdom of God as pictured in the Bible, but the true motive is enmity against God and against His Son—and the promotion of mankind as being a truly divine people.

Finally, being armed with this understanding of the spiritual war between the kingdom of God and the kingdom of the world, let's now look at the church in today's American culture in the context of Revelation 2 and 3—the letters of Jesus to the church.

CHAPTER 3

WARNINGS FOR THE CHURCH IN AMERICA
(Revelation 2—3)

BETRAYAL ARISES FROM WITHIN

One of the most eye-opening teachings in the Bible is found in the Lord Jesus' informing His disciples that when the nations commence persecuting the church prior to His second coming, many will fall away and eventually hate and betray those who remain. This is primarily the consequence of many false teachers who are solidly established within the organized church system but whose teachings continually lead their devoted followers astray.[36] Here our Commander in Chief is alerting His army that many of the enemy are within their midst, yet His words are largely ignored within the American church. This is somewhat understandable since few pastors could possibly believe that members of their congregation, or fellow pastors, would ever align with the kingdom of the world in their hatred toward the church. However, this is such a huge event that God's kingdom people will face in the near future that it simply cannot be ignored any longer. Preparation to deal with this issue will be discussed in a subsequent chapter, but for now let's address how such a catastrophic event could possibly happen.

THE LETTERS OF JESUS TO THE CHURCH

An overview of the letters Jesus dictated and that were to be given to the seven churches in Asia Minor should provide a clearer understanding of the circumstances that will cause people to fall away when confronted with life-threatening pressures. The characteristics of five of these churches will be briefly discussed within this chapter; however, I would highly recommend David Ravenhill's excellent book, *The Jesus Letters,* for those who desire additional insights.

Now, contrary to the theories of some theologians, it is extremely important to understand that these letters from Jesus to the church in Asia Minor are also meant for the entire Christian church from the first century until the present day. Jesus speaks of spiritual ailments and misunderstandings concerning sin that have historically plagued and continue to weaken the Christian churches. Christian soldiers need to stand back and take an unbiased and truthful look at the American church today, and hopefully they will see that Jesus is not only speaking to the churches in His day but is also speaking to us. Our generation needs to awaken to the tremendous weaknesses in our churches today, for the love of so many of our people has, unknowingly, grown cold.

THE CHURCH OF EPHESUS IN AMERICA
(Revelation 2:1-7)

If one were to only read the first two verses, it would appear as if the Ephesian church was a prime example of the type of church that is very pleasing to the Lord. The Ephesian church was obviously a very influential body that gave a tremendous effort to Christian ministry. However, these initial accolades from Jesus are followed by a "but," which tells us that we are about to hear what really is on Jesus' mind. There was a time many years before when the Ephesian church was passionate in their relationship with Jesus; however, their passion had now faded and been replaced by other priorities. Doctrinal purity and the letter of the Word had become more important than the Spirit of the Word, which is necessary to develop that moment-to-moment intimacy with the Lord. We the church need to understand the importance of devoting ourselves to Him. Note the following insights by Charles Stanley.

> *I believe with all my heart that it is impossible to be both goal-oriented and God-oriented at the same time. One orientation will always take precedence over the other. When our desire to achieve takes the lead, several things happen in our relationship with God. He becomes a means to an end rather than the end. We tend to use God rather than worship Him. We find ourselves seeking information about Him rather than transformation by Him.*[37]

Very subtly, the church can become like the Pharisees and their followers, who prided themselves in their hard work and doctrinal purity. Now the Ephesian church certainly baptized, fasted, paid tithes, and kept the Sabbath, which in their minds was evidence of their spirituality; yet they were blind to the presence of the Lord in their midst. This was a church that needed to pay attention to the following warning given by Jesus: *"Unless your righteousness exceeds that of the scribes and Pharisees, you will never enter the kingdom of heaven."*[38]

It was a church strong in doctrine, faithful in discipline, obviously intellectual, and abounding in the work of the Lord; yet there was a certain defect in its inner life that was so serious that it would lead the church to utter ruin before God unless it repented. Ministry was increasing, but the spiritual life of the church was ebbing away. Outwardly, the church had grown; inwardly it had become weak. Certainly, there was a remnant of those within the church who knew the love of Christ, but they no longer were the leading element within the church. The subject of spiritual growth in the knowledge of the Lord Jesus was silently becoming of secondary importance. Such routine priorities as whether the services were faithfully attended, the sacraments were properly applied, the church bulletins were read, the budget was paid—all questions that pertained to the external life and activities of the church—was its primary focus.[39]

Such churches and seminaries, with their prideful spirit of independence and the worshipping of their respective denominations, are very prevalent in the Western world today—yet, they have no idea of their lack of readiness for the coming Day of the Lord. When this type of church is confronted with persecution from a worldly government, the majority will not have the spiritual strength to stand against it and will in fact compromise the gospel message in order to maintain their status within the new governmental system. This is so serious to the Lord that He tells the Ephesian church that unless they repent and return to their first love, He will remove them from their place.

THE CHURCH OF SMYRNA IN AMERICA
(Revelation 2:8-11)

Now here was a congregation of warriors for Christ. As we contemplate the tribulation, the poverty, and the slandering that this church was experiencing day after day and year after year while maintaining their faithfulness to Christ, it should be an awakening to us in the Western world. It is probable that the Smyrna church had earlier experienced a falling away of many in their congregation as pressure was continually brought against it by the government and the worldly community. But Jesus praises the remnant who were shortly to be thrown into prison and subsequently killed. He calls them "rich" and tells them to "fear not," for He endured a similar fate, and He promises them the eternal "crown of life" if they remain faithful to the end of their lives. Notice that He didn't promise to deliver them from their tribulations but rather to stand with them and strengthen them through them. This was a victorious and conquering church in the ongoing spiritual war. They could not be hurt by the "second death." They were steadfast in their calling, and their eternal reward would be tremendous.

Paul Marshall wrote,

There are some 200 million Christians worldwide undergoing some form of persecution. The U.S. State Department cites over sixty countries where Christians face the realities of massacre, rape, torture, mutilation, family division, harassment, imprisonment, and slavery, as well as discrimination in education and employment and even death.[40]

Christians, can you imagine the shame that pretribulation raptured saints would feel when they met the Smyrna church people in the eternal kingdom? Are we more privileged, that the Lord would deliver us from a time of persecution when, historically, He strengthens most of His saints to endure it? Wake up to the reality of the times, or the oil in your lamps will be insufficient.[41]

The American churches have been relatively free of persecution and have a tendency to believe that in our "democratic country" it couldn't happen here. However, this mind-set can be a catastrophic mistake for us as the Day of the Lord approaches—for Christ Himself alerted us that before His return His people will face tribulation and death and will be hated by all nations for His name's sake.[42] Christian warriors need to remember that the kingdom of the world desires freedom to do what is right in its own eyes without being told it is wrong. Citizens of that kingdom long to rid the world of the restraining influence of the church's light in order to give free reign to deeds of darkness. There is no question that persecution will be coming to the uncompromising Christian church; it is only a matter of time as to when it will come.[43]

Ultimately, what this letter to the Smyrna church teaches us is another aspect of the spiritual character that Jesus Christ values in His people, and that is faithfulness during periods of intense trials. Here were a people who had suffered the loss of their homes and possessions, undergone rejection, blasphemies, and tribulation, and yet had remained steadfastly faithful through it all. They had experienced firsthand what it is like to "walk through the valley of the shadow of death," and they had come through victoriously. Unlike their Ephesian neighbors, they had maintained their first love despite tremendously adverse circumstances.[44] Tribulation experiences not only produce mature and strong Christians, but they also weed out the tares from within their midst. Where is Jesus when Christians are going through this time of tribulation? He's standing right alongside of us, strengthening and encouraging us to keep fighting against the powers of darkness and promising us that the finish line is fast approaching and will bring eternal rewards so great that our finite minds cannot comprehend them.[45]

THE CHURCH OF SARDIS IN AMERICA
(Revelation 3:1-6)

Of the seven churches addressed by Jesus in Revelation, the church of Sardis is the only one that did not receive a single word of commendation from the Lord. Something was seriously wrong with this one, yet the Sardis church had a reputation in the community for being "alive."

Envision this in today's commercial society: the parking lot is full every Sunday and the local police are there directing traffic; the senior pastor might host a weekly television program, as well as producing popular and well-attended events during the holiday seasons. Because of these numerous, ongoing, nonstop activities, the church gains a reputation for being "alive." It is a dynamo of activity; programs abound. But it's all done by human effort; so, in reality, it is a church that is "dead." Such churches are led by very gifted communicators—salesmen proclaiming messages of financial prosperity and easy believism and selling insurance policies guaranteeing eternal salvation. They like to call themselves champions in God's army, but they are babes; and because of their lack of spiritual maturity, most of them will flee or compromise the gospel at the first sign of persecution.

The Sardis-style ministry is simply an application of big business concepts in the guise of a spiritual move of God. The following scenario is prevalent in these deceptive churches.

When you are broken, sick, hurting, or jobless, and a local or TV preacher reaches into your hurt with tears and says, "I sense someone is hurting . . . and if you reach for your checkbook and give your best gift" . . . just dry your tears and write a check for someone or some cause that really needs it— someone worse off than you. Do it, not because you think it will trigger some divine reaction financially, or that God will feel He owes you now. Do it because it is a command to give, especially to the needy and poor. Do it to break the chain of despair and depression you may feel. Do it and laugh because God will take care of all your needs for He can create from nothing.[46]

Sardis is led by those who have lowered the standard of their message to the level of people's sensitivities and cultural norms in order to make the message nice and inoffensive, and so it remains vague. It's the opinion of many of these church leaders that they need to lure people through the doors with a happy, vague, seeker-friendly message, and then when they have their confidence, they can speak about the tougher, but inoffensive issues. They believe that being consistent and strong in the gospel message will not make friends, fill their wallets, or grow mega-churches. This is outright fraud; it is the "Gospel of Me."[47]

Yes, the Sardis community sends their children to Christian schools, listens to the latest Christian music, and attends church on Sundays, but deep within this people, there is no real hunger for the Lord, no desire to spend personal time growing in the knowledge of the Lord. Sardis believers portray an appearance of spirituality to the world, but God sees into the heart and knows that the Spirit does not reside there. All their works are dead in His sight. How easily people can become attendees of church, rather than abiders in Christ, as programs and routines replace a relationship with Him. This church is no different from any worldly club or organization that continually offers great programs to the community.[48] It is a fraudulent direction these leaders are taking, and it is leading many down the broad road toward destruction. Unless they awake and repent, they will not be prepared for His soon coming, and it will be frightening for this segment of Christianity and especially their leadership.

THE CHURCH OF PHILADELPHIA IN AMERICA
(Revelation 3:7-13)

Like the church in Smyrna, this was a church beloved by the Lord, who spoke no words of condemnation toward it. A passion for the Lord was the primary focus of their service. It was a church of "little strength," which implies that it was a small congregation with little financial resources. Yet, it was a church that remained faithful to the truth of the gospel, even when they were continually ridiculed by the legalistic Jews, who probably represented great influence and wealth within the city. It takes great spiritual strength to continually proclaim the name of the Lord in the midst of ridicule and threats of persecution. Those who will stand for His truths in such circumstances are the true "overcomers" whom Jesus encourages throughout His letters to the churches.

Jesus told these Philadelphians that because they patiently kept the word of the Lord, He would keep them from the hour of trial that is coming on the whole world. Perhaps this was a church in a province of Asia Minor that was governed by Roman authorities who were not persecutors of Christianity. If so, the church in Philadelphia would likely have been aggressively active in sending forth missionaries throughout the Mediterranean world in the early centuries of Christian growth.

On the other hand, these words of Jesus to the Philadelphians commonly have been used to support the modern-day theory of a pretribulation rapture. Our first question regarding this should be: Why should the church of Smyrna be cast into the midst of tribulation, while the church of Philadelphia is excused? This "escapism doctrine" of modern-day "rapturists" is dangerous. It puts people to sleep, and the church that expects to be received in the air before the great tribulation does not prepare itself for the battle. And in the coming hour of temptation, many will run away.

Christ continually warns His people that this hour shall come and we must remain faithful to the end; for it is the faithful church that will have the strength to endure persecution. Jesus is not saying that the faithful church will be kept from tribulation but that in the midst of persecution, when the enemy rages and the temptation to deny the Lord is strong, the Lord will be alongside to encourage and strengthen His church so that it endures to the very end. It is quite possible that the church in Philadelphia was in a phase that preceded a coming persecution, a phase that the church in Smyrna had earlier experienced.[49]

THE CHURCH OF LAODICEA IN AMERICA
(Revelation 3:14-22)

What was missing in Laodicea is very similar to what is still missing in many congregations today: a relationship with Jesus Christ. Although the Lord continues to knock on the door, the Laodicean style of church remains oblivious to His knocking, believing that He is pleased with the various activities that continually occupy its time; it has learned to excel without the abiding presence of Christ.[50] The church, not the Lord, has won the hearts of this people. Their unspoken attitude may be verbalized as follows.

Wow, thanks, God, for the gospel of Jesus Christ. We can take it from here. We appreciate the greatness of Your sacrifice, but now we want to show You what we can do. By the way, if Jesus wants to come with us, He's sure welcome. Again, thanks. We'll let you know if we need any additional help.

When it comes to relationships, lukewarmness is the last thing a lover wants from his or her beloved. Lukewarm, mediocre, or average are not the types of expressions one wants to hear, especially regarding the one a person is about to marry. This is like a woman who dates a man but refuses to marry him because she has other priorities she wants to pursue. Instead, she engages in an off-and-on, shallow relationship with him, keeping him on a string but never really committing to him.

The leaders within this form of church are Christians who know about Him and understand foundational theology, but if anyone speaks with them about pursuing a deeper relationship with Jesus, that one will quickly be labeled a charismatic fanatic. This is a very controlling leadership, and those people who disagree with their direction for the church are strongly encouraged to leave. Their inherent belief is "as long as one's sins are confessed, and the person is baptized and identified with a church congregation, that is all that is necessary." They confess a belief in Jesus, but in actuality, how can one believe in someone they don't really know? Contrary to what they say, the priorities of these church leaders are not intimacy with Christ but watching Sunday attendance climb, along with the size of the offering. More time is spent *organizing* programs than *agonizing* in intercessory prayer. Intercessors give way to intellectuals, and businessmen now run the church like a business.[51] The Laodicean church of today must awaken to the fact that baptism and church attendance is not the end but the very beginning of an ever-progressing relationship with the Lord. We need to become not only His subjects but also His children. He is our Lord and King, but He's also our Father. Yet, despite the lukewarmness of today's Laodiceans, Christ continues to knock on the door of their hearts. But, unless the individuals of this church awaken and respond to His knocking, they will remain lukewarm, and thus a terrifying time lies ahead. He will spit them out of His mouth, for this is a church that is nauseating to the Lord.

Many of the members of a Laodicean or Sardis church have common parallels with the Israelites, when they were delivered out of Egypt only to begin a challenging journey through the wilderness. They were very excited and worshipped the Lord when they were delivered across the Red Sea; but as they experienced the bitter waters in the wilderness, they grumbled and complained that the life of slavery in Egypt was far better than the wilderness journey. It is so easy to express joy when things are going well, and this is exactly the scenario that the American church attempts to maintain. We can praise the Lord during a Sunday morning worship service, but do Christians continue to praise Him in the midst of life's wilderness journey? The lukewarm church does not comprehend that it is the wilderness journey that tests and strengthens the hearts of God's people, and thus there is little equipping in these churches for the Christian wilderness journey. This form of leadership simply preaches all the good things that God will do but fails to prepare people for the certainty of a wilderness journey.

While contemplating the differences between churches like Smyrna and the Sardis/Laodicean style of leadership, I was reminded of the following experience of Al Houghton, a minister of the gospel and a former Navy pilot who flew combat missions in Vietnam.

During combat in Vietnam, most of the time is spent in routine tasks, but attack can come suddenly. When hours of routine boredom is turned into 10 minutes of panic, two very visible and dramatically different groupings of men emerged. One group (Smyrna) had already made their decision, "this war is worth the sacrifice of our lives" while the other (Sardis/Laodicea) was somewhere in "limbo land" having not yet made any real commitment. The first group functioned without the paralysis of fear and was empowered to do what was necessary to save lives. Those in the second group were literally "locked up" and looked like they were swimming in molasses. Fear is the spiritual heritage of the unprepared. Fear will be eclipsed by faith if we will embrace the covenant promises of eternal life.[52]

Semper Fi, Al!

The Laodicean church is commonplace in America today; they have repackaged God so as to make Him user-friendly. The God who deeply desires a relationship with His bride and is jealous for His holiness has been elbowed aside and replaced by a happier-faced model of Christ, who always smiles approvingly at whatever we say or do.[53] How could anyone who has met the living God, the all-consuming fire, become lukewarm about Him?[54]

THE "ATTRACTIONAL" CHURCH IN AMERICA

Most contemporary churches probably started out well. They were planted by a pastor motivated for God and in the beginning spent much time in prayer and studies. Unfortunately, many of them get caught up in their success and begin to spend less and less time in their relationship with Christ while spending more and more time building their respective ministries. As they continue down this road, they may soon find themselves loving the Bible more than the Author of the Bible. Knowing the Bible is not the same thing as knowing God, and reading the Bible is not the same thing as hearing from God. The Pharisees knew the Bible, loved the Bible, and read the Bible, but they did not know, love, or hear God.[55]

Eventually, these churches develop techniques of administration and marketing used in the business world. They develop a message of easy-believism that is inoffensive; they market salvation like a life insurance policy; they emphasize attendance and giving as most important in their walk with Christ; and they develop entertaining and fun services that will keep the people coming. Thus, the assurance of salvation is provided to seeds sown on "rocky ground" and in "thorny bushes" rather than alerting them to the dangers of the soil they reside in; it certainly smells like "Sardis and Laodicea"!

Now allow me to share a vision, not a dream, that I received from the Lord in 1982.

Early in the morning, during a period of intercession before the Lord, suddenly a trancelike vision appeared before me which depicted the church in the form of a huge, gloriously white, round rock emanating a beautiful, heavenly light. I immediately fell in love with what I was seeing, but as I began to move toward it, I discovered that a black, octopus-like demon was attached to the bottom of the rock. I suddenly became angry at this invasion on the church, and as I continued toward it, I saw its tentacles progressively moving up and throughout the rock until only a small remnant of the church (the light) remained and the black monster was continuing to go after it. At this point the vision ended, and as I came out of the trance, I was weeping uncontrollably, knowing that I was experiencing the emotions of the heart of the Lord Jesus.

Over the years, I've come to understand the deeper meaning of this vision that was received some twenty-five years ago. The "rock" is the church of the present era and the black tentacles are the world's culture, which, over the past two decades, has rapidly invaded the church and extinguished much of its glorious light. The remaining light is the holy remnant of God's people who will be prepared to stand and carry out His missions during the time of coming tribulation to the world, to America, and to the church. It will be hard to fight against this darkness and release increasingly more light into the world, but it will be fought by those passionate warriors of the Lord who are fully committed to battle against this darkness, without compromise, even to the end of their lives. These are brothers and sisters whose life purpose is to glorify the Lord Jesus and thus, are solidly committed to battle for the kingdom of light in the midst of a dark world—without regard for the personal cost.

A MARINE'S VIEW OF THE
PRETRIBULATION RAPTURE

The pretribulation rapture is a modern-day teaching that has helped create the mega-churches within America. It was originally developed in England by John Nelson Darby, who helped found the Plymouth Brethren movement back in the mid-1800s, and was subsequently popularized in this country by C. I Scofield, a wealthy American attorney who published the *Scofield Reference Bible* in the early 1900s—which contained notes that emphasized this teaching. The Scofield Bible became very popular among evangelicals, many of whom failed to see the difference between a man-made commentary and the inspired Word of God since it was all included in a single book. Today millions of books promoting this pretribulation rapture teaching have been published and sold worldwide. Also, many seminaries, bible colleges, and churches teach this as being a foundational truth to understanding God's love for His people. It is a popular teaching of mega-ministries, and it has proved extremely profitable for a few in these leadership positions—thus it is promoted in many of the Sardis and Laodicean-style churches of America. This is a teaching that has seriously weakened the contemporary American church, for it has contributed mightily to the popularity of other false gospel messages commonly known as the "easy-believism and prosperity doctrines," which also employ attractional tactics to build their respective ministries. Pretribulation rapture teachings certainly appear to be one of the "myths" that the Lord's Word has warned us about.

> *For the time is coming when people will not endure sound teaching, but having itching ears they will accumulate for themselves teachers to suit their own passions, and <u>will turn away from listening to the truth and wander off into myths.</u> As for you, always be sober-minded, endure suffering, do the work of an evangelist, fulfill your ministry. (**2 Timothy 4:3-5**)*

These pretribulation rapture teachings provide a false degree of comfort to those who correctly discern the "signs of the times" but are fearful of becoming involved, for they know instinctively that they are not ready. They certainly love reading popular books and watching various movies concerning tribulation-era events, but only if they are continually being assured that they are only reading and watching and will not be participants. Thus, they embrace the luke-warm churches and the television celebrities who emphasize this escapist doctrine. In truth, it is putting the church at ease when, in fact, it should be spiritually preparing itself for the greatest battle in the history of mankind. It is a teaching that robs the church of much of the truth of warfare, for it is embraced by those who wish to be served by God rather than be servants of God. Jesus did fore-warn His people concerning doctrines such as this when He stated that in the last days, "many false prophets will arise and lead many astray."[56]

Being a retired Marine Corps officer who spent two tours in the war zones of Vietnam, I disrespect this pretribulation rapture myth for being a wimpy sales presentation designed to please those who are scared of potential conflict. Marines don't leave people behind on the battlefield, and I do get passionately angry when I see Jesus being portrayed as a Commander who calls His people to run from the battle. Jesus Christ is the manliest of men who ever walked this earth, and "retreat" is not in His vocabulary. I can truthfully tell you that in my personal time before the Lord, I have prayerfully requested that if a pretribulation rapture is somehow true for a specific remnant, please leave me behind to stand in support of my Christian and Israelite brothers and sisters who must endure the tribulation.

Imagine being a warrior in the Army of God who was raptured before the great battle begins. How would you feel in the presence of those who, in the midst of the battle, were martyred for the testimony of God? Are those who escape tribulation by being raptured more privileged in God's eyes than they were? Personally, I believe that I would be eternally ashamed to stand alongside my martyred brothers and sisters if I were among the privileged saints who were raptured. Cowards certainly don't think like this; they are just grateful to not have to experience pain and hardships and to teach others that they too can escape the battlefield.

Warriors need to understand that the end-time tribulation is like birth pangs that bring something positive into the world. The tribulation gives birth to the second coming of Jesus, and there can be no birth without pain. The tribulation is not something for believers to enjoy; however, it is not something for us to escape from either. A wonderful purpose for a tribulation is to present an opportunity for lost people to come to repentance, for it is a period of time that will bring in the final harvest. For when God's judgments fall on the world, many will turn to righteousness.[57] Thus, God's warriors need to embrace this opportunity, for it is the most important mission we could possibly be assigned.

CONSEQUENCES OF PRETRIBULATION RAPTURE TEACHINGS

Now, this pretribulation rapture theory is more than simple error; it is a deception that can do great damage to one's faith. Generations of American Christians have been watching the early birth pangs, convinced by their teachers that the next coming event would be the rapture of the church. Yet, in reality, what is coming is intense persecution for those who hold fast to their faith in Christ. A consequence of this mythical teaching will be widespread disillusionment when tribulation descends on this nation and people will realize that they have been deceived by their teachers. There will be a great falling away, and many former churchgoers will align with the world in blaming God for allowing such catastrophe to take place and will then betray many who remain in the fellowship of the church.

Now for those teachers who have grown up believing the doctrine of a "secret rapture," consider this: It is better to warn believers to be ready for the "Great Tribulation" and then discover that they will not go through it than to tell them they need not be prepared for it and then find that they should have been. All false prophecies are dangerous, and this one carries particular risks. Consider the following testimony of Corrie Ten Boom, who was imprisoned by the German Nazis for hiding Jews from their persecutors. After the war, she spent time as a missionary to the Far East. She wrote,

I have been in countries where the saints are already suffering terrible persecution. In China, the Christians were told: "Don't worry, before the tribulation comes, you will be translated, raptured." Then came a terrible persecution. Millions of Christians were tortured to death. Later I heard a bishop from China say, sadly: "We have failed. We should have made the people strong for persecution rather than telling them Jesus would come first." Turning to me, he said: "Tell the people how to be strong in times of persecution, how to stand when the tribulation comes—to stand and not faint." I feel I have a divine mandate to go and tell the people of this world that it is possible to be strong in the Lord Jesus Christ. We are in training for the tribulation. Since I have already gone through prison for Jesus' sake, and since I met that bishop from China, now every time I read a good Bible text I think: "Hey, I can use that in the time of tribulation." Then I write it down and learn it by heart.[58]

MIGHTY MEN WITHIN THE
DISPENSATIONAL COMMUNITY

I do want to mention that several fine men of God, who have been educated in pretribulation rapture doctrines, are among the very best Christian teachers concerning ongoing current events in the twenty-first century. I truly admire and thank men like Hal Lindsey, David Reagan, Chuck Missler, Joel Rosenberg, and others for their tremendously fruitful works. These are "watchmen" in the Army of God. They have provided significant strategic information for the American church over the last thirty years. Hal Lindsey's movie *The Late Great Plant Earth* had a tremendous impact upon me when I was still an unbeliever. So, I'm very thankful for men like Hal Lindsey and Greg Laurie, who, unknowingly, pointed me in a direction leading to a tremendous born-again experience that occurred in 1979. Over the last thirty years, dispensationalists have been the most prominent teachers of the great tribulation events that lie shortly before us. They had the advantage of teaching hard truths without scaring their listeners because of the "rapture" beliefs. Unfortunately, much of their message is falling upon "itchy ears" that see no need to prepare. This is a great danger that I perceive will soon confront the American churches.

THE FRONTLINES OF THE BATTLEFIELD

Jesus is a great army Commander who is giving instructions to His soldiers; however, some of the officers under His command are giving contrary instructions, preparing for a massive retreat. A soldier preparing for war is very different from the one who thinks he will be discharged shortly before the war begins. Many believers today are like soldiers looking forward to an early discharge. Can you imagine David or Joshua preparing their soldiers to retreat when the heat turns up? Can you imagine Peter or Paul looking to escape from preaching the gospel because persecution was coming?[59] Christians must internalize this tough command of Jesus when He tells us that we need to remain faithful even unto death.[60]

Over the last fifty years in America, every war we have fought has produced three groups of people within this nation.[61]

- The first group comprises those who willingly, proudly, and bravely step up to answer the call of their country with honor.
- The second group is comprised of pacifists—those people who will not fight but neither will they protest.
- The third group is the antiwar demonstrators, who rebel against the call of their country and ridicule those who answer the call.

There is an interesting parallel between these three groups and the three groups that compose the American church of today. For example:

- The first group comprises the Army of God. They are very passionate for their Lord and are prepared to lay down their lives if called upon to do so. These are the true warriors who will journey through the wilderness in order to align with their brothers and sisters in the churches of Smyrna and Philadelphia.
- The second group regularly attends church and Bible studies, but they have little personal vision for ministry. They are content to elect leadership that will be responsible for the church's direction, and they don't feel much of a need to be personally involved. They support their pastor's vision and rely upon the words from the pulpit to guarantee their eternal destiny. They just want to sit and wait to go to heaven someday. Some belong to the church in Ephesus and others to Laodicea.
- The third group actively opposes any talk of warfare. "Make love, not war" is the motto within their hearts. However, their concept of the love of God is not a true, life-changing love but is a false love that leads people away from the fertile soil that produces true disciples of God. Their concern is to not offend people and hurt their feelings, and they repeatedly emphasize that Christ already has accomplished the victory

for us; so, we just need to be faithful in our tithing and church attendance, and He will provide for all of our needs. They love the churches in Sardis and Laodicea.

How will each of these groups respond when suddenly, like a thief in the night, catastrophic events occur that destroy this nation's economy and cause the loss of a great number of lives and robs us completely of the freedom that we once enjoyed? Will tremendous confusion abound with people crying, "Why have we not been raptured?" Which groups will be disillusioned with church leadership and begin to align with the world in blaming God for allowing such catastrophes to take place? How will they respond when, like Nazi Germany, Russia, and China, the Bible will be outlawed and those who refuse to deny the Lord Jesus will be persecuted? What will persecution look like? Historically, there has been a confiscation of assets, a separation of families into concentration camps, and execution for those who refuse to deny Christ? How are those who embraced the pretribulation rapture theory going to respond—with deep humility or more like the world because of their anger toward their rapturist-teaching pastors and their disappointment in being a part of a tribulation era? Certainly such events will cause a great apostasy, as many forsake their former beliefs and betray their former friends and family members.

Christians, a time of decision lies shortly before us: During a period of intense tribulation, will we be among those who "will fall away and betray one another?"

And then many will fall away and betray one another and hate one another. And many false prophets will arise and lead many astray. And because lawlessness will be increased, the love of many will grow cold. (Matthew 24:10-12)

Or, will our hearts respond with Isaiah's words?

My soul yearns for you in the night; my spirit within me earnestly seeks you. For when your judgments are in the earth, the inhabitants of the world learn righteousness. (Isaiah 26:9)

Will we see the persecution as an opportunity to honor Christ?

Blessed are you when others revile you and persecute you and utter all kinds of evil against you falsely on my account. Rejoice and be glad, for your reward is great in heaven, for so they persecuted the prophets who were before you. *(Matthew 5:11-12)*

We are approaching some difficult times ahead as the second coming of Jesus Christ appears to be rapidly approaching. There is a wake-up call from the Lord that is becoming louder and louder, and many are hearing it. Our Lord is searching for warriors who can hear this call and lead His people though the approaching era of end-time events. An old message is being refreshed: The church is being called to the battlefield.

GOD'S ARMY IS STRICTLY FOR VOLUNTEERS ONLY

Our Commander in Chief does not draft His soldiers, but He opens His arms and welcomes all those who volunteer. He does not employ emotional gimmickry but simply speaks out of love and calls each of us to join Him on the battlefield. Although he calls us to join Him in His battle against the forces of evil, He leaves us free to join the enemy against him if we so will. He makes no promises that we will become rich or escape pain in this life. The belief that His army will be entirely free from injuries, strife, pain, and poverty is an invention of the "health-and-wealth" gospel that is not found in Scripture or in the Christian experience. As volunteer soldiers in His army, like our Lord, we will grieve and bleed and perhaps lose our lives for our brothers and sisters who are not yet freed from the enemy. However, we are promised the ultimate victory, and if we fight, His pleasure will rest upon us. Our Lord does not encourage us to join Him simply because we want to be on the winning team, but He wants us to join because we believe in the righteousness of His cause. Volunteers also must understand that we will die in our faith, while not really receiving all of God's promises in this life.

This is not an armchair war, and it will be very difficult for many in our generation to make the adjustment from being spectators to becoming active participants. One of the consequences of television is that it turns us into "watchers" of world events so that our involvement is simply passive. Many Christians get so carried away with the final victory that they remain blind to the ongoing battle, and the oil in their lamps slowly fritters away. We all need to understand that the way to eternal life with Christ involves the way of the cross. And the way of the cross means there is a great battle to be fought. Who are they who will fall away under the pressure of warfare in these last days? They are the armchair churchgoers who refuse to enlist in the Army of God under such harsh terms. It is extremely challenging to be on the side of Christ in this life.[62]

GOD'S WARRIORS ARE NOT TRADITIONAL

Man's traditions are comfortable for many but not for the warrior spirit in God's chosen leaders. There appears to be a growing awareness among Christians who possess leadership traits (though they may not have official positions within their church) that the traditional American church is not really the frontlines of the battlefield, nor should it be. The frontlines of the battle are in all those places where Christians live out their lives: with their family, with their neighbors and friends, and in their workplaces. These places are where individuals live the bulk of their lives and thus is where the battles rage. One may spend a few hours per week within the confines of the church or in a Bible study, but this is for equipping us for the battle. The actual fight is engaged in all those places where one spends time. The equipping that is very common in the American church is simply teaching people to bring family and friends into the church so they can hear a forty-minute sermon message and, hopefully, accept Jesus as their personal Savior. Then they are released into a world where they spend from fifty to one hundred hours of their week listening and watching mainstream media presentations. Think about it: what is going to have the most effect in a person's life? The church is being increasingly invaded by the world's values and is becoming weaker and weaker, and it is time to awaken to the sound of the battle and lay aside traditional habits and equip Christian warriors for the fight. Christians need to hear and respond to this command of Jesus: "About-face!"

"ABOUT - FACE!"

Those with military experience are very familiar with the command "about-face." It is a command to immediately turn sharply 180 degrees from the direction you are currently facing. It is also a command used by our Commander in Chief, who calls us to "turn" from our sins. When we obey that command, He will remove the veil that is blinding us from the truth and put us on the path of growing in spiritual maturity. This willingness to turn in an "about-face" will suddenly cause us to see ourselves as we truly are and thus see our need for a Savior. All of God's champions occasionally will go astray and veer from the course that the Lord directs. However, like Moses, David, or Paul, they all have one thing in common: when confronted with their blindness, they will readily turn in an "about-face" and return to following their Commander.

What will Christians do when our Commander in Chief commands us to "about-face"? Will they obey Him or listen to other subordinate commanders, such as some church leaders who tell us that the Commander in Chief really meant "right-face" since it is much easier to follow that path. But a partial turn eventually will lead us away from the path that Jesus is going, and even though other leaders tell us that we are moving rightly, we are straying farther and farther from His direction. Additionally, these other commanders may convince us that the command was really "at-ease": just keep coming and giving to the church, and God will be pleased. Eventually, the time comes when the Commander in Chief gives the command, "Forward march." Only those who have heard and obeyed the command "about-face" will be equipped to follow the King of Kings and the Lord of Lords in the direction He is heading.[63]

CHAPTER 4

HORSEMEN, MARTYRDOM, AND A GREAT WAR
(Revelation 4—6; Ezekiel 38—39)

Jesus Christ, our Commander in Chief, has provided His soldiers with detailed intelligence concerning those events that will precede His return to reign over the nations of the earth. It reveals unparalleled disasters that will shortly be released upon the earth. He commanded His apostle John to record this information, and certainly one of the main objectives of this intelligence is to provide the people of this generation the opportunity to train and prepare for the raging battles that will attempt to overthrow the kingdom of God and establish a one-world government—a government designed to rid the earth of all who oppose their ungodly objectives. This also will be a time when famines, plagues, fires, earthquakes, and horrific deaths will affect billions of people throughout the nations—a time when rioting and chaos will be unimaginable—a time when the entire world will appear out of control.

Yet, this also will be a time of opportunity for that discerning Christian remnant who will *hear and believe* that He is speaking to them, telling them *to prepare* to stand for the kingdom of God in the midst of these horrendous tribulations. This intelligence primarily has been recorded in the book of Revelation, which is an inspired writing that has confused many in the church over the centuries; yet it promises great blessings to those who will believe and keep the words of this prophetic book.

*And behold, I am coming soon. Blessed is the one who keeps the words of the prophecy of this book. (**Revelation 22:7**)*

Much of the confusion that has arisen in attempts to understand eschatology over the centuries is the result of generations of Christians who could not relate these writings to their respective cultures. However, in our generation technology has developed to a degree that provides us with the ability to relate descriptive events recorded 2,000 years ago with our twenty-first century culture. Likewise, over 2,500 years ago, the prophet Daniel saw similar events that would confront our present generation, and he was so grieved in his search for understanding that a messenger from the Lord told him to seal up his visions for they were intended for those who live at the "time of the end," when mankind's *technological knowledge will greatly increase* to the point that *communications and travel throughout the world will be commonplace.*

But you, Daniel, shut up the words and seal the book, until the time of the end. <u>Many shall run to and fro, and knowledge shall increase.</u>" (Daniel 12:4)

Additionally, Daniel was told who would understand those times and who would not.

*He said, "Go your way, Daniel, for <u>the words are shut up and sealed until the time of the end</u>. Many shall purify themselves and make themselves white and be refined, but the wicked shall act wickedly. <u>And none of the wicked shall understand, but those who are wise shall understand</u>. (**Daniel 12:9-10**)*

Both John and Daniel were shown events that will soon descend upon the world like a "thief in the night," and they were told to record them so that future enlistees in the Army of God, who would use this intelligence to discern these times, would prepare to stand for the kingdom of God. The large majority of mankind in both the church and the nations will be overwhelmed by sudden and unexpected catastrophic events that will forever change their habitual lifestyles, from a life rooted in relative ease and comfort, to one of extreme hardships with many challenges that must be confronted in order to survive.

Christian soldiers need to be equipped and ready to be deployed into their respective missional assignments that await them. The following words are meant to encourage this army of warriors.

Those who are wise shall shine like the brightness of the sky above; and those who turn many to righteousness, like the stars forever and ever. (Daniel 12:3)

However, in order for Christians to voluntarily enlist in this endeavor, they need to have a foundational understanding of the battles that are coming and the objective of the mission to which they are called. The following chapters are designed to provide a clearer understanding of these challenging events, as viewed through our twenty-first-century eyes, and to provide clarity as to our missional responsibilities during this period of time. The Lord's desire for us is not ignorance of His plans but rather knowledge so that we may prepare the eyes and ears of our hearts through prayer and fasting, whereby He will draw closer to us and become our place of guidance and refuge during this period of severe hardships. Leaders in the Army of God must be committed prayer warriors if they are to have the discernment to understand the times and the commands that they will receive from their Commander in Chief.

As we move forward in the sequence of events recorded in the book of Revelation, let us now continue our quest for understanding by joining with the apostle John as he stands before the throne of God.

THE FATHER GIVES THE SCROLL TO HIS SON
(Revelation 4 and 5)

As John's adventure in the throne room of heaven begins to unfold, he finds himself standing before the throne of almighty God, the highest sovereign of heaven and earth. Obviously, John was overwhelmed by these majestic surroundings in the throne room of God, but when he had calmed somewhat, he noticed a "scroll" held in the right hand of Him who sat upon the heavenly throne. This scroll had writing on both sides, which suggests that events contained within affect both the heavenly and earthly realms; and it also was completely sealed by seven seals.[64] Suddenly a strong angel cries out, "Who is worthy to break the seals and open the scroll?" When no man was found worthy in all of heaven or earth to open the scroll, John was deeply grieved, for he realized that this scroll was of tremendous importance for the manifestation of the coming kingdom of God throughout the earth. Suddenly a Man appeared who was found worthy. It was Jesus Christ, symbolized by a Lamb as though it had been slain. This tells us it was only by His sacrificial death that even this Son of almighty God could qualify to take the scroll from the right hand of His Father and to break open the seven seals, revealing the events that precede the second coming of Jesus Christ to establish the fullness of His kingdom on the earth.

A FALSE PERCEPTION OF THE "LAMB OF GOD"

A false perception of the person of Jesus Christ has been presented by the religiosity of popular church organizations over the centuries. He is portrayed over and over as a little baby in a manger or as weak-looking, effeminate man walking around in a bathrobe with a halo over his head and little baby angels flying all around, singing to Him. The perception of heaven is a place where the "saved" sit on clouds playing musical harps and singing songs forever and ever. Disney World and some Christian movies also have joined with these phony churches in their depiction of the person of Jesus and the angels of heaven. Medieval artworks embraced by churches and cartoonists have seriously weakened the truth that Jesus Christ was the greatest and strongest of warriors who ever walked this earth. These false images certainly don't appeal to many unsaved men who are searching for a strong Leader to provide direction in their lives. The masculine spirit that has not found the true Jesus certainly does not want to follow a "wimpy lord" or live in a "heaven" like that described above. Men, this is a false portrayal of our Lord and His angelic armies. Angels under the command of Jesus Christ are not "wimpy pacifists," for they have historically killed tens of thousands of the enemies of God's people.[65] Also, the response of even the holiest men of God is one of trembling and fear when they are confronted by the glorious presence of our Lord or one of His mighty angels. He is mighty and powerful, and yet He possesses such a deep love for His people that it is just incomprehensible.[66]

A CHRISTIAN WARRIOR'S UNDERSTANDING OF THE "LAMB OF GOD"

Jesus Christ is also the "Lion of Judah," who, out of His infinite love for mankind, left the glory of heaven to experience the depths of humiliation upon the earth. He voluntarily left His throne and the presence of His Father and all the citizens of heaven who dearly loved Him in order to receive scorn, hatred, and rejection among the governmental authorities and the religious leaders of mankind and ultimately to die on a cross between two thieves. This occurred over two thousand years ago, when He pulled back the curtain of eternity and stepped out onto the stage of time for approximately thirty-three years, and then He stepped back again into eternity. But in that one brief moment of time, He sealed the fate and fixed the destiny of every man and woman. He split history and divided the ages. Jesus Christ is the "Word of God" who became flesh and dwelt among us, and now He is the only way that one can enter the kingdom of heaven and live eternally in His presence. False religions and false teachers say that there are different paths that can lead to eternal life, but He has said that there is only one way to the Father, and that is through His Son, Jesus Christ. There is no other way! He is the

Alpha and Omega, the Beginning and the End. He was dead, but He is now alive forevermore and is currently seated at the right hand of almighty God, His Father.

THE LAMB OF GOD IS ALSO OUR COMMANDER IN CHIEF

Although He is the one and only way to eternal life, and those who receive Him as their eternal Savior are redeemed by this precious blood of the "Lamb of God," He is also the "Lion of Judah." He is a truly mighty Leader who would never delegate assignments to His people that He Himself wouldn't readily embrace—a Commander whom true Christian warriors will readily follow no matter what the danger, what battles have to be confronted, or what costs have to be paid.

Now the days are rapidly approaching when a tremendous separation will take place among mankind. Soldiers in His army will walk through the valley of the shadow of death without a semblance of fear, for He will be with us. And after His victory over the kingdom of darkness, all people who have ever lived will stand before God our Father; and those who have denied Him will be cast into outer darkness, but His sons and daughters, who have been "born again" in the Spirit, will join Him in the eternal kingdom. What will this eternal kingdom be like? It is so wondrous that no eye has seen, no ear has heard, neither has it entered into the mind of man what God our Father and our Lord Jesus have prepared for those of us who are redeemed by His blood, which was shed for us.[67] Yet, during this present era of warfare, He reigns as our Commander in Chief, and His name continues to be the battle cry for those warriors who fight daily for righteousness and truth.

His name is Jesus, our Lord and our King. And true Christian warriors will follow Him anywhere and forever. These are warriors whose deepest desire in this life is to love Him with all of their hearts, all of their souls, all of their minds, and all of their strength.[68] Semper Fi, Commander Jesus!

BREAKING THE SEALS OF THE SCROLL

Now, as our Lord Jesus proceeds to break the seals of the scroll, it appears to have two effects. First, it provides us with a clearer view of the purposes of God regarding events that will usher in the kingdom of God throughout the earth, and, second, it physically launches these events in a chronological order. Thus, we observe the launching of a new era with the opening of this scroll, an era in which events will be released that eventually will climax with the coming of the kingdom of God in its fullness.[69]

Now there is a triune series of catastrophic events that are released by the power of our Lord within which much of our discussion will be centered. They are normally referred to as the breaking of the "seven seals," the blowing of the "seven trumpets," and the pouring out of the "seven bowls of the wrath of God." Now the seven seals do not retain their character as seals, for the seventh seal is revealed as seven trumpets, and the seventh trumpet is manifested as the seven bowls of wrath. Looking at the three series together, there is obviously intensification in their severity until that day when the Lord Himself descends from heaven with His army. Additionally, there appears to be acceleration as the events unfold; the seven seals seem quite spread out in time, while the subsequent series of trumpets and bowls appear to be measured in months or even days. Therefore, it appears as if the three series are successive; that is, they follow on the heels of one another.[70] Finally, there are very important interludes within this succession of events. Whereas the threefold series of seals, trumpets, and bowls are primarily concerned with what will happen to the world, the interludes give us insight into how God's people are affected during this tremendous upheaval.

THE SEVEN SEALS—AN OVERVIEW

The opening of the scroll is intended to reveal to this generation the main aspects of our future, as well as the history of the Christian era, as these forces cooperate to bring the kingdom of Christ to its perfect consummation. The spreading of the gospel of Jesus Christ has been the leading factor in shaping the course of Western civilization throughout the last two millennia. In fact, the history of the leading nations of the world is practically the history of Christianity, whereas those nations that have been uninfluenced by the gospel have had no contributing part in the development of civilization. Their condition is best described as one of age-long stagnation.[71]

The breaking of the first four seals began in the first century at the time the gospel of Christ first went out into the world, or very shortly thereafter. Their great power continues to affect the world to this day. Christ refers to these afflictions as "merely the beginning of birth pangs"; yet they appear to continue right up to the period of the great tribulation.

All these are but the beginning of the birth pains. Then they will deliver you up to tribulation and put you to death, and you will be hated by all nations for my name's sake. (Matthew 24:8-9)

As will be discussed shortly, the sixth and seventh seals have not yet been broken, but their time is rapidly approaching. First, let's look at the parallelism between the openings of these seals and the events that Jesus described to His disciples on the Mount of Olives.

THE OLIVET DISCOURSE AND THE SIX SEALS OF THE SCROLL

It was approximately sixty years since the gospel of Jesus Christ had been launched powerfully into the world when John witnesses our Lord opening the seals of His Father's scroll. As the first four seals are broken, four horsemen emerge with individual missions designed to thwart the gospel message throughout the Christian era. There is a difference among commentators as to the identity of the first horseman riding the white horse. Some believe this represents the gospel of Jesus Christ going forth into the world, and they have generally sound arguments supporting this belief. However, there is also sound argument supporting the view that this rider is going forth with the message of the false gospel. This is the most probable scenario since it appears as if the opening of the first six seals corresponds with Jesus' teachings on the Mount of Olives concerning events that would usher in the end-times.

Note the following parallelism with the opening of the first six seals with Matthew 24 and/or Luke 21:

The First Seal Releases the Rider on the "White Horse"

For many will come in my name, saying, "I am the Christ," and they will lead many astray. (Matthew 24:5)

See that you are not led astray. For many will come in my name, saying, "I am he!" and, "The time is at hand!" Do not go after them. (Luke 21:8)

White Horse Mission: To distort the message of the gospel and establish false religions.

The Second Seal Releases the Rider on the "Red Horse"

And you will hear of wars and rumors of wars. See that you are not alarmed, for this must take place, but the end is not yet. For nation will rise against nation, and kingdom against kingdom. (Matthew 24:6-7(a))

And when you hear of wars and tumults, do not be terrified, for these things must first take place, but the end will not be at once. (Luke 21:9)

Red Horse Mission: To cause continuing warring between nations and kingdoms throughout the Christian era.

The Third Seal Releases the Rider on the "Black Horse"

> *There will be famines and earthquakes in various places. All these are but the beginning of the birth pains.* (***Matthew 24:7(b)-8***)

Black Horse Mission: To cause continuing social unrest within nations and kingdoms by utilizing earthly products to maintain enmity between the rich and the poor. Seasons of famine will bring great social unrest and anger within nations. Hurricane Katrina is a modern-day example in America.

The Fourth Seal Releases the Rider on the "Pale Horse"

> *There will be great earthquakes, and in various places famines and pestilences. And there will be terrors and great signs from heaven.* (***Luke 21:11***)

Pale Horse Mission: To bring about all forms of unnatural death that will continually affect one-fourth of the world's population.

The Fifth Seal Reveals the "Faithful Remnant Who Are Martyred" Because of Their Uncompromising Testimony of the Gospel of Jesus Christ.

> *Then they will deliver you up to tribulation and put you to death, and you will be hated by all nations for my name's sake. And then many will fall away and betray one another and hate one another. And many false prophets will arise and lead many astray.* (***Matthew 24:9-11***)

The Sixth Seal Releases Great "Cosmic Disturbances"

> *Immediately after the tribulation of those days the sun will be darkened, and the moon will not give its light, and the stars will fall from heaven, and the powers of the heavens will be shaken.* (***Matthew 24:29***)

And there will be terrors and great signs from heaven. (Luke 21:11(b))

THE COMBINED EFFECT OF THE FOUR HORSEMEN UPON THE WORLD
(Revelation 6:1-8)

The four horsemen that were released with the opening of the first four seals have simultaneously been making their drive throughout the earth from the beginning of the Christian era until the present day. They have repeatedly kept the world in turmoil and will continue to do so with even greater intensity until the kingdom of God comes in fullness.

The Christian church would like to believe that the Lord would not allow His people to be affected by the wars, famines, pestilences, and deaths that are caused by the release of the powers commonly referred to as the "Four Horsemen of the Apocalypse." Obviously, this is not the case, for all these forces are sent into the world in general and they affect all of mankind.[72] However, they do appear to affect the non-Christian nations of the world more adversely than those nations that profess a belief in Christianity.

When the "red horse" appears and brings bloodshed and wars, we, as well as the unbelieving world, see our sons go into battle, where many have and will suffer and die. The same is true of the "black horse," which brings drought, famine, and economic hardships. Whatever steps mankind takes, this economic law cannot be eliminated: as soon as wages increase, the prices of commodities also rise, and the economic division among the people remains the same; rich and poor continue. This causes divisions in society in the form of strikes, protests, uprisings, and so on. The "pale horse" also enters the homes of the righteous and wicked alike and brings death in all its various forms.

Although there is a certain level of protection that our Lord provides, these horsemen appear to exercise their influence upon all mankind without discrimination. We are naturally inclined to reason that the same causes have the same effects: that what is destructive to one segment of society also must be destructive to the other and what is a blessing to one must be equally a blessing to the other. If this were actually the case, nothing positive possibly could be accomplished by the four riders. Let's now examine how differently God's people handle devastations from how people of the world handle them.

SAME CAUSES—DIFFERENT EFFECTS

The Positive and Negative Effects of the White Horse

The proclamation of the true gospel message will have different effects on different people.

Upon the elect of God, it will mean a transformation from the powers of darkness into the kingdom of light. Thus, Christ's kingdom grows and is strengthened.

However, this same gospel will harden the hearts of the worldly and increase their hatred for God and His people. It will also open the door for many who refuse to embrace the person of Jesus Christ as the Son of God to embrace other religious systems, which accept many of the doctrines of Christianity but deny that Christ is the only way to eternal life. Such compromising liberal theology found in Roman Catholicism and several Protestant denominationally-oriented churches, together with many modern cult organizations that have crept into the Christian world over the past two hundred years, is leading millions of their followers down the broad road to eternal destruction. Additionally, the Islamic faith, which does not accept Christ as the Son of God, still erroneously believes that their Allah is the same as the God of Abraham and the Father of Jesus Christ. This view also is supported by many false teachers in the "compromised Christian churches," including the pope of Roman Catholicism.

The Positive and Negative Effects of the Red, Black, and Pale Horses

What is evil to the world may not be evil to the children of God. The same adversities caused by wars, famine, and death cause some to rise in rebellion and curse God while others in the same circumstance humble themselves and patiently seek God. Thus, the same affliction can harden some while it brings others to repentance and sanctifies them. The same tribulation that brings despair to some causes others to glorify God.

In summary then, what is the effect of the four horsemen upon mankind? They tend to cause a visible separation between the people of darkness and the people of light. The true church grows stronger and purer during times of intense trials, and, conversely, the ungodly grow deeper and stronger in their hatred toward God and His people. This has been a proven effect around the globe throughout the Christian era, and these trials will become even more intense as the world moves toward the second coming of our Lord and King.

A WORLD WITHOUT THE FOUR HORSEMEN

What would be the result for this worldly kingdom if the preaching of the gospel were not followed by the horsemen released by Christ as He broke open the seals of the scroll; or, in other words, what would be the result if there were no wars, no social struggles, and no death in all these forms? Probably the kingdom of darkness would reach the height of its development prematurely. That is, the sinful world, in its attempt to establish a united world kingdom, would soon succeed in organizing into an international federation of nations and would prematurely become this formidable world power that is pictured in the later chapters of the book of Revelation. All things would be under the control of this world power, and it would force the powers of church and state, of home and school, of business and commerce, to comply with the anti-Christian order of things.[73]

Additionally, this tremendous world power would leave no room for the true church of God on earth. It would persecute and, if possible, destroy the kingdom of God in the world. However, the time for all that is not yet, for there are many who are yet to be called out of the kingdom of the world into the kingdom of God. The time will come, and probably quite soon, when the Lord allows a partial realization of this anti-Christian world power to maintain itself for a brief time, and that time is prophesied to be most terrible for the citizens of God's kingdom, for they shall be social outcasts hated by the world. So terrible will be those latter days that even the elect would not persevere were it not that those days were shortened. But as long as nation rises against nation, the world power cannot realize itself, for the simple reason that it labors continually for its own survival amidst ongoing confusion and cannot organize itself in a one-world unity.

A CHRISTIAN PERSPECTIVE ON TRIBULATIONS

Obviously, citizens of the kingdom of God also suffer according to the flesh, for we too are grieved when our sons die on the battlefield, when our homes and jobs are taken from us, or when our loved ones fall into a sinful lifestyle. However, as we continue along our journey through the wilderness of life, we discover that our Lord sees persecution from a different perspective than we do. In fact, He instructs us over and over about expecting and handling persecution, for He knows that affliction brings great strength and maturity to His chosen people.[74] Additionally, He calls us not only to endure persecution from the world but also to actually accept it with great joy, realizing that the glory that awaits us is so great that present times of suffering and persecution are not even worthy of our concern.[75] Finally, the truth that we do not stand alone but are part of a worldwide army also should bring great courage and strength. Warriors need to understand that possessing a spirit of joy in the midst of persecution certainly will have an astonishing effect on those who persecute us and may even awaken many of them to the truth of God. We must remember who the real enemy is, and it is not the ones who physically persecute us. In fact, we should pray and mourn for them, for apart from repentance the destiny that awaits them is eternal suffering. It is Satan and his dark forces that are the enemy.[76]

The life of those in God's kingdom has always been one of persecution and hatred from the world. However, it has been proved that during times of tribulation the church has grown greater and stronger, for it is a time when the body of Christ turns fully to the Lord in intercessory prayer. The modern-day churches in China, Africa, the Middle East, and other parts of the world, which continually face life-threatening persecution, reveal tremendous growth and strength among their people. Such churches are obviously much stronger in their love and devotion to the Lord than those in our nation. It is undoubtedly much more difficult for the American Christian to live a fully committed life to the Lord than it would be if they lived in countries where they underwent continual persecution.

Christians realize that all things work together for good for those who love God.[77] In the midst of devastating and grievous circumstances and even when confronted with death, we are never harmed spiritually; for by faith we cling to our Lord, who has a much greater vision for each of us. Therefore, as we experience the trials of life, the eyes of our faith need to be focused more and more on the glory that awaits us. Now it is war, sin, and suffering, but presently it will be righteousness, holiness, peace, and joy when the kingdom of Christ comes. And as far as death is concerned, the pale horse is no terror but merely an instrument to transfer us to the state of glory in the house of many mansions that He has prepared for His people.[78]

So in times of war and trouble, famine and pestilence, when the red horse drives through the earth and the black horse appears in your streets or the pale horse enters into your home, let your heart rest in the power of our Lord Jesus Christ, who holds the scroll with the seven seals and controls all things in heaven and on earth. Remember Paul's words:

For I consider that the sufferings of this present time are not worth comparing with the glory that is to be revealed to us.
(Romans 8:18)

THE FIFTH SEAL—SOULS OF THE MARTYRS
(Revelation 6:9-11)

John now sees the souls of all of the Lord's martyrs as they rest in the presence of their Father who sits upon His throne. These are all those who had been slain for the word of God since the time of creation—and most certainly their numbers will continue to grow until the return of our Lord, Jesus Christ. A chief purpose of this seal is to clearly show that the martyrdom of saints is under the control of Jesus Christ and is a necessary element in the ongoing war with the enemies of the kingdom of God. The Bible passage literally says that they had been "butchered" for the Word of God by the enemies of Christ and His church. These are committed warriors in the Army of God who did not hide their light under a basket.[79] It is a fact that they not only testified to the Word of God but they also clung to it right up to the point of death.

A very long list of names certainly exists in heaven of those who were slain for the name and the truth of God in Christ Jesus our Lord. Consider the following.

- Those churches pictured in the book of Revelation—Smyrna, Pergamum, and Philadelphia—that were hated and persecuted for Christ's' name.
- The terrible persecutions under the Roman emperors, when those who confessed the name of Christ Jesus were literally butchered and tortured to death.
- The forerunners of the Reformation who refused to return to the mother church of Catholicism and were burned at the stake by that harlot church, which was responsible for the Dark Ages of the middle centuries.
- The countless Christians that are continually murdered in various sections of countries that embrace false religions; for example, China, India, Iran, Africa, etc.

They all suffered. They all were persecuted. They were driven from place to place. They were put on the rack and tortured in every conceivable way. They were brought to the scaffold and burned at the stake. As you go through history from its very dawn to the present time, you will find an innumerable host under the altar, slain for their love for God and His Son. And what is the reason for all this? It is an inevitable consequence of the tremendous battle continually being fought between two kingdoms striving for possession of the same world.

THE SPIRIT OF MARTYRDOM

Martyr actually is the Greek word used in the Bible for "witness." A "true spirit" of martyrdom is the willingness to risk all for the benefit of others.[80] I've seen this in action on the battlefield of Vietnam; Marines will not abandon their fellow Marines in the midst of battle. At a certain point in the heat of battle, we are more concerned about the life of another than we are about our own life. The "true spirit" of martyrdom is not about dying but about faithfulness; that is, it is about dying to self in order to accomplish the risky work of living for Jesus.[81]

What about the Muslim martyrs who are sent on suicidal missions in order to kill their supposed enemies in the name of their Allah? Well, look at their motive; it is intentional martyrdom for their own self-glory and what they envision as eternal, carnal delight. Yes, it is a witness unto death, but it is the "false spirit" of martyrdom. Christian martyrs die trying to "save you"; Muslim martyrs die trying to "kill you."[82] The true martyrs are those who lay down their lives for the cause of Christ. They are not the casualties of war; they are the victors. Like champions of God throughout history, they join with their brothers and sisters in the body of Christ who continue to "crush the head of Satan."[83]

The fifth-seal martyrs are those men and women who willingly lay down their lives bearing witness for the truth of the gospel of Jesus Christ without retreat or compromise. These martyred souls under the altar of God are not crying out for vengeance against their enemies but for the glory and righteousness of God, for whom they suffered unto death, to be strongly manifested to the world.

What is meant by "laying down one's life" for the cause of Christ? Just this: Christians who are threatened with being executed will be given an opportunity by their oppressors to deny Him. Certainly many have and will continue to deny Him out of fear for their lives, but the martyrs under the altar are those warriors who made the choice to stand for Christ in the face of death. True martyrdom is a powerful witness to the world; and through such sacrifice, many people turn and come into the kingdom of God. Christians in our generation also will be confronted with this decision, but they must remember this: the reward that awaits their uncompromising witness will be great.

> *Blessed are those who are persecuted for righteousness' sake, for theirs is the kingdom of heaven. Blessed are you when others revile you and persecute you and utter all kinds of evil against you falsely on my account. 12 Rejoice and be glad, for your reward is great in heaven, for so they persecuted the prophets who were before you.(**Matthew 5:10-12**)*

How long must the martyrs wait for the judgment of God to fall on the world? Until the number of all of their brethren who are yet to be killed, even as they were, is complete. In plain language, this simply means that the time is not yet ripe for God's judgment because there are still future witnesses (martyrs) for Christ whose testimony for the gospel must go forth. No, we do not have to seek martyrdom, but we must continue to bear testimony for the Word of God and the kingdom of His Christ. If we do, we may have the hope in our hearts that presently we shall receive the white robes of righteousness, holiness, and victory. Therefore, we need to understand that the enemy who persecutes us merely serves as an instrument to bring us to that eternal state of righteousness and holiness within the kingdom of our Lord. Remember this: potential martyrs for Christ need to maintain a deep joyfulness in the midst of the world's wickedness and persecution since they are tremendously valued in the eyes of God and the eternal reward that awaits them will be great. The Lord rules! He opens the seals, including the fifth one, and so not a hair on your head shall ever be touched against His will.

SCOFFERS WILL PRECEDE THE PERSECUTION OF AMERICAN CHRISTIANS

The time of the end will witness scoffers who deride any message concerning the return of Christ. We will see this as leftist politicians, major news media, many popular movie stars, as well as numerous compromising church leaders embrace worldly socialistic values and denounce the true Christian church as being a separatist, hate-filled, and uncompromising segment of society. When the churches in America are confronted with the choice of standing for Jesus Christ or suffering persecution from the government, many will fall away and betray their former friends who will not compromise their love for the Lord. Today's scoffers will soon become tomorrow's persecutors of the true believers and followers of Jesus Christ.

> *Then they will deliver you up to tribulation and put you to death, and you will be hated by all nations for my name's sake. And then many will fall away and betray one another and hate one another. And many false prophets will arise and lead many astray. And because lawlessness will be increased, the love of many will grow cold. But the one who endures to the end will be saved. And this gospel of the kingdom will be proclaimed throughout the whole world as a testimony to all nations, and then the end will come. (**Matthew 24:9-14**)*

The "gray area" of Christianity is disappearing, and today's churches will shortly be divided by light and darkness as the events described in the above passages accelerate. These are hard truths to handle, and the majority of Christians would rather ignore them with the hope it won't happen in their lifetime rather than face the truth and prepare for it as the Lord commanded. This is the situation in the churches that Christ's warrior leadership must boldly confront.

WHEN WILL THE LORD'S JUDGMENT COME?

The world has not yet shown its real character in the fullness of its hatred of God the Father and His Son, Jesus Christ. In the past, when witnesses for Christ were butchered, the human enemy was not so directly conscious that they rose up against the name of Jesus Christ. However, the time is coming when the world populace will be fully conscious that it is the hateful name of Jesus Christ that is the great obstacle for all their plans of globalization. This will be a time when more than just specific nations rise up against our Lord; it will be the entire world that visibly manifests its dark character. Tribulation and persecution of the saints in the future will become more universal in its character. In other words, the world will attack the true body of Christ fully conscious that it is making an attack on the holiness and the truth of God. There will be no more gray area between good and evil; one either stands with Him or against Him. Separation of the two kingdoms will become completely visible to all. It is at this point that the world is ripe for judgment.[84]

Yet, it will not occur in the United States until the government of this country, which was founded upon Christian values and later became the most influential and strongest nation on earth, joins with the rest of the world in its hatred toward true Christianity and the nation of Israel. Those with discernment understand that contemporary America is currently on the precipice of uniting against the Lord's people.

OPENING THE SIXTH SEAL
(Revelation 6:12-17)

This coming event certainly has to be the greatest and most frightening scenario in the material universe since the days of Noah and that great flood that engulfed the entire world. Yet, this modern-day catastrophe is much different from the flood in Noah's generation, since most of the world's population will initially survive, even though several million people undoubtedly will be killed. Obviously this event is yet future, since nothing as extraordinary as this has occurred in human history since the time that John received this vision. The opening of the sixth seal certainly will cause many of us to wonder how anyone can survive such a catastrophic event, and yet it is just the beginning of numerous catastrophic events that will soon follow.

Observe those who are hiding themselves and trembling in fear of almighty God and His Son, Jesus Christ, whom they now recognize as the King of the universe.[85] They are the mighty ones of the world, who controlled the world's finances and held positions of authority and thus dominated the social and political world. They are also strong in wisdom and learning, people who have always denied the Christ in their worldly philosophies and who, in their imagined strength, opposed and ridiculed the people of the Lord, who believed the message of the gospel.[86]

Eventually this powerful group of worldly leaders will acclimate to this season of chaotic events and will organize, like ancient Babel, to fight against the Lord and His people. But this time they will understand that they are aligning with the world and fighting against almighty God, who is their Creator. This scenario will be discussed in a subsequent chapter.

THE ENTIRE WORLD WILL ACKNOWLEDGE THE REALITY OF GOD

In the past when significant disasters struck different nations of the world, the great majority of people did not see the hand of God in them; they simply assumed them to be natural disasters that continually occur in the world. So what is it about this catastrophe, other than it is so much greater and widespread, that causes mankind to realize that it is a consequence evolving from the wrath of God and not simply a natural disaster?[87] An obvious answer is that this sixth-seal catastrophe is triggered by another event designed to strike at the heart of the Lord—a worldly assault against the kingdom of God so massive and powerful that only the Lord Himself could possibly bring about its defeat.

First, for better understanding, let's take a brief historical look at a time when the Lord delivered His people from the bondage of the world. He brought ten plagues against the most powerful nation in the known world and subsequently drowned their mighty army in the Red Sea in the process of delivering His people from the hand of the world's bondage. This deliverance was known throughout the Middle Eastern countries, and they came to know that the God of Israel was truly God. Although this awareness of God brought about a great fear upon these nations, the great majority of them continued to oppose the people of God rather than unite with them.

A similar, but much greater, event is about to take place. It will grab the attention and concern of the entire world and may possibly trigger the opening of the sixth seal and the subsequent trumpet judgments. A mighty army, greater than the world has ever seen, will soon descend upon the nation of Israel.

INTRODUCTION TO A GREAT WAR

A large percentage of people around the globe do not doubt that a terrible darkness is rapidly creeping into the world. Currently there is no major world war waging between nations, yet the continuing threats of upheavals in the Middle East or terrorist attacks here at home seem to dominate the news in today's mainstream media. The word *nuclear* is becoming more and more commonplace in our daily news stories. Even Hollywood appears to be profiting from this mind-set by producing bloodcurdling movies of wars and dark forces threatening the world. They are certainly scary but also quite entertaining; and they blindly encourage masses of moviegoers as their movie-star champions arise to protect the people against these dark forces and thus provide a happy, comfortable ending that allows people to sleep at night.

In truth, there is a growing evil in the world that will continue to gather its forces and strike against the kingdom of God. A remnant of God's people certainly understands that catastrophic times are rapidly approaching, but we need to be active in our preparations. We certainly can learn much by looking through the lenses of politics and economics, but this only provides us with a two-dimensional understanding. We need that third dimension, and this can be found only in the Scriptures, where a much clearer picture emerges. God has provided us with tremendous amounts of information for our generation, but we must search for it. Just because millions of Americans say they believe that Bible prophecy is coming true before their eyes or that they are living in the last days does not mean that they are truly aware of or preparing for events that are right around the corner. The watchmen of God who are burdened to warn the people need to anticipate how, when, and where these forces of darkness will strike next.[88] Now let's look at a coming war that could well be the event that launches the end-times tribulation era.

A GREAT WAR BEGINS IN THE MIDDLE EAST
(Ezekiel 38 and 39)

Approximately 2600 years ago, the Lord spoke to his prophet Ezekiel concerning a great army from the north that was going to descend upon the nation of Israel in order to rid the earth of a people that are despised by the majority of the world's population. This is an army made up of a coalition of several nations, and led by one of the largest and most powerful nations in the world. Ezekiel was told that this attack will occur in the "latter days," when the inhabitants of Israel have been gathered from many nations and have resettled in the land. It is also a time when its citizens live "securely" in the land. During a recent interview with Joel Rosenberg, the author of the book *Epicenter,* General Amidror, a former head of Israeli Military Intelligence stated,

> Unless or until Iran gets nuclear weapons, Israel today is more strategically secure than at any other point since her birth.[89]

Since 1948 Israel has been an established nation whose citizens of Jewish descent have been gathered from various other nations around the world. Israel is quite a small nation, with a population of approximately seven million, yet it is also a prosperous nation that is well armed and nuclear capable, thanks to the United States, who, together with Great Britain, has been its chief ally since its formation sixty years ago. This "recently established" and "living securely" scenario, together with other current events seems to indicate that this could well be the time of Ezekiel's war; which is commonly referred as the Gog-Magog war.

Regarding their relationship with God, today's Jewish people are primarily secular or legalistically religious like the Pharisees of Jesus' time; yet in the midst of the people, there are approximately six thousand messianic Jews, who embrace Yeshua (Jesus) as their Messiah. However, as a nation, the great majority of the Jewish people and their government are essentially ignorant of the God of Abraham or don't really care. Some folks may wonder, then, why does God care for them as a nation? Well, primarily, it goes back to His covenant over four thousand years ago, when He made the following promise to Abraham, the father of the people of Israel.

> *I will make of you a great nation, and I will bless you and make your name great, so that you will be a blessing. I will bless those who bless you, and him who dishonors you I will curse, and in you all the families of the earth shall be blessed." (Genesis 12:2-3)*

However, that covenant was not made because the Lord holds Israel to be a righteous nation, for He says,

> *And I will vindicate the holiness of my great name, which has been profaned among the nations, and which you have profaned among them. And the nations will know that I am the Lord, declares the Lord God, when through you I vindicate my holiness before their eyes. I will take you from the nations and gather you from all the countries and bring you into your own land.*
> *(Ezekiel 36:23-24)*

This has been the historical purpose for establishing Israel as a people of God: that through the Israelites and their testimony and/ or their circumstances, God will reveal Himself to all the peoples of the earth. Additionally, there are "numerous prophecies" that tell about a coming time when all of Israel will be saved and ungodliness banished from the land.

The Lord Himself will initiate this great war by putting "hooks" into the jaws of the enemies of Israel and dragging them to a place where He will pour out His wrath to such an extent that the entire world will tremble, and, like the ancient Egyptians, they come to know that the Lord of Israel is surely the one true God.[90]

A GREAT ARMY DESCENDS FROM MAGOG

Although Ezekiel's prophecy was written more than 2500 years ago, chapters 38 and 39 provide us with extraordinary intelligence concerning who will be involved and when it might occur. First let's look at the nations that comprise this massive coalition that descends upon Israel with the intent of wiping out the Jewish race. Of course, the Bible uses ancient names when describing these enemy nations, but most scholars agree on who they are. Rosenberg's book gives great clarity by providing a table matching the biblical names with the modern names.[91]

Russia is described as the leader of this "Axis of Evil," and Iran is mentioned first among the countries that align with Russia. A summary of the nations follows.

1. Russia	2. Iran	3. Sudan	4. Ethiopia	5. Libya
6. Algeria	7. Tunisia	8. Turkey	9. Gomer = possibly Germany & Eastern Europe	10. Many peoples after you = possibly Palestinians, Jordan, Lebanon

Note that these nations are mostly Islamic and are nations that have harbored a deep hatred for Israel since their formation as a nation. Ezekiel's description of this army suggests that it will be the largest and best-equipped military force ever assembled and, in modern terms, will consist of a countless number of infantry troops, tanks, and aircraft, all armed to the maximum. They will advance on Israel like a "storm" and like a "cloud covering the land." This certainly sounds like a massive onslaught of ground and air forces.

Additionally, it is interesting to note that two nations that have historically been enemies of Israel are not on the list; they are Iraq and Syria. One can surmise that this war will occur when these two countries no longer have the military capability to join their allies in their mission to destroy the nation of Israel. Now the absence of Iraq is understandable if this invasion is to occur in the near future, since their armed forces were dismantled during the war with the United States. However, the absence of Syria presents a very interesting scenario for those who are familiar with the "oracle of Damascus," where Isaiah prophesies that a future time is coming when Damascus will cease to be a city and will become a "heap of ruins." The oracle goes on to describe the terror that will confront Israel and what will happen to their enemies.[92] It certainly appears as if a war between Israel and Syria will precede the invasion of Israel by the military forces led by Russia and Iran. In fact, the destruction of Damascus and the defeat of the Syrian army may be the episode that ignites the Gog-Magog invasion of Israel. This could well be another "hook" in the Russians' jaws, for there currently exists a Syrian-Russian treaty whereby Russia has pledged to provide military support in the event that Syria becomes engaged in battle with Israel over the Golan Heights.

RUSSIA'S MOTIVE FOR INVADING ISRAEL

Why would Russia be motivated to commit all of its forces to assist the Middle Eastern countries against their enemy, Israel? Ezekiel tells us that Russia desires "to seize spoil and carry off plunder," which in our day makes a lot of sense since the Middle Eastern countries control the majority of oil resources, which drive the world's economy. Russia has been struggling economically for decades, and if they can successfully align themselves with the Middle Eastern countries, of which Iran is the key power, they will have significant control over the world's oil reserves. Additionally, Russia certainly wants to regain its superpower status among the nations of the world, and this alliance with the Middle Eastern nations may be considered an opportunity to unseat the United States as the strongest and most influential political and economic power in the world. Russia, which had lost its place as a superpower when the communist government disintegrated, is struggling economically but not militarily. Now comes an opportunity to become the greatest and wealthiest nation on earth. This is definitely a "hook" that the Lord uses to draw Russia into this devastating conflict.

IRAN'S MOTIVE FOR INVADING ISRAEL

Iranian President Ahmadinejad has said that he believes the end of the world is only a few years away. He also has said that the way to hasten the arrival of the Mahdi (Islamic Messiah) is to launch an apocalyptic holy war against the Christians and Jews. Ahmadinejad boasts that the Imam gave him the presidency for a single task—to provoke a "clash of civilizations" in which the Muslim world, led by Iran, takes on the "infidel" Western world and defeats the United States. Iran's goals for the war are certainly different from Russia's, so why would Iran and other Middle Eastern countries embrace this Russian influence? No doubt it is because Russia possesses the military capability and technology that these countries need in order to subdue Israel.[93] The Islamic nations have warred against Israel since its formation and have met with hardly any success. They need military help.

These enemies of Israel could easily work together, but Russia is playing with fire. Islamic teaching says, "Listen to the good news about the Mahdi! He will rise at the time when people will be faced with severe conflict and *the earth will be hit by a violent quake.* He will fill the earth with justice and equity as it is filled with injustice and tyranny. He will fill the hearts of his followers with devotion and will spread justice everywhere."[94] Additionally, it is said that those who persist in their disbelief and wickedness shall be killed by the soldiers of the Mahdi. Islam will be the religion of everyone and will enter all the nations of the world. The Mahdi will offer the religion of Islam to the Jews and the Christians; if they accept it, they will be spared, otherwise they will be killed. It seems unlikely that this catastrophe can be avoided. Warfare and bloodshed are inevitable.[95]

WHY THE UNITED STATES WILL ABANDON ITS SUPPORT OF ISRAEL

In his intelligence report, Ezekiel rules out the possibility that any country will come to Israel's defense once Russia and Iran and their allies launch their invasion from the north. Now the United States, England, and other European countries have been staunch supporters of Israel since its formation as a nation in 1948. So what is it that will cause our country to abandon its support for Israel at the moment of their greatest crisis?

Unfortunately the United States is now a politically divided country. As Americans tire more and more of our Middle Eastern conflicts, the leftist voices grow louder in their support of a Palestinian state with no concern for the consequences to Israel. In fact, there is a rapidly growing belief that if we abandon our support of Israel, we will no longer be endangered by Muslim terrorists. Today, our country has all but abandoned its support of Israel, as we see fewer and fewer Americans supporting the Jewish state. We're starting to hear comments like, "Why should we spend a dime to save Israel?" and "Let the Jews fight their own battles" and "The only reason we as Americans are getting attacked by Muslims is because we support Israel—the sooner we stop, the sooner there will be peace."[96]

It is most probable that the Gog-Magog war will occur when the United States is completely governed by the leftist Democrats and we have a government much like Europe, which may decry an invasion of Israel but would not militarily attempt to stop it. Additionally, the war could be launched at a time when the U.S. is fighting for survival in the throes of unparalleled economic collapse; or perhaps it may come at a time when the U.S. is fighting against chaotic situations in our own country as a result of increased terrorist activity that may render us virtually impotent on the international scene. Actually, all three of the above scenarios could exist simultaneously, feeding off one another. Obviously, this is our current scenario, and I do believe that this war against Israel will be launched during our present administration.

The real test, of course, will come when Russia, Iran, and all their allies begin to move forces toward Israel.[97] Ezekiel's intelligence indicates that there will be a verbal protest from Saudi Arabia and nations in the West but obviously they will not lift a hand to interfere.[98]

WHY THE EUROPEAN UNION ABANDONS ITS SUPPORT OF ISRAEL

Unfortunately, Europe is a continent where anti-Semitism is rapidly increasing. Jewish schools and synagogues throughout Europe are constantly vandalized and burned, and individual Jews are continually verbally abused and assaulted. Rockwell Schnabel, the U.S. ambassador to the European Union, stated that anti-Semitism in Europe "is as bad as it was in the 1930s."[99] In November 2003, a European poll revealed that the majority of Europeans actually named Israel as the greatest threat to world peace, ahead of Iran and North Korea.[100] Therefore, we can safely assume that Europe would not militarily lift a hand to save Israel.

It is obvious that without the intervention of the United States or a united Europe, there is no one else on the planet who could possibly stand against these tremendous forces that will soon be mustered against the nation of Israel. In short, the kingdom of this world hates the nation of Israel and its citizenry wherever they are living; but in reality, it is a hatred for the God of Israel. Israel is the nation that God uses to make His name known throughout the world.

And my holy name I will make known in the midst of my people Israel, and I will not let my holy name be profaned *anymore. <u>And the nations shall know that I am the Lord, the Holy One in Israel,</u> (Ezekiel 39:7)*

THE INVASION FROM THE NORTH AND THE LORD'S RESPONSE

Ezekiel's intelligence reports that this military alliance will descend toward the mountains known today as the Golan Heights, which is Israel's northern border adjacent to Syria, Lebanon, and northern Jordan. It is at this place that the Lord launches His offensive against this enemy by causing a great earthquake to explode in their midst—an earthquake greater than any the world has ever known. The mountains and cliffs fall upon this invading army, hailstones, fire, and sulfur rain down upon their heads, and pandemic diseases sweep through their ranks as well as through many other peoples who supported these troops in their war of annihilation against Israel.

Tremendous panic and confusion will eliminate discipline among the troops; and during this confusion, they will begin to fire their weapons against one another, resulting in a great massacre within their own ranks. This sudden devastation is so great that all the nations of the earth, together with all animal and sea life, will quake at the presence of the Lord as His fury is poured out on the armies of the enemies of His people. There no longer will be any doubt that the God of Israel and of the committed Christians in the body of Christ is the one and true God.

This is a very similar scenario to that ancient time when God delivered His people from Egypt and provided safe passage through the Red Sea. Then He wiped out the entire Egyptian army, which was, in that period of history, the most powerful military force in the world. All the nations of that day knew that the God of Israel was God, but this future event will be so much more catastrophic. All the nations shall know that the God of Israel is the Lord and that He will not allow His name to be profaned anymore. That doesn't mean that they won't hate Him, but they certainly will be more careful in their future plans for world domination. This will be the most catastrophic event ever witnessed by mankind since the flood, but this is not the end, for things will soon intensify.

A TIME OF CLEANSING OF THE LAND

Following the earthquake and the devastation that takes place on the Golan Heights, the people of Israel who are unharmed will go out to clean up the land and gather all the wreckage of the weaponry for burning. It will take seven years of constant fires to cleanse the land of the residue of the planes, helicopters, artillery, tanks, trucks, jeeps, trailers, small arms, supplies, and all other equipment that is destroyed. Additionally, the Israelites will gather up many valuable assets that are abandoned from a remnant of survivors who have fled. Much wealth will be accumulated during this cleansing process.

The birds of the air and the beasts of the field will eat the flesh of this once mighty army and drink the blood of those previously considered "princes of the earth." As for the remaining carcasses, we are told that all the people of the land of Israel will assist in burying the bodies in a massive graveyard cast of the Dead Sea. Even though the entire population of Israel will be locating and transporting the bodies to this burial site, it will be seven months before the land will be completely clean of all the carcasses. The former leader of this army, identified as Gog, also will be buried. Gog is not a personal name but more likely a title such as prince, or czar, or president, or general. The burial site will be called the Valley of Hamon-Gog.

It appears as if several million soldiers and civilians will be killed during this coming day when the Lord magnifies His holiness as the Defender of His people in Israel. All the house of Israel shall know that the God of Abraham, Isaac, and Jacob is their God. There will be no more secular Jews in Israel.

THE GOG-MAGOG WAR—A SECOND ONE COMING?

The book of Revelation does speak of another Gog-Magog war that occurs at the end of time.[101] However, this is a second war that is yet farther into the future, not the war that is recorded by Ezekiel. We know this for several reasons.

- First, Ezekiel's war occurs relatively soon after the rebirth of the nation of Israel and the ingathering of the Jewish people from around the world. The second Gog-Magog war occurs after Jesus has reigned on earth for one thousand years.
- Second, Ezekiel's war involves a fearsome, but limited, coalition of countries that surround Israel. The war in Revelation involves all the nations from "every corner of the earth" coming to attack Israel.
- Finally, after Ezekiel's war, life continues; bodies are gathered and buried for seven months, and weaponry is gathered and burned for seven years. By contrast, the war in Revelation is followed immediately by the end of the world. Satan and his followers are judged and thrown into the "lake of fire." The heavens and earth are destroyed, and a completely new heaven and new earth are created, and the followers of Jesus Christ will live on this new earth for the rest of eternity.[102]

A CATASTROPHIC EVENT FOLLOWING THIS GOG-MAGOG WAR

There is another very significant event that takes place following the devastation resulting from this great earthquake. The Lord is not yet done, for Ezekiel receives this additional intelligence from the God of Israel:

> *I will send fire on Magog and on those who dwell securely in the coastlands, and they shall know that I am the Lord.* *(Ezekiel 39:6)*

In addition to the destruction of the armies, "fire" is sent north onto the Russian heartland, as well as upon those who dwell "securely" on the coastlands. This implies a sending of "fire" between two groups of people, which sounds very much like a *nuclear exchange*.

A Plausible Scenario

When God's earthquake hits Israel, fear, confusion, and chaos will cause exchanges of fire within the Russian forces. Escalation will ensue, and the Russians may well think that the West is attacking them. Most likely a nuclear exchange will begin inadvertently. Ezekiel also does not identify the people inhabiting the "coastlands in security"; but he does say they will also be on the receiving end of this nuclear war. The Western alliance, led by the United States, is the only group of nations capable of engaging the Soviets in a major nuclear war, and thus it appears that the heartland of Russia will launch the first strike against the West, which will then retaliate.

A Second Plausible Scenario

Muslim terrorists on both Western and Eastern continents could detonate nuclear "suitcase bombs" in various cities in retaliation for what they see as an attack upon the Middle Eastern world.

Experts say that the blast from a single ten-kiloton nuclear bomb (suitcase size) in a major city would destroy everything within a half mile of ground zero, contaminate 3,000 to 5,000 square miles with toxic levels of radiation, and kill 300,000 people within a matter of minutes.[103]

Now, concerning the second scenario, I wish to share something very interesting yet largely unknown in the West. The chief sign that announces the coming of the Mahdi is a "massive earthquake," which will launch a global war to kill and/or to subjugate Jews, Christians, and other "infidels."[104] This Islamic belief may very well cause them to launch an internal nuclear attack on various cities around the country following the great earthquake that the Lord releases in the Golan Heights.

GOG-MAGOG: THE WAR THAT LAUNCHES
THE GREAT TRIBULATION

It is highly probable that this "earthquake" described in the book of Ezekiel is the same "earthquake" that strikes the earth when the Lord opens the "sixth seal." If so, this Gog-Magog war in Ezekiel is what will launch the great tribulation upon the earth, which will affect all the nations.[105] Finally, the catastrophic effect of a nuclear attack may be what John describes in greater detail in the series of judgments known as "the seven trumpets."

GOG-MAGOG AND THE CHRISTIAN ATTITUDE

True followers of Jesus Christ may be the only friends Israel and the Jewish people will have left as this terrible war approaches. We need to remain faithful in praying for the peace of Jerusalem on a daily basis. Additionally, the Jews in America undoubtedly will be persecuted during this scheme of events. We must, with all of our heart, align ourselves with them and show our solidarity for their people and their nation.

At the same time, we must remember that God loves the Muslim people of the Middle East as well as the Russians and others living in the former Soviet Union. Lovers of Christ must love and show compassion to all people. This doesn't mean excusing the actions of anti-Christian governments, but it is the believers' hard work to demonstrate and communicate Christ's love during mankind's darkest hours.[106]

CHAPTER 5

TRUMPETS, NUKES, AND A LITTLE BOOK
(Revelation 8—10)

SUMMARY OF THE SIXTH SEAL

The "great earthquake" launched by the Lord against the mighty enemies of Israel will soon rock the entire planet. It will not occur at some unforeseen moment, but will come at a time when the entire world is watching a tremendously large army led by the Russians coming against the nation of Israel in order to purge them from the land once and for all. The events following the opening of the first "five seals" were all initiated by the Son of God, but the world did not recognize them as such. However, with the opening of the sixth seal, the Lord's presence will be manifested to all the nations of this modern era. His concern for His people and His anger toward their enemies will leave no doubt that the God of Abraham, Isaac, and Jacob is truly God.

Many in the church might ask, "Why is the Lord revealing Himself through Israel, a predominately secular nation, and not through His church, who believes that Jesus is the Messiah?" Certainly the church exists worldwide and has in various times and places been under persecution, but the Jewish people also have suffered under continual persecution. Yet, the world does not recognize the reality of God through those events that have continually occurred throughout the last two thousand years of history. So what event could possibly initiate such a catastrophic response by the Lord that the entire world would not doubt His existence and His commitment to oppose the forces that intend to annihilate His people? It would be an event that, if not stopped, would forever destroy Israel from the face of the earth, an event so impressive that it would clearly reveal that the God of Abraham, Isaac, and Jacob is true to His covenant and that He will deliver His people from the hands of their enemies. It would be an event that would occur at a time when the entire world would witness it and an event that would turn many in Israel back to their Lord—perhaps not yet to recognizing Jesus as the coming Messiah, but back to the God of their fathers.

THE DAWNING OF THE "DAY OF THE LORD"

The opening of the "sixth seal" appears to be the launching of the Day of the Lord; this is not a twenty-four-hour day but a period of time when the Lord will continually manifest Himself through His people in the midst of the greatest devastation in the history of mankind. It is a day of warfare between the forces of light and darkness.[107] It is a time when "seven trumpets" and "seven bowls" will successively alter world events and continually usurp the world's vision of peace and brotherhood without God. These plagues will fall directly upon those of mankind who do not have the "seal of God" on their foreheads. The purpose of this "sealing," as well as the identity of those who will be sealed (protected) from being casualties of the "trumpet events," will be presented in the following chapter.

The "trumpet events" will cause the powers of unbelief and hostility toward God to break into the open in the person of the Antichrist, and then every person's loyalty will become plain. The "end times" is an era when the forces of both righteousness and evil will be so open and clear that all persons must declare themselves either for Christ or for Antichrist. Thus, these plagues being poured out upon the earth are not simply judicial but also have a merciful purpose: they are designed to turn men, women, and children to God while the time for decision remains.[108] The Day of the Lord eventually will culminate with the second coming of Jesus, the Son of God, and the Commander in Chief who will lead His army of warriors in the final battle.

A NUCLEAR RESPONSE TO THE GOG-MAGOG WAR

The sixth-seal events also appear to include additional devastations that quite possibly result from the earthquake. As mentioned in a previous chapter, it is very possible that this "great earthquake" creates such panic and confusion among the world powers that a nuclear war is triggered between Russia and "those who dwell securely in the coastlands."[109] In his book, *Today's Technology in Bible Prophecy*, Charles W. Miller sees events in the sixth seal from a nuclear perspective.

> *When he opened the sixth seal, I looked, and behold, there was a great earthquake, and the <u>sun became black as sackcloth, the full moon became like blood</u>, and the <u>stars of the sky fell to the earth</u> as the fig tree sheds its winter fruit when shaken by a gale. <u>The sky vanished like a scroll that is being rolled up</u>, and every mountain and island was removed from its place. (Revelation 6:12-14)*

John's vision of "falling stars" could well be the fiery streak of a rocket exhaust from nuclear tipped missiles as they soar through the atmosphere at speeds up to 8,000 miles/hour. This is followed by a tremendous nuclear blast, which drives everything away from its superheated center with 4oo miles/hour winds. After a few seconds, the winds reverse, in what is called the suction phase, and rush back along with dust and smoke into the vacuum created when the bomb initially exploded. These inflowing winds produce strong updrafts just seconds after the explosion. A column of fiery dust and smoke-filled air promptly forms and rises at a speed of nearly 300 miles/ hour several miles into the darkening sky. Eventually a gigantic mushroom shaped cloud is formed. The early ascent prior to the mushroom cloud forming gives the visual impression of the "sky departing like a scroll that is being rolled up."[110]

THE RESPONSE OF THE VICTIMS
(Revelation 6:16-17)

Unlike conventional wars, where the privileged people, such as generals, politicians, and the wealthy, often manage to avoid personal catastrophe, all classes of people in the target zones will be victimized. Survivors of the initial blast and heat wave will head for the hills, since staying in the vicinity of the nuclear blast will result in severe and painful radiation poisoning.

"Fall on us" reveals the victims' numbed state of mind and utter hopelessness. When they take stock of injuries, exposure to radiation, and lack of food, water, and medical support, they will consider death from falling rocks a better fate than what they are about to face. They had been rooted in the belief that they were able to live life as their own god. They intended to build their own kingdom of righteousness and peace as viewed by their own concepts and they intended to accomplish all this without any interference from almighty God and His beloved Son. They never knew that His kingdom already was realized in the hearts of His people. They laughed at the idea that this world was principally wicked and that the earth would one day pass away. Their hope was in the stability of the eternal universe, and now that hope is frustrated in a moment.

Additionally, this will be a wake-up call to many professing believers who knew that God's judgment was inevitable but were living as if they would never have to experience it. These are people who voiced a belief in Jesus but lived a life that separated themselves from Him, and thus they were overwhelmingly fearful of seeing His face. This initial calamity will be so severe that they will suppose that the end of the world is upon them. However, this assumption will be incorrect, for it is simply the beginning of the Day of the Lord. Despite the numerous movies and books depicting the horrors of nuclear war, the Bible teaches that the great majority of people will be unprepared to cope with the aftermath of a worldwide nuclear war.[111] However, the remnant among the people of God who will be "prepared" for the Day of the Lord will have understanding of the times and thus will not be filled with fear or consternation, even though this will be a dreadful period from a natural point of view. These are the mighty leaders who will arise and be knighted from on high and will guide many down the narrow road leading into the kingdom of God.

THE OPENING OF THE SEVENTH SEAL
(Revelation 8:1)

With the breaking of this final seal, the entire prophetic book of Revelation is opened for all to see. Viewing this newly opened book leaves those in heaven in stunned silence, for it reveals that the tremendous devastations to be released by the sixth seal is merely a glimpse of an infinitely greater chaotic series of events that are about to descend upon the world. Many in heaven, like the martyrs under the throne, have to be wondering why the Lord would not quickly step in to halt man's senseless violence and put an end to misery. When the book of Revelation is opened to their understanding, they are speechless, for the horrors of this post-nuclear world war will continue on for a much longer time than anyone anticipated. This stunned silence will be the same emotional reaction of the Christian church when they finally come to understand the destructive forces that are about to engulf the world and realize that they are right in the middle of it. Then, the church will finally recognize that we are indeed in the age of the end times and that the judgments of the trumpets and bowls are on the way.

There also will be a large segment of unbelievers who will not harden their hearts and will begin to seek answers from the people of God. However, the great majority of mankind, who have hardened their hearts against God and His Son, eventually will recover from their fear and begin to unify more quickly in their endeavor to create their own kingdom. The coming trumpet judgments will harden them even more, and they will unite to create a world empire much like that in the ancient city of Babel, only instead of Nimrod as its ruler, they will select the Antichrist.

This seventh seal has no plague or judgment content, but its opening actually launches the sounding of the seven trumpets. Thus, the first six seals relate to the forces leading up to the time of the end, while the seven trumpets relate to the beginning of the events of the end.

SILENCE IN HEAVEN AND THE PRAYERS OF THE SAINTS
(Revelation 8:1-5)

During this silence in heaven, seven angels are standing before the throne of God, and they receive seven trumpets. They do not immediately commence blowing these trumpets, but they reverently keep silent until something else has been finished. Subsequently, another angel approaches the altar and receives incense, along with the prayers of the saints. This angel then kindles the incense with the fire from the altar; he stands before the throne of God and causes the incense and the prayers of the saints to ascend up to the Lord almighty. It is very evident that the all-important elements in this period of silence are the prayers of the saints rising up before the Lord. What is the object of these prayers? "Our Father, who art in heaven; blessed be thy Name; Thy kingdom come; Thy will be done upon earth as it is in heaven." This is the cry of the saints who have been calling for His kingdom to come for more than four thousand years. The time has come for the launching of judgments that will prepare the world for the second coming of our Lord to set up His kingdom across the entire earth. Now comes the beginning of God's answer to our prayers.[112]

Then the angel took the censer and filled it with fire from the altar and threw it on the earth, and there were peals of thunder, rumblings, flashes of lightning, and an earthquake.
(Revelation 8:5)

It is quite possible that this is the heavenly event that launches the great earthquake in the Gog-Magog war. That is when the prayers of the saints over the centuries are united together with the prayers of those interceding today for the protection of Israel from the enemies that are coming against them. A mighty earthquake is coming that will soon shake the entire earth, an earthquake that will ignite an unprecedented, continent-smashing nuclear war.[113]

Christian prayer may delay the start of this war, but it will not prevent it. However, it could allow those who understand the times to personally prepare and to warn others that nuclear war is knocking at our front door. This "period of silence" in heaven most likely will be when the world sees that Russia and Iran are preparing to invade Israel, while the Western world is weakly voicing their opposition to it. And we may very well be in that "period of silence" today. The great earthquake and subsequent nuclear war is then launched when the angel suddenly casts the fire burning with the prayers of the saints down to the earth.

THE FIRST FOUR TRUMPETS
(Revelation 8:6-12)

Trumpets are used in Scripture to awaken people to matters of extreme importance or to summon them to prepare to resist an approaching enemy. Here they are used to alert the world that the Day of the Lord is at hand and will be accompanied by great distress. Listen to the prophecy of Joel concerning this time.

> *Blow a trumpet in Zion; sound an alarm on my holy mountain! Let all the inhabitants of the land tremble, for the day of the Lord is coming; it is near, a day of darkness and gloom, a day of clouds and thick darkness!* (**Joel 2:1-2**)

It is likely that the trumpet prophecies foretell seven major events that will occur in the closing period of this nuclear war. Collectively, they document the ferocity of the sixth-seal nuclear war, the war's immediate aftermath, and the continuing, long-term repercussions.

These trumpet plagues fall into two separate groups. The first four are directed against the elements of nature and the heavenlies, while the last three, which are called "woes," fall directly upon mankind. A similar division is seen in the breaking of the seals, where there also, the first four were clearly distinguished from the last three.

The First Trumpet Sounds = A Burning of the Land

> *The first angel blew his trumpet, and there followed __hail__ and __fire__, mixed with __blood__, and these were thrown upon the earth. And a third of the earth was burned up, and a third of the trees were burned up, and all green grass was burned up.* (*Revelation 8:7*)

Nuclear hail is formed when large quantities of earth and water are sucked into the fireball and become vaporized. Subsequently, they gradually descend to earth in what we call fallout. John described this nuclear fallout as hail, since it does look like ordinary hailstones. The fallout of hail that falls quickly back to earth within one day is generally the size of marbles. Lighter particles continue to fall like dusty snow, and eventually invisibly, for weeks afterwards. This affects the food crops that are subjected to severe contamination, and they cannot be harvested for decades.

Fire is naturally mentioned, for a single megaton bomb can set ninety-five square miles on fire at the same time. The blood refers to the vaporized remains of people and animals falling back to earth following the blast. Those in the vicinity of an airburst nuclear explosion would be instantly reduced to superheated gases and would eventually fall to the earth as vaporized blood, along with other burning debris. Studies have indicated that a large-scale nuclear war (5,000-10,000 megaton yields) would result in 750 million immediate deaths from the blasts alone. Another 300 million also would die from the heat and radiation coming out of the explosion. But, that's not all. Another billion or so undoubtedly would require medical attention for burns, lost limbs, and other injuries, and yet such overwhelming medical needs could not be met.[114]

Note also that the effect of the first trumpet is imagery from the seventh Egyptian plague during the days of Moses.[115]

The Second Trumpet Sounds = A Burning of the Sea and Marine Life

The second angel blew his trumpet, and something like a great mountain, burning with fire, was thrown into the sea, and a third of the sea became blood. A third of the living creatures in the sea died, and a third of the ships were destroyed. *(Revelation 8:8-9)*

This appears to be the naval side of the nuclear war. The great mountain burning with fire is not easy to identify. Some commentators think it may be a fiery meteor. However, undersea naval combat with nuclear submarines undoubtedly will be part of this war and thus, the naval vessels at sea will be under attack since that is where the large portion of nuclear weaponry is launched. Thus, like the landmasses, one-third of the seas will be destroyed with much death.

Note also that the effect of the second trumpet is imagery from the first Egyptian plague during the days of Moses.[116]

The Third Trumpet Sounds = A Burning of the Fresh Water

The third angel blew his trumpet, and a great star fell from heaven, blazing like a torch, and it fell on a third of the rivers and on the springs of water. The name of the star is <u>Wormwood</u>. A third of the waters became wormwood, and many people died from the water, because it had been made bitter. (Revelation 8:10-11)

Wormwood is a bitter herb that Scripture employs as a symbol of bitterness and sorrow that God gives to those who forsake Him.[117] Here it is probably used to describe extreme bitterness in the waters caused by radioactive fallout. This certainly pictures the nuclear radiation effect upon the interior of the continents, where the world's rivers and lakes are found. Many survivors will be faced with the dilemma of drinking irradiated waters or dying of thirst. Thus, many undoubtedly will die from these embittered waters. Drinking of irradiated waters will result in a slow, painful death from radiation sickness. Starting with nausea, vomiting, and diarrhea, victims will experience internal bleeding, ulcerations of the lips, and loss of hair within two weeks.[118]

The Fourth Trumpet Sounds = A Darkening of the Heavens

The fourth angel blew his trumpet, and a third of the sun was struck, and a third of the moon, and a third of the stars, so that a third of their light might be darkened, and a third of the day might be kept from shining, and likewise a third of the night. (Revelation 8:12)

A future nuclear war involving the incineration of one-third of the earth will not be the result of a detonation of a few nuclear bombs. Even the twelve-kiloton atomic bomb dropped on Nagasaki in 1945 blocked the sun's rays for a short period of time. However, when we consider the explosion of hundreds of nuclear warheads, each a thousand times more destructive than the Nagasaki bomb, the distinct possibility of there being enough smoke launched into the earth's atmosphere to cause this amount of damage becomes chillingly apparent. Once high-altitude nuclear smoke clouds encircle the earth, they will become a miles-thick, dark curtain throughout the skies. In addition to keeping one-third of the sun's rays from reaching the earth, the thick clouds literally will shorten the length of daylight by a third and the nightlight likewise. Studies of the post-effects of nuclear warfare reveal that the lands would experience subfreezing temperatures over most of the northern hemisphere. These temperatures could remain below freezing for months. No area of the globe could be counted on to be free from this "nuclear winter."[119]

Note also that the effect of the fourth trumpet is imagery from the ninth Egyptian plague during the days of Moses.[120]

THE EAGLE'S WARNING

At the completion of events resulting from the first four trumpets, one-third of mankind's entire physical universe has been decimated. The land, the oceans, the lakes and rivers, and the skies have all suffered tremendous devastation. Sickness and epidemics from a poisoned environment will abound worldwide. However, it is about to get worse. Suddenly, John is shown an eagle flying across the heavens and proclaiming that the next three trumpet judgments will be delivered directly against mankind rather than the environment.

Then I looked, and I heard an eagle crying with a loud voice as it flew directly overhead, "Woe, woe, woe to those who dwell on the earth, at the blasts of the other trumpets that the three angels are about to blow!" (Revelation 8:13)

FIFTH TRUMPET WOE: THE NEED FOR MARTIAL LAW

The typical survivor's first reaction to these events will be panic, but this eventually will be replaced by anger. As we have seen in the aftermath of the Twin Towers and Hurricane Katrina, many people will rise up against local authority, angry that government would allow this to happen to them, and demand that something be done to help them. Undoubtedly, there will be a huge outbreak of crime, including robbery and murder among the citizenry. Young people in the prime of life, aware of the lethal effects of radiation, will be angry that they may die in a matter of weeks or months and will want to strike back at the authorities who failed to protect them. Food and water will be scarce, and supplies, transportation, and fuel will be nonexistent. There will be a frantic hoarding of food; neighborhood homes will be attacked by gangs and small groups of criminal bands seeking food and other goods. Eventually, this will be organized by gang leadership, who will recruit these bands to steal for them in order to gain items to sell on the black market. Crops will be highly valued for food, and trees will be highly prized for heating, cooking, and building shelters. Thus, martial law will be the initial measure taken by an existing government to protect the food supplies and to restore order among the survivors to insure their nation's survival.

FIFTH TRUMPET WOE: LOCUSTS
STINGING LIKE SCORPIONS
(Revelation 9:3-10)

To begin with, we need to remember that there is an ongoing spiritual war in the heavenlies, as well as in the world. Recall that John saw two sides of the scroll, representing the spiritual heavenly reality and the physical worldly reality. The scroll has been opened and the decrees of the Lord are being released in both the spiritual and physical worlds, revealing that the Lord is controlling the entire situation. Angelic beings are restrained until the time of the Lord's command, and then, in His perfect timing, they are released to carry out their individual missions in this war. This fifth trumpet scenario is designed to reveal what this event will look like from a worldly perspective in the twenty-first century.

Now within this passage there is again the imagery of the smoking aftereffects of a nuclear detonation. However, out of the aftermath of a nuclear strike, something will arise to attempt to control and subsequently take advantage of this catastrophic situation.

*Then from the smoke came locusts on the earth, and they were given power like the power of scorpions of the earth. They were told not to harm the grass of the earth or any green plant or any tree, <u>but only those people who do not have the seal of God on their foreheads</u>. They were allowed to torment them for five months, but not to kill them, and their torment was like the torment of a scorpion when it stings someone. (**Revelation 9:3-5**)*

The Bible has previously referred to locusts as vast destructive armies.[121] In this instance, it is conceivable that the locusts are representative of a vast, perhaps global, military force. This army will not be sent to destroy but to protect environmental property like the trees and crops that survived the nuclear strike. They are allowed to torment mankind but not to kill them. This is not a conquering army but a military peacekeeping force. Their supposed mission is to establish law and order in those communities struggling to survive the chaotic aftermath of the nuclear war. Their initial orders are not to kill anyone, even if violating martial law, which is a typical order given to combat troops sent to restore order during national emergencies. This command is important in preventing an armed revolt from arising among the masses. However, concentration camps certainly will be employed.

These troops will be characteristic of a scorpion army. Scorpions are so bad-tempered that they will lash out at anyone or anything that dare to cross their path. The weaponry used by this peacekeeping force will be like the tail of a scorpion. Although they are ordered not to kill the masses, they certainly will inflict pain and torment, and thus it appears that Taser-gun weaponry will be involved. This is weaponry that will inflict pain like the sting of a scorpion but will not cause death.

The "sealed ones" of God will be exempt from being harmed by this force. It appears as if these are the Christians who are protected from this chaotic environment, and through their leadership, they will be active in bringing peace and understanding to the situation. These are those Christian warriors who have prepared themselves for this "Day of the Lord" and thus are not among the scared, chaotic, and rebellious masses.

THE APPEARANCE OF THE LOCUSTS

In appearance the locusts were like horses prepared for battle: on their <u>heads were what looked like crowns of gold</u>; their <u>faces were like human faces</u>, their hair like women's hair, and their <u>teeth like lions' teeth</u>; they had <u>breastplates like breastplates of iron</u>, and the <u>noise of their wings was like the noise of many chariots with horses rushing into battle</u>. They have tails and stings like scorpions, and their power to hurt people for five months is in their tails. (Revelation 9:7-10)

The shape of the locusts described in the fifth trumpet scenario easily can be identified with helicopter gunships, which undoubtedly will be utilized by this peacekeeping force. The whirring noise of the rotor blades and the thump, thump, thump sound of a chopper passing overhead certainly can be identified with the sound of locust wings and the sound of chariots of many horses running to battle. The "crown" of rotor blades, the "faces of men" in the cockpit, the locust-shaped body of the chopper, and the "lion's teeth" armament all foretell the use of numerous helicopter gunships to police the countryside, provide support for the ground troops, and transport Taser-wounded prisoners to concentration camps.

FIFTH TRUMPET WOE: NUCLEAR WINTER

These peacekeeping efforts will last for five months, which seems to coincide with the length of a nuclear winter, a period of time when temperatures are below freezing and a third of the light from the sun and moon has been darkened. Tests reveal that for a ten-thousand-megaton-yield exchange, which is enough firepower to burn up a third of the earth, subfreezing temperatures could last almost six months. John is describing five months of widespread famine and political upheaval in the midst of arctic-type temperatures. It is a period of such grief and hopelessness for the world citizenry that many will seek death, but death will flee from them and they will have to continue in their deep suffering for a time.[122]

Five dreadful months is reemphasized. Why? Christians should pay close attention to its significance in light of God's past warnings regarding major calamities and those who listened and acted. For example, Joseph stored grain for seven years in Egypt before a seven-year famine arrived. We also can look at this example in Noah and the building of the ark. We must respond to John's seven trumpet warnings and make the preparations and commitment necessary to survive as well as minister during the coming nuclear holocaust. We definitely need to store up food and water and other provisions that will last for at least five months.

FIFTH TRUMPET WOE: THE ARRIVAL OF APOLLYON

They have as king over them the angel of the bottomless pit.
His name in Hebrew is Abaddon, and in Greek he is called
Apollyon. (Revelation 9:11)

Now we are introduced to the military commander over this so-called peacekeeping force. It appears that this person will arise from a position of relative obscurity to international importance in the post-nuclear war period. The reference to this "king" being the "angel of the bottomless pit" describes this world leader's dark character and mission. Both *Abaddon* and *Apollyon* mean "destruction" or "to destroy." His name exposes this demonically empowered leader's evil character and hidden agenda. Perhaps this is the coming world leader who will be claiming that his mission is to bring about world-wide peace. This will certainly be welcomed among the masses that have survived this nuclear war. If this is the Antichrist who is yet to be revealed, he will need to gain the backing of the world's military establishment as his first step toward world power. Possibly he is a military leader who has been chosen by the European Union to bring order out of this chaotic situation. Subsequently, if he is the chosen one, once he gets control he will overthrow those kings who oppose his dominance and take over the leadership of the world government.

SIXTH TRUMPET WOE: 200 MILLION KILLERS
(Revelation 9:13-18)

Five of the seven trumpets have now sounded, and the world is now fully aware that these are judgments emanating from the throne of almighty God. During this period, numerous people throughout the world will have repented and committed their lives to serving their Lord Jesus Christ; yet the vast majority will continue in their rebellion and hatred toward Him. Now a voice calls out from the golden altar before the throne of God, indicating that the time finally has come for vengeance against those of mankind who have trampled under foot and despised the blood of the Savior. Thus, with the sounding of the sixth trumpet, demonic forces are released that will mobilize a murderous army numbering 200 million that will kill approximately two billion of the world's inhabitants.

Many commentators believe this to be an organized army from the East, perhaps from China, that rises up out of the turmoil in order to conquer and control the remainder of the earth. The People's Liberation Army of China (PLA), which is the world's largest military force, comprises approximately three million active soldiers.

Another possibility is that these are organized Islamic terrorists who reside in countries around the world and may well believe that this long-awaited "great earthquake" launches the coming of their Mahdi; thus, they may launch a worldwide war for their god, Allah.

Now would these Islamic terrorists number 200 million? Certainly not, but consider the following possibility: The actual number of men composing this murderous army may be far less than 200 million since this vision describes 200 million demonic horsemen. It is quite possible that these are demons which possess members of a smaller size army of Muslin terrorists. Recall the "legion" of demons that possessed one man which Jesus released into a herd of 2,000 pigs. Perhaps it could be that similar demonic "legions" control members of a worldwide terrorist army with the mission to wipe out one-third of the world's population. If so, then it is possible that this is a 100,000 man army controlled by 200 million murderous demons.

Regardless of the identity of this army, it does appear to be a nuclear onslaught that kills one-third of mankind.

*And this is how I saw the horses in my vision and those who rode them: they wore breastplates the color of fire and of sapphire and of sulfur, and the heads of the horses were like lions' heads, and **fire** and **smoke** and **sulfur** came out of their mouths. (**Revelation 9:17**)*

If the trumpet series is indeed nuclear, as previously described, and a third of the earth is destroyed or polluted, then surely that will result in a tremendous loss of lives. The three plagues of fire, smoke, and sulfur certainly sound like the three devastating effects of nuclear devices.

For example:

- Fire = Blast in the immediate proximity.
- Smoke = Heat that travels much farther out than the blast.
- Sulfur = Radiation that travels great distances from the initial explosion.

One can only speculate concerning the specifics of this destructive scenario; however, it is a certainty that these plagues are a supernatural force led by the four demonic angels who have been waiting for centuries for this murderous opportunity to unleash their hatred against humanity. A very clear description of this breathtaking demonic army and its destructive intent is very similar to what is also described by the prophets Joel and Isaiah.[123] Finally, we know that because of the reference to the Euphrates River, where the dark angels are released, that this great war probably will originate in the Middle East.

Certainly the possibility that our generation will experience these trumpet judgments should be an awakening among those in the body of Christ who have ears to hear. The devastating events are obviously punitive in nature, but they are also intended to bring many to repentance.[124] Like the Israelites who were protected against the plagues that came upon their Egyptian captors, the 144,000 who are sealed also will be protected. Nevertheless, they too will be indirectly affected by these plagues, as hardships abound worldwide and unsealed family members and friends become victims. Yet, they are the ones who will not fear and will continually praise the Lord in their circumstances.[125] As a result, the light of Jesus will shine mightily through them, and this will create an astounding, dual effect upon mankind. That is, many will repent and turn to the Lord who protects and provides, but the large majority will be more deeply embittered toward God and the church, whom they will blame for the devastation.

No matter how the scenario unfolds, Christians must be prepared not only to endure but also to minister in the midst of this chaos. Much fear and confusion will be present among the majority of the people of God throughout this period of the trumpets. Such gloom and doubt will cause many to begin to lose sight of their Lord and His revelation as they begin to cry out, "Why does God allow this to happen?" It is at this point that John witnesses the coming of a mighty angel into the midst of this devastation, one who will bring understanding to these times.

A MIGHTY ANGEL BRINGS A LITTLE BOOK
(Revelation 10:1-11)

The identity of this mighty angel who comes down from heaven should be obvious to His people. He appears glorious and very powerful, perhaps as He did when he first appeared to John on Patmos and to Daniel at the Tigris River.[126] Now He comes again in a time of trouble never before experienced upon this earth, and He stands upon the sea and the earth, revealing His control over all things. Nothing happens against His will; the war and the famine and the pestilence and tribulation cannot happen outside of His authority. And He tells us by the rainbow over His head that in the midst of mighty judgments, He will never forget His covenant with His people. This is certainly our Lord Jesus Christ, who is our King and Lord of the entire earth.

He brings with Him a little book, which contains instructions and warns us beforehand what we must do during the tribulation times that are yet to come. That little book must not be merely read and copied; it must be eaten, for it is symbolic of all that John still has to prophesy. Special preparation on the part of John was necessary for this book contains the message of the seventh trumpet, revealing how the kingdom will come and how the purposes of the Father will be done in accomplishing the destruction of the powers of the kingdom of darkness and establishing the eternal kingdom of God upon this earth. Special preparation certainly was needed, for this is not a pleasing message, at least for that period of time leading up to the establishment of His earthly kingdom.

It is a message that reveals (1) severe battles, destruction, persecution and vengeance; (2) the fate of Jerusalem and the temple; (3) the ministry and fate of the two witnesses who are killed for their testimony; (4) the conflict between the woman and the dragon, who attempts to destroy her Child; (5) the beast that arises out of the sea and the beast that arises out of the earth, plus the terrible things they do upon the earth; (6) the overwhelming power of Antichrist and his war upon the people of God; (7) tribulation and oppression for the sake of Christ's kingdom; (8) mystery Babylon and her greatness as well as her destruction; (9) the pouring out of seven vials of wrath, which devastate the entire earth; (10) the coming of the Lord Jesus with his army of saints; (11) the establishment of a millennial kingdom; (12) the binding and subsequent loosing of Satan; (13) the coming down from heaven of the new Jerusalem; and (14) the creation of a new heaven and a new earth where righteousness prevails.

Thus, this little book contains a tremendous, terrible message that has a glorious finale — at least for the people of God. Therefore, John, as well as all the ministers of the gospel in this generation, must be prepared. The seven thunders spoke plainly, but John could not be prepared by simply writing down what he had heard.[127] He must not be merely informed; he must eat the little book, swallow it, and thus make it a part of himself. Here we have the symbolic significance of the preparation of John and every true witness of Christ in the world as a prophet. The message he was to bring was not going to be sweet to the taste of the world but one of tremendous difficulty and sorrow and judgment. Because of this, it will be contradicted and opposed, not only by the wicked world of Antichrist, but also by much of the church as it currently exists. Many who do not truly belong to Christ but are in the church will hate and deny and oppose the message of tribulation and judgment. They will shout, "Peace, peace when there is no peace."[128] Even more, the message may sometimes be opposed by the true people of God, who do not always see and understand that in this world the church must expect tribulation and judgment in order for the kingdom to come. It takes spiritual courage, the courage of a warrior with great faith, to be a prophet of this message. And in order to stand against this opposition, the prophet of this message must "eat" the book of this prophecy.

The prophet Ezekiel had a very similar experience for he also had to "eat" the scroll before he was prepared to proclaim God's message of tribulation and mourning upon the house of Israel. He was told that the house of Israel is stiff-necked and rebellious, so he must expect opposition; and in order to stand for the Lord with this message, it must be part of his very system.[129]

PROPHETIC WARRIORS MUST "EAT THIS BOOK"

If John had simply read the little book, its contents would have remained outside of him and would not have influenced his heart and mind. Thus, he would not have been a true prophet of this message who could stand for the truth in the midst of the world and uphold its testimony in spite of opposition and suffering and tribulation. It had to become part of his flesh and blood, his soul and spirit. It had to transform him, change him, and make a different man out of him. The truth of this message had to so dominate him that he could never believe anything else and could never be silenced about it.

Now, this was not merely revealed to John, in which case the passage would have no significance for us. It contains a lesson for us. It teaches what we must do with the testimony of God in general, but especially with the book of Revelation. We can study the book and listen to various interpretations, and we might find intellectual enjoyment in its interpretation. Perhaps our curiosity will be some-what satisfied; but that is not sufficient, for the message of this book demands a positive stand.

The question is: Do we believe these things? Is this really true that:

- The world is in iniquity and will fight to the last against Christ and His kingdom?
- There is an apostate part of the church that will align itself with the Antichrist?

- That the kingdom of Christ can come in no other way except through worldwide wars, judgments, and tribulations?

If you believe these things, the book of this prophecy will determine your stand against the world and prepare you for opposition within the church and for a great falling away. Are you ready? If so, you must eat it, appropriate it; it must become part of your entire system and control the direction of your life so that you know only one life, the kingdom of God.

The little book speaks of many woes and tribulations, but it also speaks of joy, peace, and everlasting life. The book tastes sweet to the mouth, but afterward we realize the bitter element, for it is bitter in the belly. Commitment to "eat" this little book does not mean that the Word has no bitter after-effects when it reaches the belly. The process of assimilation and digestion is often painful, for the Word has to battle against the influence of the flesh and its lusts; and it is a painful battle, no matter how sweet it was when first eaten. It causes bitterness and struggle until the medicine of the Word of God has done its work and transformed us.

This is especially true in the book of Revelation for this little book speaks of salvation, redemption, heavenly glory, eternal life, everlasting joy, and a new creation, where our tears are wiped away. This is also the popular, continuing message of the church. But, the little book speaks of this only after self-denial and suffering and great personal sacrifice has occurred. It holds before us the glory of the future but only at the end of a dark and terrible road to travel.

*Beloved, do not be surprised at the **fiery trial** when it comes upon you to test you, as though something strange were happening to you. But rejoice insofar as you share Christ's sufferings, that you may also rejoice and be glad when his glory is revealed. (**1 Peter 4:12-13**)*

It is a road of battle for those on earth who are citizens in the kingdom of God. It is a road of persecution and mockery on the part of the world. Jesus Himself tells us, "He that shall save his life will lose it, but he that shall lose his life for My sake shall save it." This is a truth that is hard to grasp. Yet, as it begins its work of transformation, the truth of the "little book" may at first seem painful as it mortifies the old man. But more and more, it leaves nothing but one desire, the coming kingdom of God. This should be the effect of our assimilating this little book of prophecy.[130]

MIGHTY LEADERS WILL ARISE TO GUIDE MANY INTO THE KINGDOM

The time is rapidly approaching when warrior-type leaders, many of whom are outside the traditional American church, will need to network with one another in order to stand together and confront the dark challenges that await this generation. This is a time when numerous disciples of the Lord Jesus, like Peter, Paul, and John, will arise from among His prepared remnant to lead His people toward their respective callings; a time when many true prophets, like Ezekiel, Jeremiah, and Zechariah, also will arise to provide understanding and direction to those with ears to hear; and a time when leaders are called to mobilize the Lord's people into military-type fighting units, such as squads, platoons, and battalions, composing an army that will strongly and without compromise stand for the name of Jesus Christ and His kingdom all across this world. These are the 144,000 who have been sealed prior to the sounding of the trumpet judgments. There has been much written concerning the identity and purpose of those who are chosen for sealing. Yet, most of those writings have directed attention away from the church, and therefore individual Christians have not been motivated to prepare for a sealing that will anoint them to stand in the midst of tribulation.

The next chapter will address such issues as:

- Who are the 144,000 who are sealed?
- What does being "sealed" look like in the midst of these judgments?
- Where does this "sealing" take place?
- What is the true purpose for this sealing?

CHAPTER 6

GODS WARRIORS IN THE END TIMES = 144,000
(Revelation 7)

HOPE CONTINUES TO SHINE IN THE MIDST OF DARKNESS

Tremendous devastation will take place on the earth during the coming period of "trumpet judgments." One-third of the earth, the seas, and human beings are targeted for destruction, yet two-thirds will survive. However, if it were God's purpose to destroy the entire earth, He wouldn't do it in stages. These trumpet judgments are unbelievably devastating, yet they are still warnings to mankind and a call for repentance. In fact, God will plant His chosen warriors among the nations to be powerfully anointed ministers for Christ during this time of great suffering. Before the first trumpet sounds, the Lord will send an angel to seal these "servants of God" in order to protect them from the trumpet judgments that will soon descend upon the earth. These comprise the "Knighthood of Christian Warriors" whose light will continue to shine in the midst of great darkness. They will bring the hope of salvation to millions of people who are scared and searching for answers. These "servants of God" are commonly referred to as the 144,000 from the twelve tribes of Israel.

Then I saw another angel ascending from the rising of the sun, with the seal of the living God, and he called with a loud voice to the four angels who had been given power to harm earth and sea, saying, "Do not harm the earth or the sea or the trees, until we have sealed the <u>servants</u> of our God on their foreheads." And I heard the number of the sealed, <u>144,000, sealed from every tribe of the sons of Israel</u>. (Revelation 7:2-4)

"144,000 SERVANTS" = ARMY OF GOD IN TRIBULATION

Servants is an English word that really doesn't fully communicate the character of these men and women who will receive the seal of God prior to the launching of the trumpet series of events. The Greek and Hebrew words for "servants" are *doulos* and *gibbar* respectively. It is a description applied to the apostles,[131] to the prophets,[132] to Moses,[133] to the true worshippers of Christ,[134] and to anyone who gives himself wholly to another without regard for personal interests.[135]

Thus, these "*doulos* and *gibbar* servants" are the warriors in the Army of God who are totally sold out to the Lord Jesus Christ and will glorify His name with their lives throughout the latter days of God's judgments. They are the Lord's disciples of the twenty-first century who have heard and obeyed the Lord's command to "be ready."[136] They represent the "Knighthood of Christian Warriors" that, in the author's view, are the disciples who will be empowered and dispatched by Jesus Christ to minister in the midst of the Great Tribulation.

WHO ARE THESE "SONS OF ISRAEL" REFLECTED BY THE TWELVE TRIBES?

There are primarily two opposing views that need to be briefly addressed, since both are widely held in the Western church.

First, there is what many call the "pretribulation dispensational" view. Adherents of this view believe that the twelve tribes of Israel who are sealed prior to the trumpet series are the latter-day people of "natural Israel." Furthermore, they also assume that natural Israel is simply today's "Jews." They teach that this passage describes the beginning of salvation for all Israel (or Jews) recorded by the apostle Paul.[137] Furthermore, this view teaches that only Jewish people will comprise the earthly church during the great tribulation, since the present-day Christian church will have been raptured. Thus, only the Jewish nation in the land of Israel will be the chief object of wrath from the Antichrist.

However, this raises an interesting question: Why are the "lost tribes" of Israel included among those sealed prior to the trumpet judgments? Today's Jews are descendants of only four tribes (Judah, Simeon, Benjamin, and Levi). Yet those who are sealed prior to the trumpet series are the Lord's servants from all twelve tribes of the sons of Israel. Adherents of these dispensational teachings believe the Jews to be the sole representatives of the sons of Jacob. This infers that since the descendants of the northern tribes can no longer be visibly identified, they cannot be counted among the sons of Israel. It is true that descendants of the former northern tribes no longer exist as a single nation, yet they do exist worldwide. God has hidden them among the nations, but He is about to anoint and seal many of them for a future purpose.[138]

A second view is what is commonly known as the "spiritual Israel" view. That is, the twelve tribes of Israel represent the New Testament church, composed of both Jews and Gentiles. There are some good arguments as to why the present-day church may be identified with Israel; for instance, some New Testament verses address the similarity between Israel and the Church.[139] Yet, many adherents of this teaching tend to misinterpret Scripture when they teach that the Church has totally replaced Israel as the people of God.

Thus, the two most prevalent views of the identity of the 144,000 that is being taught by Western church theologians are:

- *Pretribulation dispensational view,* which teaches that the 144,000 who are sealed consists solely of the Jewish nation who will experience the hardships of the great tribulation, while the more privileged church will be celebrating their rapture experience in the heavenlies.

- *Spiritual Israel view,* which teaches that the church has replaced Israel as the chosen people of God. This is commonly called "replacement theology" and has been embraced by many in the church for centuries. This is a false theology that has resulted in a deep hatred toward the Jews, whose descendants are continually blamed for the crucifixion of Christ. This biased teaching has produced many terrible holocausts over the last 1500 years, as millions of Jews have been persecuted by the church, who believed they were doing a service for their God. Roman Catholicism as well as several Protestant denominations continues to adhere to this theology, believing they are truly God's chosen people.

There are elements of truth and deception in both of these views; however, there is another perspective that is much more rational and biblically sound than those teachings outlined above. Because this list of those sealed includes tribes within the northern kingdom of Israel, which were scattered among the nations of the world over 2700 years ago, there remains a nagging sense that the identity of the 144,000 runs much deeper than those traditional views of modern-day theologians, who erroneously teach that Israel means either "the church" or "the Jews." Let's take a look; perhaps you will find the following both intriguing and enlightening.

A BRIEF HISTORY OF THE NORTHERN KINGDOM OF ISRAEL

The Bible records that King Rehoboam, the son of Solomon, caused the northern tribes to rebel and establish a separate nation. Surprisingly, the Lord commanded the tribes of Judah and Benjamin not to resist that secession.[140]

Thus, approximately 930 BC, Israel was divided into two separate kingdoms composed of the following tribes.

Tribes in the Northern Kingdom of Israel

1. Reuben	2. Gad	3. Asher	4. Naphtali	5. Manasseh
6. Issachar	7. Ephraim	8. Zebulun	9. Levi (partial)	10. Dan

Tribes in the Southern Kingdom of Judah

1. Judah	2. Benjamin	3. Simeon	4. Levi (partial)

Over a period of two hundred plus years, nineteen kings, all of whom "did evil in the sight of the Lord," ruled over the northern kingdom. The Lord allowed Assyria, an enemy of Israel, to conquer the northern kingdom in 722 BC. It was a brutal massacre of men, women, and children, but those who survived were all deported from the land and forced to assimilate into other nations and cultures, where they completely lost their religious and national identity. Thus, the northern kingdom of Israel was gone and these ten tribes never reappeared in the pages of history after their defeat by the Assyrians.

The southern kingdom continued to remain in the land, although 130 years later, they too were conquered by the Babylonians and went into captivity for 70 years, after which approximately 50,000 people returned to the homeland and Jerusalem. These were the people of Judah, who came to be known as the "Jews." Yet, as many as 95 percent remained in Babylon and were assimilated into the Babylonian culture.

Why is this important? Well, for one thing, it helps us to understand where today's "Jews" come from. This means that the descendants of the northern tribes, as well as those who remained in Babylon, are "not" considered "Jews." Isn't it somewhat ironic that today's "Jews" are continually referred to as national Israel, yet they represent a very small fraction of Abraham's descendants?

Now this does raise some interesting questions; for example:

- Didn't God make His covenant with "all" the descendants of Abraham, Isaac, and Jacob?
- Because of the disappearance of the northern tribes, does this covenant now apply only to the house of Judah?
- Was the prophet Jeremiah mistaken when he said that God was going to make a new covenant with the house of Judah "and" with the house of Israel?
- Were the prophets mistaken when they heard from the Lord that He was going to forgive and restore (not replace) the house of Israel as a people of God? There are numerous biblical prophecies predicting the restoration and uniting of the twelve tribes once again into one nation who will eternally serve the God of Abraham, Isaac, and Jacob.[141]

ISRAEL (EPHRAIM) NOW LIVING AMONG THE NATIONS

Four thousand years ago, Jacob laid his hands upon his grandson Ephraim (a son of Joseph) and prophesied that the descendants of Ephraim would become a multitude of nations.[142] As most Bible scholars know, the name of Ephraim in Scripture frequently refers to the entire northern kingdom. Certainly, Ephraim was the largest tribe, but as big as it got, it never became a multitude of nations before it disappeared in 722 BC. Since it didn't happen before the disappearance, then Ephraim must have become a multitude of nations after its disappearance. Well, where are they? Where has the Lord hidden them? Obviously, they don't even know themselves.[143]

Just before the fall of the northern kingdom in 722 BC, the Lord sent the prophet Hosea to Israel to prophesy concerning the coming captivity. In his writings, Hosea foretold what was to take place for Ephraim (the ten northern tribes) after their disappearance into captivity.

- The number of their descendants would be more than the "sand of the sea which cannot be measured."[144]

- They were to be rejected and become "wanderers among the nations."[145]
- However, the Lord was not finished with Israel (northern tribes), nor would He ever be finished with them.[146]
- In order to illustrate His long-suffering nature for Ephraim, the Lord told His chosen prophet Hosea to marry a harlot. Subsequently, she was unfaithful to Hosea, which broke his heart, and she left him for other lovers. After a period of time, the Lord told Hosea to forgive her and take her back and restore her as his wife. Likewise, the Lord stated that Ephraim would someday be restored and become His bride.[147]

Now comes another surprise. Not only will the descendants of Ephraim (northern kingdom) suddenly reappear, but after thousands of years of separation, they will once again be united with Judah (southern kingdom).[148] The prophet Ezekiel speaks clearly of this future uniting of Judah and Ephraim, and we also learn from Scripture that when Ephraim returns to the land of Israel, from which they were once cast out, they forever will be called "sons of the Living God."[149]

The fact that we have lost track of these descendants of the northern kingdom is irrelevant. Our Lord has made promises to those people that will be kept. Don't believe these "replacement theologians" who teach that the church has replaced Israel. This is a very misleading doctrine that will confuse a sound understanding of biblical prophecy. A day is coming when a remnant of the descendants of Ephraim will be brought back to the land of Israel, and there they will be reunited with their Judean brothers. That day probably will take place at the second coming of Christ, when He gathers His army together for the Battle of Armageddon. Then we'll reign together with Him in the land of Israel.

AMERICA—A HOME TO THE
DESCENDANTS OF EPHRAIM?

Now let's take a look at where these descendants of Ephraim may currently live. There are many stories concerning how descendants of the ten lost tribes migrated to Europe. Although this cannot be conclusively proved, suffice it to say that many of the heraldic symbols used by the great houses of Europe have their roots in the titles Jacob gave his children. Those coats of arms that people so proudly hang on their walls are straight out of Genesis 49:1-27.[150] Certainly many of these peoples migrated into Europe and subsequently to America. It is interesting to note that the prophet Hosea says that at the time of Ephraim's return to the land of Israel, many will come from "the west."[151]

It is a strong probability that a great number of the descendants of Ephraim are Christians living in the United States. Note the following.

- The covenant of circumcision was required of ancient Israel. Up until the 1980s, babies were routinely circumcised in the United States and millions still are today. This was one of the few nations on earth, besides Israel, to do so. Why us?
- The United States was the first nation to have a five-day workweek, thus observing the Sabbath as well as Sunday. Where did that originate?
- It appears from the prophet Zechariah that Ephraim would be the only ally that Judah will have in their war against the "Greeks."[152] At the time of this prophecy, Ephraim had been lost for two hundred years, but here they are united with Judah. Judah is seen as the bow of war and Ephraim as the arrows. They are fighting against the "sons of Greece." From 332 BC until 65 BC, the Greek Empire included the Middle Eastern countries that are now Lebanon, Iran, Iraq, Syria, and Egypt. Today, these are the homes of the Shiite Muslims.[153] Today the United States is the sole ally of Israel. Perhaps this is the Ephraim of the northern kingdom aligning

with Judah of the southern kingdom against their enemies, the sons of Greece.

Finally, Paul tells us in Romans that "all Israel will be saved" when the "fullness of the Gentiles has come in."[154] Perhaps this is because the ten northern tribes are mixed in with the Gentile nations. Think about this! When you consider our own genealogy, can we trace our roots back 200 years? 500 years? How about 2700 years? Modern Israel boasts immigrants from 180 nations. Ephraim, comprising many more peoples than the Judeans were also dispersed some 800 years earlier and therefore, their descendants would be far greater. So, whether one is Hispanic, Asian, African, Indian, or Caucasian, it's more than probable that many of us are physical brothers and sisters descended from Abraham. God knows with certainty. Now, this doesn't mean that every Christian is a descendant from Ephraim, although certainly many are. But, like Rahab, Ruth, and Jethro, many Gentiles are also grafted into the promises of Israel.[155]

THE MEANING OF THE NUMBER 144,000

The delineation of the 12 tribes with that of 12,000 from each tribe can be viewed as a method to universalize the totality of God's elect people residing on the earth at this time. Note that numbering is very significant to understanding much of the symbolism in Scripture.

The number twelve in the bible frequently represents the people of God. For example:

- 12 tribes of Israel in the Old Testament
- 12 apostles of Christ in the New Testament
- The 24 elders before the throne of God in Revelation 4 are probably representatives of God's people from both the Old Testament and the New Testament.

The New Jerusalem will have 12 gates bearing the names of the 12 tribes of Israel and also will have 12 foundation stones bearing the names of the 12 apostles. Also note that the New Jerusalem is laid out as a perfect cube, just like the most holy place in the tabernacle and the temple. The length, width, and height are each 12,000 furlongs or 1500 miles. This is the city that will house the entire people of God.[156]

- 144,000 will be sealed with the names of both the Father and the Son written on their foreheads. Now 144,000 = 12 x 12 x 1,000. The use of the number 144,000 does not necessarily imply an exact number of those who are sealed; it is probably symbolic of a perfect totality of those God has chosen to be sealed.

THE IDENTITY OF THE 144,000 SEALED SERVANTS OF GOD

These are the mighty leaders in the Army of God who will lead His people during the reign of terror that will descend upon the earth. They are the men and women who heard and obeyed the command of Jesus to "be prepared" for His coming.

Just who are they, and where do they come from?

- They are Christians descended from the tribes of the southern kingdom (Jews).
- And they are Christians descended from the tribes of the northern kingdom (Israelites or sons of Ephraim).
- And they are Christians descended from the Gentile nations who have been grafted into God's people.

Currently, they reside in every nation around the world, but a day is coming when they will all gather together with their Commander in Chief, Jesus Christ, on Mount Zion.[157]

144,000 IS A REMNANT OF THE CHURCH, NOT THE WHOLE

The sealing of the 144,000 does not mean that the entire church is sealed. This section of prophecy is not speaking of eternal salvation; it is an anointing of discipleship for those who will be a powerful light in the midst of the darkest period in the history of the world. Many will be eternally saved but not sealed. We see a sign of this immediately after the sealing of the 144,000, when John is shown a numberless multitude from every nation worshipping before the throne of God. These are those coming out of the great tribulation who have been cleansed by the blood of the Lamb.[158] This great multitude will be composed of those Christians who were within the church at the launching of the latter-day judgments, as well as many others who are among the great harvest that will take place within the midst of the great tribulation. Most will have died of natural causes, but they will reign forever and ever because they have truly repented and were reborn into the kingdom of God. Death may be a blessing conferred on people for their faithfulness and to deliver them from evil times. They may be killed, but they do not suffer because the Lord has historically gathered together His faithful people before disaster struck.

> *Therefore, behold, I will gather you to your fathers, and <u>you shall be gathered to your grave in peace, and your eyes shall not see all the disaster that I will bring upon this place.</u> (2 Kings 22:20)*

Yet, it is a special privilege for some believers, granted by the Lord Himself, that they might suffer for the sake of Christ.[159]

> *Only let your manner of life be worthy of the gospel of Christ, so that whether I come and see you or am absent, I may hear of you that you <u>are standing firm in one spirit, with one mind striving side by side for the faith of the gospel,</u> and <u>not frightened in anything by your opponents.</u> This is a clear sign to them of their destruction, but of your salvation, and*

that from God. For it has been granted to you that for the sake of Christ you should not only believe in him but also suffer for his sake, (Philippians 1:27-29)

"Striving side by side" is perhaps, two-by-two proclaiming the gospel in the midst of evil darkness, which has come upon the entire earth. This is publicly proclaiming Jesus Christ without fear of the enemy, even though you are in the midst of severe persecution. Joy remains in the hearts of these warriors. They love Jesus Christ, and they love others more than they value their own lives.

Now the 144,000 who have been sealed for the mission of discipleship during the great tribulation will be greatly challenged. As it was with the apostle Paul, hardships, persecution, and imprisonment await this sealed army of Christian knights. Yet, wherever they go proclaiming His name in the midst of chaos, they will go in a powerful anointing that will greatly impact many people across the earth.[160] A great harvest lies ahead, but contrary to much modern-day teaching, the greatest harvest will come in the midst of the greatest tribulation.

The 144,000 will be those with the faith of Caleb and Joshua, who were the only two among hundreds of thousands of adult males who were ready to go up against an enemy of giants that appeared unbeatable. They believed that God would give them the victory. Thus, they were the only two among that entire generation who were commissioned to lead God's people into the Promised Land. The remainder of that adult generation perished in the wilderness.[161] Surely many of those who perished in the wilderness received eternal life, but they didn't have the commitment to their God to stand strong in the face of a great enemy. They were not the leaders with the warrior spirit that could lead others into the Promised Land amidst the greatest and most dangerous of circumstances. This is the spirit that resides in the 144,000 who will be sealed prior to the coming trumpet judgments.

LEADERSHIP QUALITIES THAT IDENTIFY
THE 144,000 REMNANT

These 144,000 are Christians who continually deny themselves and take up the cross daily and follow Christ.[162] They are His true disciples in the latter days, who view chaos as the greatest opportunity for the light to shine in the midst of darkness.

They are among those historical champions of God who were willing to lay down their lives for the gospel of the kingdom. They understand that they will be persecuted by the world, but it doesn't deter them. Likewise, pressure may be applied to members of their family in order to force them to back off, but their love for the Father and His Son and for the body of Christ will strengthen their commitment to "continue to march."[163]

They are warriors who continue to rejoice in the midst of trials, for they know that it is through the bootcamp in the wilderness that faith and purity of heart is greatly strengthened. Their military mindset understands that there is no victory without a battle and one is not equipped for battle without the training received in the bootcamp of life's tough challenges.[164]

Today, these are those in the body of Christ who recognize the challenging times that are coming quickly, and frequently they can be found strengthening their relationship with the Lord in their respective prayer closets. They are habitual intercessors who understand that in order for true faith to be exercised one needs to let go of the world (in fasting) and lay hold of heaven (in prayer). They are the "watchmen" who are prophets in the Army of God.[165]

These are those who deeply sigh and groan over the sinful abominations that are committed in the midst of the nations. They are being sealed like their brothers and sisters were prior to the destruction of Jerusalem in the days of Ezekiel.[166]

They are also identified with the "overcomers" or "conquerors" Jesus was calling for when He spoke to the churches in Revelation 2 and 3.

Finally, they are the "firstfruits" for God, who follow the Lamb wherever He goes, and in their mouths no lie is found for they are blameless.[167] They will be an anointed light, reflecting the glory of the Lord in the midst of darkness. This is the future glory of Israel.

> *Arise, shine, for your light has come, and the glory of the Lord has risen upon you. For behold, darkness shall cover the earth, and thick darkness the peoples; but the Lord will arise upon you, and his glory will be seen upon you.*
> *(Isaiah 60:1-2)*

Now many readers may believe that this is not for them, but it is for all who will hear His voice and begin to prepare spiritually. These leadership characteristics are not the result of a bible college or seminary education, nor do they describe the majority of those in present-day, full-time ministry. They are the result of one's quest to become more and more like the Lord Jesus Christ, and we must never settle for a lesser vision in our daily journey.[168] Those who actively and strongly pursue this quest in the daily affairs of life likely will be among those who are sealed.

In summary, the 144,000 "servants of God" do not include the entire church but are the firstfruits of His people, those anointed disciples of Jesus who walk with Him for three and a half years during His latter-day's ministry. Their ministry is addressed in greater detail in chapter 8.

CHAPTER 7

THE "SEVENTY WEEKS" OF DANIEL
(Daniel 9:24-27)

If the twenty-first-century knighthood of warriors within the body of Christ is to have a clear overview of their mission during the period of the great tribulation, it is important to have a solid grasp of a prophecy that was shown to the prophet Daniel over 2500 years ago. This prophecy, which is revealed in just four verses of Scripture, is one of the most difficult and controversial passages in the Bible. But it is very foundational for a proper understanding of events that appear to provide a timetable for both the first and the second comings of Jesus Christ; as well as the objectives that will be accomplished at both comings.

A HISTORICAL BACKGROUND OF THIS "SEVENTY WEEKS" PROPHECY

It was a time in the history of Israel when the southern kingdom of Judah had been in captivity in Babylon for almost 70 years. Approximately 536 BC, Daniel, a prophet of the Lord, understood that Jeremiah, some 50 years earlier, had prophesized that this captivity would last only 70 years.[169] Additionally, some 150 years earlier, Isaiah had prophesized that a leader by the name of Cyrus would decree their deliverance from captivity and allow them to return to Jerusalem.[170] Daniel's heart must have leaped as he heard reports of this chosen Persian leader who was making a name for himself throughout the Middle East. Therefore Daniel, realizing that a man by the name of Cyrus was coming into power, knew that a crucial time was approaching; thus he began to pray fervently that the Lord would soon deliver His people from the bondage of Babylon.[171] This prayer of Daniel primarily acknowledges the sin and guilt of the nation of Israel and its forefathers as he vehemently pleads for the mercy of God and for deliverance from Babylonian captivity.

It is important to understand that the primary issue in Daniel's mind was that the large majority of the Israelite people had become worshippers of the Babylonian gods, which allowed the Babylonian populace to equate the God of Israel with their own gods. Now that the Jewish people were in captivity, they were a reproach before the nations of the world, and thus the God of Israel was considered to be weaker than the pagan gods. Now to Daniel, and surely to a remnant of other Judeans, it was more important that Yahweh, the God of Israel, be manifested as the only true God than it was for guilty Israel to escape the consequences of their infidelity. This was a similar concern that Moses had some nine hundred years earlier, when the Israelites were delivered from Egyptian bondage and shortly afterwards, turned from their God to worship a golden calf.[172]

Daniel understood that if the Lord allowed His people to remain in exile forever and allowed Jerusalem, His holy city, to remain in ruins, that no one would ever believe that this God of Israel was the one and true God, the holy Sovereign of the universe. This was Daniel's burden during this time of prayer. Thus, the stakes were high, and Daniel's prayer received an immediate response from the Lord as He dispatched His holy emissary, Gabriel, to personally communicate His message to Daniel. In one of the most challenging passages in the Bible, the Lord responds to this prayer of Daniel with a mysterious prophecy that addresses both the first and the second comings of the Messiah. It is a prophecy that is frequently referred to as "the seventy weeks" of Daniel.

SEVENTY "WEEKS OF YEARS" WILL BRING ABOUT SIX RESULTS

Seventy weeks are decreed about your people and your holy city, to finish the transgression, to put an end to sin, and to atone for iniquity, to bring in everlasting righteousness, to seal both vision and prophet, and to anoint a most holy place. (Daniel 9:24)

Here Daniel was told that "seventy weeks" had been decreed by the Lord to accomplish six results. The first group of *"three negative results"* appears to be identified with the *first coming* of our Lord Jesus Christ.

<u>To "finish the transgression"</u>: Because of their transgression, the Lord previously had decreed that the Judeans were to be in captivity to the Babylonians for seventy years. Now He says that "seventy weeks of years" will put a complete end to transgression of the law of God. In other words, there is a time coming when the Lord's people will be delivered from the curse of the law.

<u>To "put an end of sin"</u>: This conveys the truth that a time is coming when all sin will be put away from before the face of the Lord.

<u>To "atone for iniquity"</u>: This suggests that a perfect Sacrifice will be made in order to accomplish the first two items.

In summary, transgression, sin, and iniquity represent the nature of the curse, which has separated mankind from the Lord since the fall of Adam in the garden. The crucifixion of Jesus Christ is definitely in view here, even though His people will not experience the fullness of putting away all sin from the earth until His second coming.

The second group of *"three positive results"* appears to be identified with the *second coming* of our Lord Jesus Christ.

To "bring in everlasting righteousness": This refers to the state that will exist between the Lord and mankind when sin has been completely removed from the earth.

To "seal both vision and prophecy": This is the final goal of God's plan for the ages and will culminate when Jesus Christ receives His earthly throne. Then all prophecy, including that dealing with the second coming, will be fulfilled.

To "anoint a most holy place": This appears to refer to a future temple from which our King, Jesus Christ, will reign over the nations of the earth. Perhaps this is the New Jerusalem discussed in chapter 14 of this book. A detailed description of this coming temple can be found in the book of Ezekiel.[173]

Remember that these six elements will be accomplished at the completion of the "seventy weeks of years"; therefore, it appears as if both the first and the second comings of the Son of God are in view.

SEVENTY WEEKS = SEVENTY WEEKS OF YEARS

Know therefore and understand that from the going out of the word to restore and build Jerusalem to the coming of an anointed one, a prince, there shall be **seven weeks**. *Then for* **sixty-two weeks** *it shall be built again with squares and moat, but in a troubled time. And* **after the sixty-two weeks, an anointed one shall be cut off** *and shall have nothing.* **(Daniel 9:25-26)**

For those who are unfamiliar with Hebrew, each of the "weeks" referred to in this prophecy are actually representative of "seven" Hebraic years, which consist of 360 days each. For example, 70 "weeks" equates to 490 "years." There are three groups of weeks in this prophecy, which total "seventy weeks." These are *sixty-two weeks* (= "434 years"), *seven weeks* (= "49 years"), and *one week* (= "7 years").

Both the "sixty-two weeks" and the "seven weeks" refer to a period of time between the issuing of a decree to rebuild Jerusalem and the coming of the Messiah. The "one week" is a little more difficult, but it appears to be the time frame in which the Messiah, Jesus Christ, ministers upon the earth in order to accomplish the six tasks. The "one week" also is believed by many to be the length of time for the reign of Antichrist. Perhaps this is also true since Satan's purpose for the Antichrist is to replace Jesus Christ in the world as the true messiah. Therefore, he attempts to imitate some of the prophetic events regarding the ministry of Jesus Christ, such as performing great miracles, including resurrection from the dead.

The decree to rebuild Jerusalem appears to originate with the Persian king Artaxerxes in 457 BC. Although this decree by this Persian king emphasizes adorning the temple and enforcing the law of Moses, Ezra took this commission as approval to rebuild the walls of Jerusalem.[174] Now if one were to add the "7 weeks" to the "62 weeks," it would total 483 years, which, using the *solar calendar,* would bring it to AD 27, the approximate beginning point of Jesus' ministry. However, there was a second decree of Artaxerxes that came in 445 BC, when the king granted permission to Nehemiah to rebuild the walls of Jerusalem.[175] If one were to measure 483 years with the *Hebraic calendar,* this would approximate the time of the crucifixion of Jesus—that time when the Messiah was "cutoff" following a three-and-a-half-year ministry.

MYSTERY IN THE NUMBERING OF THE WEEKS (AD 2016?)

This calculation raises a somewhat mysterious question: If 483 years was the supposed time frame, why did Daniel say "sixty-two weeks" and "seven weeks" instead of "sixty-nine weeks"? Something else appears to be involved here. We must remember that both the *first and second comings* of Jesus Christ are involved in this prophecy. It is conceivable that the "seven weeks" also is to be used for calculating a time for the *second coming* of Jesus, the Messiah.

Another interesting scenario that addresses this mysterious *sixty-two-plus-seven-weeks* issue comes from Sir Isaac Newton, a devoted student of the book of Daniel, who, using the *Julian calendar,* calculated 434 years from the decree given to Nehemiah until the birth of Jesus.[176] Thus, approximately 300 years ago, Newton understood that "sixty-two weeks" was appointed for the first coming of Jesus and that the "seven weeks" must represent a time when there would be a second decree to rebuild Jerusalem.

Thus, it appears that the "seven-week" or "forty-nine-year" period, which is a Jubilee period, has to occur subsequent to the restoration of the Jews to the land of Israel. With this understanding, those in our generation know that on June 7, 1967, the Jewish nation gained control of Jerusalem following the Six-Day War, whereupon they began to rebuild this city. This "forty-nine-year" period of time will then end in 2016, which may very well bring us to the final three-and-a-half-year ministry of Jesus—only this time He ministers through His body; the 144,000.

A SUMMARY OF THE MATHEMATICAL CALCULATIONS

Artaxerxes' Decree in 457 BC:

- 62 weeks + 7 weeks = 483 *solar years,* which would end in AD 27, the beginning of Christ's ministry.

Artaxerxes' Decree in 445 BC:

- 62 weeks + 7 weeks = 483 years, which, using the *Hebraic calendar,* would end in AD 32, the time of Christ's crucifixion.

Sir Isaac Newton's theory using the *Julian calendar*:

- Beginning in 445 BC: 62 weeks = 434 years which would end with the birth of Christ.
- ½ week = 3 ½ years: this is the first ministry of Christ ending in His crucifixion.

Jerusalem restored to the nation of Israel on June 7, 1967:

- 7 weeks = 49 years; this would end in 2016.
- ½ week = 3 ½ years: this may be the second ministry of Christ through His body of 144,000, which would end in 2020, when they too will be cut off.

A STRONG COVENANT FOR "ONE WEEK"

And he shall make a strong covenant with many for one week, and for half of the week he shall put an end to sacrifice and offering. And on the wing of abominations shall come one who makes desolate, until the decreed end is poured out on the desolator. (Daniel 9:27)

The first coming of Jesus Christ was through a supernatural birth in the natural world. He came to confirm the covenant of His Father and to lay down His life to atone for the sins of His people. His second coming also will be with a supernatural birth, only this time through the spirit indwelling the "firstfruits" within the body of Christ.[177] This knighthood of warriors will be filled with the Spirit and will powerfully minister throughout the world. These are the 144,000 who are pictured as standing with the Lamb on Mount Zion.[178] Like their King before them, they will be cut off after three and a half years, and, then, three days later, they too will be resurrected and will arise to the heavens to be joined with their Commander in Chief, with whom they will return together in a mighty army that will defeat the kingdom of darkness and establish the kingdom of God throughout the earth. These men are the vanguard of the Lord and will fulfill in their lives the second half of the seven-year ministry of Jesus Christ, which occurs during the great tribulation period.[179]

A COUNTERFEIT COVENANT

The first coming of Jesus Christ in His natural body and His soon second coming in His spiritual body fully confirm the true covenant that the Father made with His people. However, the prince who is to come, the Antichrist, also enters into a seven-year covenant with the nation of Israel. That too will be cutoff after three and a half years, when he sets up the abomination of desolation in the physical temple in Jerusalem. Satan will now reign for three and a half years in the hearts of his people. Satan always has attempted to counterfeit the works of the true Messiah; thus he creates his own covenant with Israel, and his false messiah also confirms the covenant for seven years. This covenant will be a peace treaty the nation of Israel will sign with her enemies.[180]

The next chapter will address the mission of this "knighthood of the Lord" during the period of great tribulation.

CHAPTER 8

WARRIORS FOR CHRIST IN THE MIDST OF THE GREAT TRIBULATION
(Revelation 11)

Going to war for the kingdom of God is very different from going into Iraq or Vietnam. Soldiers in the Army of God are fighting to save people, not kill them. In fact, God's warrior soldiers are fighting to help free and save many of the very ones who will be used to fight against them. Christians are not warring against other people but against the spiritual forces that are using them. Soldiers in the Army of God love their enemies because they are fighting for them, not against them. This is a tough truth that requires a higher vision than just looking at things in the natural; believers must have their spiritual eyes opened to see and live this reality.[181]

Spiritual insight into the events recorded in chapter 11 of the book of Revelation is essential if we are to have a foundational understanding of our leadership role in the Army of God within an evil world system—a system that is committed to erasing the name of Jesus Christ from the earth and establishing its own eternal kingdom. Revelation 11 is not intended to be chronological but presents us with an overview that will enable us to understand much that is to follow in subsequent chapters, which provide more specific details. Here we are presented with (1) a graphic picture of the

164

church in the end-times generation; (2) an overview of the battles to be fought during this time; (3) a powerful gospel message that the Lord's chosen people will take throughout the earth; and (4) several truths that Jesus taught His disciples concerning the events that will precede His second coming.

THE TEMPLE AND THE HOLY CITY

Then I was given a measuring rod like a staff, and I was told, "Rise and measure the temple of God and the altar and those who worship there, but do not measure the court outside the temple; leave that out, for it is given over to the nations, and they will trample the holy city for forty-two months." (Revelation 11:1-2)

There are three significant areas being addressed here. First, there is the temple, which includes the altar where the people of God gather together to worship their Lord. Second, there is the outer court, which is that area that surrounds the temple and where many gather together but do not enter the temple itself. Finally, there is the holy city, which, together with the outer court, will be surrendered to the world's forces for a period of forty-two months (1260 days). Now regarding these three separate areas, John is commanded to measure only the temple with the altar and those who worship within.

Warriors, it is important to remember that the book of Revelation was written to the church in order to provide understanding of coming events so that Christian leadership will be equipped to lead the Lord's people through these tremendously challenging battles that lie before us. Therefore, it should be apparent that it is the church that is in view when this text speaks of both the temple and the holy city.

Passages in the New Testament clearly reveal that the "temple of God" is a spiritual structure composed of every true Christian who trusts only in the blood sacrifice of their Lord Jesus Christ. Jesus Himself is also part of this spiritual temple, for He is the "corner-stone" upon which the entire temple is built. The ancient prophets and apostles of the Lord also are described as being the foundation of this temple. Over the centuries, this temple has continued to be built as our brothers and sisters in Christ have stood uncompromisingly to the point of death for the glory of the Father who sits upon the throne and for His beloved Son. The building of the temple continues today as Christians in this generation proclaim the majestic glory of the Word of God, which allows His light to be manifested in the midst of the darkness of today's world. This holy temple of God will not be completed until the gospel of Christ has gone out to the peoples of all the nations around the globe.[182] Its completion appears to be finished at the time of the sounding of the seventh trumpet.[183] There is nothing more holy to the Lord than this spiritual temple, and all who attempt to destroy it will themselves be destroyed.[184]

Now this spiritual temple resides in the "holy city," which is also a spiritual city whose inhabitants are all those who profess the God of Israel to be their God. In fact, Jesus Christ Himself also has been called the "City of the Lord."[185] Yet within this city reside many rebellious citizens who confess the Lord but do not live in righteousness.

> *Hear this, <u>O house of Jacob, who are called by the name of Israel,</u> and who came from the waters of Judah, who swear by the name of the Lord and confess the <u>God of Israel</u>, but <u>not in truth or right. For they call themselves after the holy city,</u> and stay themselves on the God of Israel; the Lord of hosts is his name. (Isaiah 48:1-2)*

"God here admonishes the faithless hypocrites among his chosen people. These seemingly pious Israelites practiced idol-worship on the side and yet, had the audacity to invoke the name of Yahweh as their God also, pretending that they were true citizens of his holy city."[186] Also note that it is Israel, the house of Jacob, and not simply Judah (the Jews) who are mentioned here. These are those who confess the God of Abraham, Isaac, and Jacob throughout the entire earth, not simply those residing in the land of Israel. This city also has been referred to as the "oppressing city" that is rebellious and defiled and will accept no correction or draw near to the Lord.[187]

IDENTIFYING THE TEMPLE AND THE HOLY CITY

The temple and the holy city described in these verses is the contemporary church of the end-times generation, and the altar of atonement within the temple represents the person of Jesus Christ and that place where God's people are redeemed within the holy city. It is on this basis that we should understand that the "holy city" described in this text is representative of the entire world of Christianity—that is, all who have been baptized in the name of Jesus. Recognize the parallelism here: just as many of the ancient citizens of Jerusalem were supposedly inhabitants of the city of God, so also the spiritual Jerusalem of this dispensation is inhabited by nominal Christianity. Therefore, within this great city of the Christian world are three broad classes of Christianity.

There is the false church that calls itself Christian. It performs Christian labors and believes it is responsible for mankind's redemption, but it denies Jesus Christ as the true Son of God and the one and only way to eternal life. This is the false church, similar to those in ancient Jerusalem who continued to worship their man-made theology. This is a city serving the purposes of Satan.

There is also a segment of the church that resides in the outer court. They represent the "show church"—that part of Christianity that outwardly pretends to belong to the true church and feigns to believe in the atonement of Christ but are inwardly hypocritical. These are the tares among the wheat; they go with God's people to His temple for worship, but they never enter that spiritual sanctuary of fellowship with God. They are invited into the temple, but they choose to remain in the outer court. They love to attend the churches in Sardis, Ephesus, and Laodicea. This is where the money changers hang out.[188]

Finally, within the temple reside the true people of God who worship at the altar of Christ in spirit and in truth. These are those who have truly committed their lives to the Lord and are frequently found in their prayer closets alone with God. They have a heart burdened for justice, righteousness, and integrity, and they long to see the name of Jesus Christ glorified throughout the earth. They also have a heart deeply burdened for those who stay in the "outer court" and in the "city proper." Although their words may sound somewhat harsh and cruel to many, they are meant to awaken righteousness among those residing outside the temple.

Just as there were three distinctions in old Jerusalem—the city proper, the outer court, and finally the temple—so there are three distinctions in spiritual Jerusalem of our day: the Christian world, including the false church, the show church, and the true church of God.[189]

A TRUE PHYSICAL TEMPLE WILL SOON BE BUILT IN JERUSALEM

Finally, I do want to emphasize my belief that a new physical temple will soon be built by the Jewish citizens of physical Jerusalem, which definitely will be a sign of the times. The building of this temple probably will take place following the victory of God's people in the Middle Eastern war described earlier in the sixth-seal event. While Israel is rebuilding their temple, the Lord will be in the process of completing the building of His temple, a spiritual temple made without hands in the hearts of His people.[190] Thus, as we observe these things occurring in the natural, we need to be able to discern what is simultaneously occurring in the spiritual and to be fully prepared to recognize all that will soon follow.

MEASURING THE TEMPLE

Now John was commissioned by the Lord to measure only the temple and not the outer court or the holy city. This is a spiritual act of separating the true church from the false. Here we are taught in symbolic language not only the condition of Christianity within this generation but also how it will undoubtedly manifest itself as the end of the age approaches. Those who remain outside the temple eventually will reveal themselves as enemies of Christ and His true church. We are also told that this will continue for forty-two months; a period of time that the true body of Christ will be in the wilderness outside the reaches of Satan.[191] This is also a designated time for the Antichrist to exercise his authority upon the earth.[192]

Within the context of measuring the temple, John is told that two witnesses of the Lord will prophesy for three and a half years.

THE TWO WITNESSES

*I will grant authority to my two witnesses, and they will prophesy for 1,260 days, clothed in sackcloth. (**Revelation 11:3**)*

The identity of these two witnesses is one of the more controversial and difficult questions in this section of Revelation. Many modern interpreters believe them to be Enoch (or Moses) and Elijah, who shall literally return to earth to fulfill their ministerial calling and then be killed by the Antichrist. Certainly this interpretation possesses an element of truth, but it also limits our understanding of this passage if we think that it literally refers to two men. Enoch and Elijah were great witnesses of the Lord in their day, and as such they should be viewed as types of those who will be called to proclaim a powerful gospel message in the coming days. Scripture reveals numerous champions of the Lord who stood strong for Him throughout their lives on earth; but their earthly mission has been accomplished, and now they reside eternally with the Lord. Other witnesses soon will arise to be anointed by the Lord to proclaim a great and powerful gospel message to the world in the coming days. The two witnesses in this text are not two single persons, for they have universal influence throughout the entire world. They are also universally hated, and their eventual death brings universal joy among all the citizens of the world's kingdom. It is certainly not conceivable that two single individuals in a single city could cause so much commotion throughout the world. Then who are these two witnesses?

These are the <u>two olive trees and the two lampstands</u> that stand before the Lord of the earth. (Revelation 11:4)

TWO OLIVE TREES AND TWO LAMPSTANDS

The reference to two olive trees and two lampstands harkens back to a similar vision given to the prophet Zechariah centuries earlier.[193] Zechariah received a vision from an angel of the Lord in which he beheld a candlestick containing seven lamps. Above the candlestick he saw a golden bowl filled with oil, which had pipes connecting to each of the seven lamps, providing each lamp with the oil needed to give light. Now on each side of this oil-filled bowl stood an olive tree. These two olive trees were the source of oil supplied to the golden bowl, which then passed it on to the seven lamps. Thus, we have a candlestick receiving its oil from a bowl above it, which in turn receives its oil from the two olive trees. If the candlesticks, which are representative of the Christian church,[194] are to give true light, then oil must be provided by the two olive trees. These olive trees are symbolic of the Holy Spirit of God, who provides the oil of knowledge necessary to allow the light to shine through the people of God. In summary, what John is seeing is symbolic of God's chosen disciples as they minister in the midst of darkness in the power of the Holy Spirit.

THE POWER OF TWO

It is always the testimony of two that must confirm the Word of God.

<u>If I alone bear witness about myself, my testimony is not deemed true</u>. There is another who bears witness about me,

*and I know that the testimony that he bears about me is true.
You sent to John, and he has borne witness to the truth.*
(John 5:31-33)

Jesus is always present wherever two or more are gathered
together in His name.

*Again I say to you, <u>if two of you agree on earth about anything
they ask, it will be done for them by my Father in heaven.
For where two or three are gathered in my name, there am I
among them.</u>* ***(Matthew 18:19-20)***

When Jesus dispatched His chosen ones to minister among the
masses in His authority, it was always two by two. Jesus sends out
the apostles two by two.

*And he called the twelve and began to <u>send them out two
by two, and gave them authority over the unclean spirits.</u>
. . . And if any place will not receive you and they will not
listen to you, when you leave, shake off the dust that is on
your feet as a testimony against them. <u>So they went out and
proclaimed that people should repent.</u>* ***(Mark 6:7, 11-12)***

Jesus also sent out the seventy-two.

*After this the Lord appointed seventy-two others and sent
them on ahead of him, <u>two by two</u>, into every town and place
where he himself was about to go. And he said to them, "The
harvest is plentiful, but the laborers are few. Therefore pray
earnestly to the Lord of the harvest to send out laborers into
his harvest. Go your way; behold, <u>I am sending you out as
lambs in the midst of wolves.</u> Carry no moneybag, no knap-
sack, no sandals, and greet no one on the road. Whatever
house you enter, first say, 'Peace be to this house!' And if a
son of peace is there, your peace will rest upon him. But if
not, it will return to you<u>. . . . Heal the sick in it and say to
them, 'The kingdom of God has come near to you. . . . The</u>*

one who hears you hears me, and the one who rejects you rejects me, and the one who rejects me rejects him who sent me." (Luke 10:1-6, 9, 16)

IDENTITY OF THE TWO WITNESSES IN THE MIDST OF THE GREAT TRIBULATION

Just as Jesus dispatched His chosen disciples two by two throughout the land of Israel, so He will again send out His disciples of this last generation two by two throughout the entire world. These end-times disciples are the 144,000 (witnessing two by two), who are sealed following the Middle Eastern war and prior to the sounding of the trumpet judgments. We see them gathered together with their Commander in Chief on Mount Zion. They are the firstfruits of God's people, and they follow His Son wherever He goes.[195]

Mount Zion, in the literal sense, was the hill in the city of Jerusalem upon which the temple was built and where the Lord dwelt with His people in Israel. However, Mount Zion also is used to describe the true church, where Christ dwells in the hearts of His people. These 144,000 who have been sealed with the name of God on their foreheads come from far countries all around the world, but they will be gathered together with their Lord on Mount Zion. Perhaps this is a literal gathering prior to being sent out two by two throughout the earth, or perhaps it is a spiritual gathering with their Lord as He speaks to them individually within their hearts. Additionally, this scene also may be a literal gathering together of His disciples following their martyrdom, which will take place following their three-and-a-half-year ministry throughout the earth. At any rate they will receive their marching orders and be commissioned with authority from on high prior to being dispatched into a world that is in the midst of great tribulation. This is the time when His chosen knights will minister in even greater power than was witnessed in the ministry of the Lord Jesus Christ during His three-and-a-half-year ministry two thousand years ago. Such great power has never been consistently manifested since the days when the Lord Jesus walked with mankind.

*Truly, truly, I say to you, whoever believes in me will also do
the works that I do; and <u>greater works than these will he do,
because I am going to the Father.</u> Whatever you ask in my
name, this I will do, that the Father may be glorified in the
Son. If you ask me anything in my name, I will do it. (**John
14:12-14**)*

Their power won't be greater in quality than that revealed in the
ministry of Jesus, but it certainly will be greater in quantity since it
will be manifested throughout the entire earth.

Their power over people and the environment will be like that
reflected in the ministries of Moses and Elijah. It also may be that
they participate in the calling of the trumpet plagues upon the earth.
Note the similarity.

*They have the <u>power to shut the sky, that no rain may fall</u>
during the days of their prophesying, and they have <u>power
over the waters to turn them into blood and to strike the earth
with every kind of plague</u>, as often as they desire. (**Revelation
11:6**)*

The gospel message of these 144,000 witnesses will reach every
nation and people upon the earth. They also are described as being
clothed in "sackcloth," which denotes that their message primarily
will be a call for repentance from sin.

*Go therefore and make disciples of all nations, baptizing
them in the name of the Father and of the Son and of the
Holy Spirit, (**Matthew 28:19**)*

*And this gospel of the kingdom will be proclaimed throughout
the whole world as a testimony to all nations, <u>and then the
end will come</u>. (**Matthew 24:14**)*

*<u>The glory that you have given me I have given to them</u>, that
they may be one even as we are one, I in them and you in me,
that they may become perfectly one, so that the world may*

know that you sent me and loved them even as you loved me.
(John 17:22-23)

They will go forth in the fullness of the tremendous glory of the Son of God during a time when worldwide technology and transportation will allow all inhabitants of the earth an opportunity to respond.

And those who are wise shall shine like the brightness of the
sky above; and those who turn many to righteousness, like
the stars forever and ever. But you, Daniel, shut up the words
and seal the book, until the time of the end. Many shall run to
and fro, and knowledge shall increase. (Daniel 12:3-4)

144,000 WILL REPRESENT THE THIRD COMING OF ELIJAH

Approximately 430 years before Christ, The Lord told the prophet Malachi:

Behold, I will send you Elijah the prophet before the great
and awesome day of the Lord comes. (Malachi 4:5)

The Jewish religious community continues to await the return of Elijah, seeing it as a sign preceding the coming of their Messiah. They believe it to be the literal, physical presence of Elijah rather than one coming in the spirit of Elijah. However, the New Testament shows that it was John the Baptist who came in the spirit of Elijah for the purpose of "preparing the way of the Lord."[196]
As previously shown, the spirit and power of Elijah are also found to be present within the two witnesses. Therefore, as John the Baptist was anointed by God to call the people to repentance and to declare the coming of the Lord, it appears as if many with the anointing of Elijah, who are commissioned to call people from among all the nations to repentance, also shall be the voice of one

crying in the wilderness, "Prepare the way [for the second coming] of the Lord; make His paths straight."[197]

These anointed messengers of God will be found in the wilderness, even as John the Baptist came before the first coming of Jesus. Like John, they too will be rejected by the religious leaders and sent instead to the poor and the outcasts, who will hear the true words of God in the midst of tribulation. However, it will not be just one voice this time.[198]

144,000 WILL CHARACTERIZE THE TRUE PROPHETIC SPIRIT

The prophets of God are the eyes of the body of Christ. They are the seers who announce to the people the warnings of the Lord. The true prophets always have had the spiritual discernment to understand their times. It was their assignment to warn, admonish, and call for repentance. The prophets are also called as watchmen. They stand upon the walls of Zion to blow the trumpet and warn of coming danger.

A.W. Tozer also spoke of the tremendous need for the true prophetic ministry.

If Christianity is to receive rejuvenation, another kind of religious leader must arise among us. He must be of the old prophet type, a man who has seen visions of God and has heard a voice from the Throne. When he comes (and I pray God there will not be one but many), he will stand in flat contradiction to everything our smirking, smooth civilization holds dear. He will contradict, denounce, and protest in the name of God and will earn the hatred and opposition of a large segment of Christendom. Such a man is likely to be lean, rugged, blunt-spoken and a little bit angry with the world. He will love Christ and the souls of men to the point of willingness to die for the glory of the One and the salvation of the other. But he will fear nothing that breathes with mortal breath.[199]

The life of the messenger with a genuine prophetic call is not immune to valleys of depression. This is all part of the package. He lives a life that is lonely. The revelation of Christ can come only in the solitary place, away from the crowds and noise of the vendors and their religious wares. These are true prophets who receive their prophetic office directly from the Lord. The prophets are burdened vessels, for they see the vision and the lateness of the hour. The prophet's character is likely to be one of shifting moods, unpredictable at times, and he is not likely to be found mingling with the religious. When a prophet of God speaks a true word of the Lord, it will definitely produce hatred and scorn in the minds of numerous listeners.[200]

The true prophet of God is serious, sober, and not easily persuaded to compromise. His lot is most likely found hidden away on the backside of the desert alone with God. He is the one with a heart for justice, righteousness, honor, and integrity. His words may come across as harsh or cruel, but to the one with spiritual perception, his words are received to awaken righteousness. The higher the calling into his purposes, the hotter the fires required to purify the servant. The greater the responsibility, the greater and more intense are the fires that perfect. This is the cost of prophetic ministry.[201]

THE GOSPEL MESSAGE OF THE TWO WITNESSES

The two witnesses of Christ, who symbolize the 144,000, will boldly and fearlessly stand united against the apostasy of this age as they bear the testimony of Jesus Christ and His truth among all the nations of the earth.[202] As to the contents of their message, this army of "two witnesses" will continually stand before the Lord of the whole earth and will speak nothing but that which their Lord has commissioned them to speak. They will speak of Christ and His atoning blood, which is the witness of the righteousness and holiness of God in the midst of a sinful world. They will openly condemn all efforts to seek salvation outside of that atoning blood, and this will infuriate the false church and the worldly leadership that is attempting to establish a one-world kingdom. This will be a time of tremendous miracles, as the gospel message goes forth in a power greater than the world has ever seen: the blind will see, the deaf will hear, and many of the afflicted will be healed throughout the world.[203]

But this also will be a time when waters turn to blood, the skies are shut so that no rain may fall, and plagues strike throughout the earth. The kingdom must come through tribulation and through all kinds of plagues and calamities. Do not think that this is strange; Moses delivered his people from Egypt by bringing great devastating plagues upon the land, which brought Egypt to its knees. During Elijah's day, the kingdom again was strengthened when he prayed that God would withhold rain from an apostate nation. It also will be that the people of God in the last days will consciously refuse to pray for blessings on the wicked world, and they will beseech God for plagues and judgments that His kingdom may come. And it shall become plain to the entire world, even as it was plain to Pharaoh in the case of Moses and to Ahab in the case of Elijah, that it is the two witnesses of God, ministering throughout the world, who bring about these plagues upon the earth.[204]

The mission of these end-times witnesses for Christ is not to bring peace to the world but to bring division and war, not just among nations but within neighborhoods and families.

> *Do not think that I have come to bring peace to the earth. I have not come to bring peace, but a sword. For I have come to set a man against his father, and a daughter against her mother, and a daughter-in-law against her mother-in-law. And a person's enemies will be those of his own household. Whoever loves father or mother more than me is not worthy of me, and whoever loves son or daughter more than me is not worthy of me. And whoever does not take his cross and follow me is not worthy of me. Whoever finds his life will lose it, and whoever loses his life for my sake will find it. (**Matthew 10:34-39**)*

This is a hard teaching that is never heard from the pulpits, but separation has to take place. The pure light of holiness will not compromise with darkness. There can be no middle ground in the kingdom of God. This truth of God is 180 degrees opposite of that which is embraced by the worldly system, which emphasizes "tolerance" as a requirement for world peace. Not surprisingly, the world's government will once again unite with the false church of Christianity to persecute the true church with the objective of erasing the hard gospel message of Jesus Christ from the earth.[205]

However, if we keep our eyes upon the Lord, our attitude in the midst of persecution and suffering will be one of great joy, knowing that the eternal rewards that await us will be great.[206]

Yes, this will be a time of great tribulation never before seen since the creation of the earth, yet this also will be a time of a great harvest of souls such as the world has never before seen. And there will be no more grey areas; one stands either with Christ or against Him. Love and hatred will be clearly visible among all the inhabitants of the earth.

The enemies of Christ will not be able to stop the two witnesses until the end of the forty-two-month period. At that time, when their testimony is complete, the Beast will be allowed to rise up against the two witnesses. The power of the Antichrist may not be fully manifested until the message of the gospel has been preached among all the nations and the testimony against the wicked world and against the false church has been finished. The world must hear the gospel message proclaimed by the church and must hear it repeatedly so that they become fully conscious of their sin and the redemptive work of Jesus Christ. Those who reject Him will do so willingly and deliberately. Then the testimony is finished and may be silenced. At this point the Antichrist will overcome the witnesses and kill many of them but not all, for there will be a remnant of saints who are alive at the second coming of Christ. But for most of the saints of God, this will be a time of terrible persecution as the Antichrist rises up to silence their testimony. Then the Antichrist will reign supreme, and the world will rejoice and send gifts to one another because the church, which spoke of blood and judgment, has finally been overpowered; or so they believe. The world's hatred of God's people, spoken of by Christ, will reach its zenith.

If the world hates you, know that it has hated me before it hated you. If you were of the world, the world would love you as its own; but because you are not of the world, but I chose you out of the world, therefore the world hates you. Remember the word that I said to you: "A servant is not greater than his master." If they persecuted me, they will also persecute you. If they kept my word, they will also keep yours. But all these things they will do to you on account of my name, because they do not know him who sent me. (John 15:18-21)

A SECOND DEATH FOLLOWED BY
A SECOND RESURRECTION

These witnesses will have completed their worldwide testimony after forty-two months. During that time many among the world's population will have experienced tremendous "true revival"—yet, the majority of the world who rejected the message will be exploding with anger toward those who have hindered their plans for establishing a worldly kingdom. Now the final three-and-a-half-year ministry of the Messiah has been completed through His body, which fulfills the last three elements spoken by Daniel in his renowned "seventy weeks" prophecy.[207] The earthly ministry of Jesus Christ is almost complete; there remains one more event that will be even more glorious than all that preceded it, an event that will bring finality to the gospel of the kingdom. That is the resurrection of the body of Christ. Jesus' first, physical resurrection two thousand years ago initiated a worldwide ministry that has resulted in millions of people entering into eternal life as sons and daughters of God. Now this second, spiritual resurrection, through His body of 144,000, will complete His ministry in this age.

Here we see the first mention of the Antichrist, who at this point in time is the ruler of the kingdom of the world. He is leading the charge to trample the blood of Christ under foot. Prior to the completion of their forty-two-month ministry, the world was not allowed to hinder the 144,000, and certainly many were "burned" who tried to stop them.[208] Just as the veil of protection was removed from Jesus Christ following His three-and-a-half-year ministry, it is also removed from His body of 144,000 chosen prophets following their three-and-a-half-year ministry. They will be slain in view of the entire world in the streets of "the great city that symbolically is called Sodom and Egypt where their Lord was crucified."[209]

Is this "great city" literal Jerusalem? Some commentators say that the city is symbolic of all cities worldwide that are immoral and rebellious against God (Sodom), that enslave God's people (Egypt), and that continually trample the blood of Jesus underfoot (where the Lord was crucified). Thus, they believe that these end-times witnesses are killed in cities throughout the world. Perhaps this scenario is true, but also consider the following possibility that this glorious event will take place in the literal city of Jerusalem with the entire world watching. Recall that Jesus voluntarily went to Jerusalem, knowing that it was time to lay down His life. Likewise, it is highly probable that the 144,000 also will be called by the Lord to travel to Jerusalem, knowing that they too are about to lay down their lives. It appears to be at a time when the Antichrist sets up the "abomination of desolation" on the temple mount and demands that the entire world bow down and worship it. This abomination undoubtedly will be challenged by the people of God, just as Shadrach, Meshach, and Abednego refused to bow down to the image of Nebuchadnezzar in ancient Babylon.[210] Therefore, I perceive that this 144,000 remnant of true Christianity will simultaneously ascend to the temple mount in Jerusalem and refuse to worship this image of the Antichrist. Subsequently, they will be beaten and killed with the entire world watching and cheering and celebrating by giving gifts to one another. Like a Fourth of July party, they will probably set off fireworks around the world, celebrating their supposed victory over the kingdom of God.

However, this is not the end of the ministry of these witnesses, for after three days the entire world will witness the resurrection of this great and numerous body of Christ and watch in horror as they ascend to heaven. Subsequently, a great earthquake rocks the city of Jerusalem, killing seven thousand people. This will result in tremendous worldwide fear and perhaps many, like the Roman soldiers who crucified Jesus, will finally have their eyes opened and will give glory to God and to His Son. Hopefully, these are people who have not yet taken the "mark of the Beast."

This is the second resurrection, and hopefully it will cause more people among the nations to finally have their eyes opened to the truth of the atoning blood of Jesus so that they repent and begin to seek the Lord with their whole heart. It would appear to be the last opportunity for mankind to respond to the gospel of Jesus Christ and enter into the kingdom of God.

CHAPTER 9

CONFRONTATION BETWEEN THE WOMAN AND THE DRAGON
(Revelation 12)

A n overview of over six thousand years of spiritual warfare between the kingdom of God and the kingdom of Satan is depicted in Revelation 12. The object of this stage of John's vision is to provide Christians with a summary of the war that has been taking place between the kingdom of God and the kingdom of Satan since the fall of mankind, a war that will continue until the second coming of our Messiah. Much of what is presented here is revisited in greater detail over the next five chapters. Hopefully this section of the study will provide the Army of Christ with greater insight into the tactics of Satan and his armies of darkness.

THE IDENTITY OF THE WOMAN
(Revelation 12:1-2)

The appearance of this woman is so mighty and glorious that the sun, moon, and stars of heaven all serve as signs to bring out the beauty and the authority that she has been given from on high. John sees her exalted among these heavenly bodies of light, which were all created to rule over the day and the night. Obviously, she is of tremendous importance to the Lord and His kingdom. So, who is this woman? Well, to begin with, listen to the Lord speaking to Satan shortly after he enticed the fall of Adam and Eve into sin:

"I will put enmity between you and the <u>woman</u>, and between your offspring and her offspring; he shall bruise your head, and you shall bruise his heel."
(Genesis 3:15)

This is commonly referred to as the first covenant promise that our God made with mankind. Yet, even with all her glorious appearance, the woman has not yet reached her purpose for existence, which is twofold.

To the <u>woman</u> he said, "I will surely multiply your pain in childbearing; <u>in pain you shall bring forth children</u>". (Genesis 3:16)

First, she is anointed to give birth to the Messiah, the Son of God, who will destroy the effects of sin on mankind. Second, she will give birth, together with the Holy Spirit, to all those who will eternally inhabit the kingdom of God. Thus, this woman is the symbolic mother of the people of God. She can be identified with true Israel in the old dispensation and with the true Christian church in the new. According to various Old Testament Scriptures, the heavy afflictions upon Israel that preceded the birth of the Savior are represented by these severe birth pains.[211] This woman, in all her glory, is also in a state of tremendous suffering, supported only by the hope of a male offspring she painfully awaits. Suddenly, she sees a terrifying dragon, ready to devour her child as soon as He should be born.

THE DRAGON
(Revelation 12:3-4)

Throughout the four thousand years of the old dispensation, Satan had been totally committed to identifying and annihilating all offspring originating from this woman, who was commissioned to establish a kingdom of God upon the earth. Conversely, God's kingdom, being led by the great King, has been commissioned to destroy the dragon's kingdom, which is very powerful, as indicated by his appearance, having seven heads, ten horns, and the seven crowns upon each of the heads. It is a picture of a monstrous serpent of hideous appearance, terrible power, royal authority, and a bloodthirsty and destructive nature. He is especially focused on the Promised One whom God said would have the power to crush him and destroy his plans for the world. Initially, he probably believed that Abel was the chosen one, and so he had Cain murder him. But then Seth was born, and the spiritual seed of the woman began to multiply in the line of Seth. When Satan realized that his problem was not so simple, he changed his strategy. He got the "sons of God," who were angelic beings, to marry the natural "daughters of men" in order to merge together the human and angelic race and thus eliminate the possibility of a human seed arising from a woman.[212] Again, God counterattacked this tactic through the great flood and saved the seed of the woman through the family of Noah. And so Satan's efforts continued throughout the history of the old dispensation, as he sought to control the population of the entire world at the tower of Babel, to enslave the nation of Israel in Egypt, and to annihilate them as a nation using the Assyrians and the Babylonians. When those early tactics eventually failed, Satan attempted to rule over God's people through the mighty Grecian and Roman empires. Throughout this entire period, Satan was intent on either preventing the birth or murdering the child, yet he did not know who the Child would be or when the woman would give birth to Him.

THE BIRTH OF THE MALE CHILD
(Revelation 12: 5)

The long-awaited time finally arrived when the woman, through the Holy Spirit of God, gave birth to the Savior, who had been promised some four thousand years earlier. Satan didn't know who the natural mother would be, but he did know through earlier prophecies that the birth would be in the town of Bethlehem. When he received intelligence from his sources that the birth had recently occurred, he enticed the Judean king, Herod, a servant of the dragon, to take whatever measures were necessary to have this newborn child slain. Herod then dispatched his soldiers to Bethlehem who murdered all the children under two years of age so that he might be sure of destroying the one hated Child.[213] But in spite of all this, the Promised One appeared— Christ was born.

The angels of heaven loudly proclaimed the glory of the birth of Christ, and thus Satan learned who He was and directed all his efforts to thwart the purposes of the Son of God throughout His short life among us. The dragon was not certain how Christ intended to gain the victory over him, although he did recognize Him as the Promised One, as he heard the heavenly angels rejoicing over His birth. Therefore, he employed two different methods to usurp the plans of God for His Son. First, Satan attempted to subject Him spiritually by offering Christ the kingdoms of the world if He would only bow down and worship Satan.[214] When this failed, he aroused the enemies of Christ, the religious leaders of the day, to continually come against Him throughout His three-and-a-half-year ministry. This tactic only caused many within the nation of Israel to come to the knowledge of the truth of their Lord and to recognize the hypocrisy of these religious leaders. Yet, a time had been ordained from the beginning when Jesus was to be cut off after three and a half years of ministry, and thus His enemies were allowed by God to seize Him. Those enemies vented all their anger and jealousy by severely mocking and beating Him. Eventually they crucified Him between two thieves, intending to display Him as simply another criminal in Israel.

Obviously Satan had to be joyously celebrating while Christ was suffering on the cross, for he certainly believed he had finally won. He thought that he had "crushed the head" of God's chosen Champion and thus turned the tables on God's promise to crush his head. What he didn't realize was that the victory for the people of God's kingdom lay in the way of the sacrifice of the perfect Lamb of God. Sin is what gives the devil his claim for the possession of mankind, and now sin itself has been cast out of those of mankind who embrace the sacrificial Lamb that the Lord Himself has provided. The deceiver himself has been deceived! And now he is about to reap what he has sown, as Michael and his angelic army are about to throw him and his demonic army out from the heavens and from the presence of the Lord and down to earth.

THE WAR IN HEAVEN
(Revelation 12:7-12)

The Scriptures of the Old Testament clearly reveal that Satan had access to the courts of heaven and could stand in the presence of almighty God.[215] It is very probable that throughout the four-thousand-year period of the old dispensation, a battle raged in the heavenlies for the souls of those who entered into paradise before the death and resurrection of Christ. Historically, Christ had not yet "crushed the head" of the serpent and thus had not yet assumed dominion over the citizens of the kingdom of God. Satan was still the sovereign ruler of this world, and he argued that all of mankind came under his dominion due to their sin, which disallowed them access before the presence of almighty God.[216] Therefore, according to Satan's view, all the saints of the old dispensation, including Abel, Enoch, Noah, Abraham, Moses, Job, and David, entered into heaven as sinners over whom he had a righteous claim, and they deserved to go to hell, for their sins had not been properly atoned for.

However, the counsel of almighty God countered Satan's argument. That counsel established that Christ's atoning sacrifice applied not only to people who are born on earth following the sacrifice of Christ but also to those who had been born before the crucifixion. Thus, a spiritual war was continually being fought for the souls of the saints of the old dispensation. The head of the Lord's army was Michael, an angelic general who appears in Scripture to be in command of the entire angelic army that is assigned to protect God's chosen people during their life on earth and to confront the claims of Satan for the souls of the Old Testament saints.[217] Finally, when Christ came, suffered, paid the death penalty for the sins of His people, and ascended to heaven to sit at the right hand of almighty

God, the battle was finally decided in favor of Michael and his army of angels. The great voice sang out,

> *Now the salvation and the power and the kingdom of our God and the authority of his Christ have come, for the accuser of our brothers has been thrown down, who accuses them day and night before our God. (Revelation 12:10)*

This was the deathblow to Satan; it was probably shouted by Michael and his entire army at Satan and his army in a power so great that the mighty enemy was finally cast out of heaven.[218]

Satan has lost the battle in the heavenlies, but he will never surrender; he must be completely defeated. Now that he has been cast down to earth, his wrath is directed toward the woman and her offspring, who remain upon the earth; and the conflict continues to this present day.

THE WAR BETWEEN THE WOMAN AND THE DRAGON
(Revelation 12:6, 13-17)

Now the scene shifts back to the earth, where the woman dwells and continues to bring forth offspring.

> *And when the dragon saw that he had been thrown down to the earth, he pursued the woman who had given birth to the male child. (Revelation 12:13)*

The remainder of this chapter is a prophetic picture of all that has and will take place in the Christian era. Satan failed to prevent the birth of Christ, and he failed in his centuries-long war with Michael; and now, being filled with a raging fury, he is intent on pursuing and wiping out Christianity from the face of the earth. His initial and favorite tactic is one of murderous persecution of those who truly profess Jesus as their Lord. However, it isn't just his raging fury that governs his pursuit of the woman; it is his intent to oppose the will of almighty God. The church, symbolized by the woman, is not only the mother of Christ; she is also the mother of all true, spiritual children of God. These are the citizens of the kingdom of God, who continue to oppose Satan and his purposes among mankind. Therefore, he is committed to annihilating true Christianity from the face of the earth.

Satan pursued the woman, but the Lord intervened and enabled the woman, with two wings of the great eagle, to fly into the wilderness, where Satan could not go. This wilderness is representative of that spiritual place where God's people are nourished from on high and, therefore, where neither Satan nor his legions can enter. It lies right in the midst of the world, yet it is separated from the world.[219] Although the people of God reside in the world, they are spiritually separated from the worldly lifestyle. Those in the wilderness live by the principles of God. This wilderness, which is the invisible kingdom of God, is spread all across the world among all nations.

BATTLEFIELD TACTICS EMPLOYED BY SATAN

Although Satan cannot pursue the woman into the wilderness, he certainly can employ military tactics against her in his attempts to destroy her or render her impotent on the battlefield. His initial tactic in the first centuries of Christianity was one of persecuting Christians, using segments of the Roman government. It was Satan's plan to murder the leaders of the early Christian movement and to create fear of persecution among the masses, but this tactic backfired on him. Certainly great numbers of Christians were martyred, but the gospel continued to go forth on the soaring strength of the "eagle's wings," and this period of intense martyrdom by secular government only resulted in the kingdom of God growing greater and stronger than ever before.

As long as the Christian church remained in a state of separation from the world, the armies of Satan were impotent against it. Thus, he employed a second tactic designed to unite the church with the world. He opened his mouth and cast a huge stream of water into the wilderness, designed to wash the church out of the wilderness and unite it with the world. He can then use that segment of the church that washes back into his world to align with him against those who remain in the wilderness. Like the exodus wilderness in the days of Moses, there is a large segment of people who would rather enjoy the comforts of the world than the hardships of the wilderness, which is designed to prepare His people for entry into the Promised Land. Therefore, a large segment of the church that initially entered the wilderness is now brought out on the floodwaters of Satan. These are a people who verbally profess faith in Christ but actually worship the things of the world. They are used by Satan to establish religious organizations, mock the theology of true Christians, and persecute those who remain faithful in the wilderness. This began with the formation of the Roman Catholic Church, and it continues to this day. The Roman Catholic Church, with the exception of a small believing remnant in its midst, is very much of the world. Her popes have built an unrivaled worldwide empire of property, wealth, and influence. In order to amass their earthly empire, they have repeatedly engaged in spiritual fornication with emperors, kings, and princes. Claiming to be the bride of Christ, the Roman Catholic Church has been in bed with godless rulers throughout eighteen centuries of history. This demonic organization also has been responsible for the murder of millions of men and women dedicated to Christ who would not adhere to the pagan theologies of the pope and his religious leaders.[220]

When the fires of persecution waxed hotter and hotter over the European continent, the Lord again provided a refuge where His people might be nourished from the face of the serpent: the "wilderness" of the Western Hemisphere. He supplied them with "eagles' wings" to the land of America, where they were delivered out of the abyss of Roman Catholicism and where Protestantism was allowed to grow.[221] Immediately thereafter, Christian missionaries were dispatched to take the gospel of Christ to foreign nations all around the globe. Thus, over the last three hundred years, Christianity grew stronger and stronger around the world as Christians in the midst of this Western wilderness proclaimed the gospel protected from the persecution of the enemy.

Again, Satan was forced to change tactics when he failed to merge all the Christian institutions with the world. He now turns to individual believers. He does this by "mouthing" a flood of false doctrines and heresies throughout the Christian institutions in both Europe and America.[222] Such is the present method of satanic attack in the West, as lies from the mouth of Satan have become popular teachings, not only in our country's school system, but also in many false churches that claim to embrace Christian doctrines. For example, Satan, appearing as an "angel of light," has convinced the majority of American institutions that:

- Jesus Christ is not really the Son of God but merely a good man who sets a fine example for us to follow.
- Man is basically righteous, and we must stop listening to those who proclaim that all are born sinners.
- God is really not our Creator; we are merely a product of evolution.
- The Bible was written by ancient men as they perceived the world of their day; and, although it contains many good lessons for us, it really is not the "Word of God."
- Whether we are evangelical Christians, Catholics, Muslims, Buddhists, or Hindus, we all serve the same god.
- Eventually all persons will have eternal life, and we will all become like god.
- Vocalizing that Jesus Christ is the only way to eternal life is detrimental to society and should be outlawed.
- The elimination of both Jews and uncompromising Christians certainly would be helpful to the establishment of worldwide peace.

Now we are approaching the generation of mankind when Satan is preparing his military forces to completely erase the name of Jesus Christ from the face of the earth and defeat the plans of God, our almighty Father, for His sons and daughters among the human race.

REVIEWING SATAN'S MISSION AND TACTICS FOR THE END TIMES

Satan has been thrown out of the heavenlies, and he knows that his time is short; but he is not about to give up. In fact, the six-thousand-year-old war between the armies of light and darkness is about to intensify. Satan knows that if he can prevent mankind from professing loyalty to God the Father and His Son, then Satan himself would become the recipient of all worship and glory throughout the earth. Thus, he could claim that he is now in control of all those initially created in the "image of God." Perhaps then Satan could argue before both the angelic and earthly populations that he is much more qualified for rulership over creation and should occupy the throne of almighty God. The mission that drives his evil heart may be summarized as follows.

Satan's Mission Statement: *"To ascend into the heavens, where I will raise my throne above the stars of God and make myself like the Most High,* [223] *(and where I will continue to challenge His sovereign rule over all of creation.)"*

For four thousand years, Satan attempted to make a frontal attack against God by claiming his authority over all of mankind, both living and dead, because of their sin. But he found that to be an absolute impossibility. The difference between the Creator and the created angelic beings is so vast that Satan's challenge was ludicrous, as proven by the life, death, and resurrection of the Son of God. Of all the living beings created by God, the closest to His heart was mankind. Being "in the image of God," mankind has the capacity for the likeness of God, something Lucifer as an angel did not possess.

Beloved, we are God's children now, and what we will be has not yet appeared; but we know that when he appears we shall be like him, because we shall see him as he is. (John 3:2)

Now Satan obviously possesses a heart of immense pride, coupled with a deep bitterness toward our Lord God; yet he was not powerful enough to overthrow Him. However, the "children of God" can be very vulnerable to the supernatural power of Satan.

SATAN'S PRIMARY OBJECTIVES IN HIS WAR ON MANKIND

First, Satan intends to show the entire angelic realm that he is a leader to be worshipped, and he will prove it by controlling those of the Lord's creation who were created in "His image." The principal tactic used to accomplish this was and still is "deception." Satan deceives mankind into believing that the tremendous potential that resides within us can be more fully realized by living life under our own guidance rather than under God's. Thus, Satan convinces the majority of mankind that they have no need for God and that they can be their own gods, doing whatever is pleasing to them, even if it is harmful to others. This self-centered nature is really the nature of Satan.

Second, Satan intends to rid the world of all those who are not deceived and are totally committed to God the Father and to His Son, Jesus Christ. He does this by convincing world governments, together with false religions, that God's people are the only obstacle that keeps them from achieving their worldly goals—so they must be either converted to the world's belief system or killed.

If Satan can defeat the Army of God on earth, then he certainly will claim that God's Word concerning earthly redemption has been voided by the powers of darkness and that he alone is worthy to rule over all of creation. Thus, his commitment to destroy God's beloved witnesses from the face of the earth is tremendously strong.

SUMMARY OF REVELATION 12

Two thousand years are compressed into a few verses in this chapter of Revelation. The intent was to reveal the purposes of Satan, as well as the protection and purposes of God with respect to the war between the kingdoms. This brings us up to the time when the final battle will be fought, but this battle will be greater and more powerful than any previous event in history. One last supreme effort awaits release of a powerful gospel to peoples of all nations. This will be a gospel released through the body of Christ, His 144,000 witnesses for three and a half years throughout the days of great tribulation. These are those who "keep the commandments of God and hold to the testimony of Jesus" right up to that day of their martyrdom. The next chapter presents an overview of this final battle and the tactics that will soon be released by Satan and his dark forces in both the human and spiritual realms.

CHAPTER 10

THREE BEASTS – AN UNHOLY TRINITY
(Revelation 13)

The purpose of this chapter is to prepare and strengthen the warriors in the Army of God by providing advance intelligence concerning the dark and terrifying leadership that soon will arise from among the nations of the world. This will be a time of great trouble as evil leaders who have been anointed by Satan will be obsessed with eliminating the kingdom of God from the face of the earth and establishing an anti-Christian kingdom that will reign forever and ever.

Since the creation of man, Satan has been totally focused on wiping out the people of God from the earth and setting up a kingdom totally devoted to himself. Yet to date, he has been unable to complete this evil mission, as Jesus Christ continues to reign in the hearts of millions of His people. Knowing the purposes of the enemy, our Commander in Chief now provides His army with information regarding Satan's future attempt to establish an anti-Christian power throughout the earth. This phase of John's vision begins with Satan, the dragon, standing alongside the sea, knowing that his time is rapidly running out.[224] If he is to successfully complete his mission of worldwide conquest, he must quickly rally the entire world to unify under his lordship. So far he has been unable to destroy the woman in the wilderness, but he has developed a terrible new plan.

He is about to establish the greatest and most powerful kingdom in the age of mankind. This kingdom will be led by two men anointed with monumental satanic power, and their primary mission will be to rally the world to rise up and devour all those who faithfully proclaim the name of God the Father and His Son, Jesus Christ.

A BEAST RISES UP FROM THE SEA
(Revelation 13:1)

John is a witness to this yet future event, when he sees a dreadful beast possessing tremendous power rising up out of the sea. The sea here is symbolic of agitated and troubled peoples and nations who are controlled by the power of sin.[225] Therefore, this beast arises from the midst of tumultuous nations that have been experiencing tremendous devastations and are crying out for a worldly savior. It is quite probable that this troublesome period on the earth is the aftermath of the "trumpet series" of events—a time of famine, plagues, and a terrified populace resulting from a short but devastating war that has wiped out a third of mankind and the natural resources of the earth.

Beasts in Scripture are frequently symbolic of great world empires.[226] These empires all have different characteristics, even as wild beasts are different. They may differ in strength, courage, speed, ferocity, and crushing power, just as leopards, bears, and lions differ from one another. Some are nobler than others, and some are more despicable. This final beast combines all the characteristics of the great empires that have historically ruled parts of the world. It will have the courage and ferocity of a lion, it will conquer with the speed of a leopard, and it will possess the merciless, crushing power of a bear. This terrible beast is symbolic of that last evil kingdom that will reign during the time known as the great tribulation. This final world power does not consist of just one nation and one people; rather it combines within itself all the evil character and powers of every worldly kingdom that has historically arisen in opposition to the kingdom of God.

In the previous chapter, Satan, the dragon, was symbolized by seven "crowned heads" and ten horns.[227] Here in this chapter, the beast from the sea is described as having seven heads and ten "crowned horns." This beast from the sea is not Satan, but it resembles him and is submissive to Satan's authority. The dragon is the most ferocious of all beasts, and here we see that he intends to give his power and authority to his "beastly son" (the Antichrist), who will use it in an attempt to carry out his father's purposes. Satan is a spirit, and as such he cannot establish an earthly throne in person. He needs a human agent to be subject to him as a world ruler. However, there is a condition that must be fulfilled: this ruler has to worship and bow down to him; otherwise Satan would lose the very dominion he sought. Thus, the Antichrist is about to receive what Jesus Christ refused when Satan offered Him all the kingdoms of the world in exchange for His allegiance.[228]

Let's now briefly analyze some of the bodily features of this Beast in order to obtain a deeper insight into the character of the Beast and his evil designs for God's chosen people. This will provide soldiers in the Army of God with additional understanding of the battles we will shortly be facing from a worldly society committed to ridding the name of Jesus Christ from the earth and replacing Him with their messiah, the Antichrist.

SEVEN HEADS OF THE BEAST
(Revelation 13:1-2)

The seven heads are representative of great empires that rise above all other nations of the world. These are mighty kingdoms that historically have risen to oppose the kingdom of God. John was told that there is a succession in these seven empires. At the time that John received this vision, around AD 90, he was told that five of these empires already had fallen, one was currently ruling; and the last one was yet to come.[229] The five that had already fallen were the Egyptian Empire, the Assyrian Empire, the Babylonian Empire, the Persian Empire, and the Grecian Empire. The sixth empire that currently was ruling during John's vision was the Roman Empire.

A brief background of the history and character of each of these first six empires is provided in appendix A. The seventh head of this beast, together with the ten horns, represents the "end-times" kingdom, which collides with Jesus Christ and His mighty army in the final conflict preceding His second coming.

Now, none of these previous six "beast empires" ever actually ruled the entire world, but each was the greatest oppressor of God's people during its historical reign. Obviously, these were not the only nations that had been enemies of the Lord and His people. Nations such as Philistia, Edom, and Moab continually despised and warred against God's people, yet none of these nations were of great size or worldly influence. On the other hand, there were other large and powerful empires in the ancient world—China, India, and Mongolia, for example—but these had little if any contact with God's chosen people. There were only six empires that were of such size and influence in the ancient Near East that figured prominently in the history of God's people up to the time of Christ and the early years of Christianity. All of these empires not only were powerful politically and commercially, but they also were strongholds of idolatrous polytheism. Satan, the dragon, had authority over each of the empires, and he attempted to use these worldly powers to defeat the kingdom of God.

Although these six historical empires have all been great and powerful, none has ever succeeded in attaining universal power over the entire earth or been able to overcome the kingdom of God. Since the discovery of the Western Hemisphere, this has become even more difficult; thus, a worldwide kingdom must be established in an entirely different way. The last kingdom will come by a confederation of prominent nations rather than by military conquest. This is represented by the "ten horns," which are symbolic of a final manifestation of united nations that will all be of one mind.[230] It will be understood that one nation cannot accomplish world domination. It needs to be a league formed of the "seventh head," made up of the "ten horns" who will eventually give their power over to one man, who is the "eighth" and one of the "seven."[231] This is the Beast in its entirety; a confederation of world powers being of one mind and giving all of their power over to a man. This is also the resurrection of the old kingdom of Nimrod's Babel, a united confederation, in modern form.[232]

ANTICHRIST—THE FINAL WORLD RULER

From within this seventh kingdom will arise a leader who will perfectly personify the darkness of Satan in the flesh, an "anointed one" whom Satan has chosen to rule over this final demonic kingdom. This is the Antichrist, Satan's messiah to the world, who possesses his father's image and will require all the earth to bow down and worship his spiritual father. Just as Christ is the Son of God who came in the flesh to redeem His people out of the world, now the Antichrist is the son of Satan who comes in the flesh to eliminate the people of God from the face of the earth. Satan believes that by overcoming the people of God, he will have a legitimate claim to be the greatest and most deserving ruler over all of creation. Here we see this dragon in the world working to overthrow the kingdom of God, but his ultimate ambition is to defeat God's plan for His people and thus argue that he is more qualified to rule over all creation.[233]

Antichrist will emerge on the world political scene, bringing new hope through a multitude of promised "changes." He will honor all who acknowledge him and set them up as rulers and reward them with land and wealth taken from among the people.[234] Because of the apparent relationship of the ten horns to the Roman Empire revealed in the book of Daniel, it appears as if the Antichrist may arise out of a modern culture that is descended from the ancient Roman Empire.[235] However, he may or may not presently be a citizen of any contemporary European, Middle Eastern, or northern African nation that was once a part of the Roman Empire. It's possible that he could even be an American whose ancestors came from a region that was once under the control of the Roman Empire.

ANTICHRIST—HIS POPULARITY

That person who will one day fill the role of the Antichrist is likely a national political figure somewhere in the world today and viewed by his constituents as another popular and successful politician. He will emerge on the world's political scene in the aftermath of worldwide economic, environmental, and military disasters. He gains control by stepping up at this time and mesmerizing the masses into believing that he alone is the one who can lead the world into peace and prosperity through a multitude of promised "changes." He probably is quite handsome and certainly has a charismatic personality that can mesmerize the masses like a popular rock music celebrity. He will seduce many with flatteries to the point that even the wise among the people will stumble and be led astray.[236] These are people who have been raised on "Hollywood stuff" and are schooled in a godless public education system. They have very little conception of the history of the United States or the Middle East. All they know is that when they see and hear this man speak, it makes them feel "warm and fuzzy" inside. They relish hearing vague terms such as *hope* and *change*.

Although the man known as the Antichrist will be charismatic, he also will be very firm in his speech and probably with eyes that appear hypnotic, along the lines of Adolph Hitler's. Being possessed by Satan, he also will have the fierce countenance of a lion—flattering but very dangerous to those who will not idolize him. He will be perceived by the masses as their true savior.

ANTICHRIST—THE APPEARANCE OF INVINCIBILITY
(Revelation 13:3, 14)

Somewhere in his rise to absolute power, Antichrist receives a mortal wound to the head that appears to be fatal. It is possible that he will physically suffer an assassination attempt, which is published in the media as having been fatal. This probably will occur when his popularity is growing, for it appears as if the entire world is aware of this apparently fatal incident. Suddenly he will "miraculously" recover, and the world will marvel as if their heroic messiah has been raised from the dead. They will see this as some sort of divine approval on this man's life. Now the masses will embrace their "savior" with more vehement energy than ever before, and they will begin to see him as a god. This wound may be faked, or it may be real; but nevertheless this perceived resurrection will result in much loyalty from the world. This supposed death of Antichrist and his miraculous recovery is intended to paint a parallel picture with the death of Christ and His resurrection. This tactic of the dragon is designed to weaken the gospel message that the death and the resurrection of Jesus Christ is the only path to eternal life.

Many commentators do not believe that this "wound that was healed" pertains to a human being. They write that it is symbolic of the reincarnation of ancient Babel, or the Roman Empire, or some other power. However, we must ask the question, "Why does the Lord provide so much information concerning this man?" It seems this detail is recorded so that His loyal soldiers will know who and what they are up against. Thus, being familiar with his tactics, we will not be seduced like many in today's church who will be blinded by his hypnotic speech and "miraculous resurrection."

Additionally, he will certainly convince the world that he is invincible when he brings down three powerful nations in his rise to power.[237] Perhaps the assassination attempt will emanate from among these three nations. At any rate, the world will shout, "Who is like the beast, and who can fight against it?"[238]

THE COMING OF THE TWO-HORNED BEAST
(Revelation 13:11-17)

There is a second agent through whom Satan will carry out his war against the kingdom of God. He is symbolized as a beast with two horns like a lamb but one who speaks with the mouth of a dragon. This second beast is less terrifying in appearance, but he will be anointed by Satan with miraculous power. He is commonly referred to as the False Prophet. He will personify the tenderness and love of a lamb, yet it will be a deceptive form of love, for he will soothingly preach comforting lies intended to gain the loyalty of mankind through trickery.

The primary mission of the False Prophet will be to bring all of mankind to worship the Antichrist. He will have supernatural skills of persuasion, which he will use to promote the Antichrist as a great man with a tremendous love for his people and one who will bring peace and prosperity to the world. The False Prophet is the workhorse who causes the people to turn to Antichrist. Both delude the masses and exercise their authority over the world. Antichrist represents the kingdom of the world in the political and military realms, while the False Prophet deals with the religious, moral, and commercial aspects of this society.

Together with Satan, the Antichrist and the False Prophet will constitute an unholy trinity of malicious evil. As Christ received authority from His Father, so Antichrist receives authority from the dragon; and as the Holy Spirit glorifies Christ, so the False Prophet glorifies the Antichrist.

THE FALSE PROPHET—HIS THREEFOLD MINISTRY

Signs and Wonders

The False Prophet will publicly perform incredible signs and wonders before the world for the purpose of demonstrating his supernatural authority. This will cause the world to embrace him as a true prophet who deserves great respect and obedience to his every command. These miracle workings of the False Prophet also will persuade the vast majority of people that the god of the False Prophet is greater than all other gods. The result of these "showy miracles" will surely shift the focus of many away from the works of Christian disciples to the person of the Antichrist. He intends to undermine the works and miracles of the disciples of Jesus Christ, who will be sharing the gospel and also performing miraculous works during this period of time. The healing and other miracles of our Lord through the work of His disciples will be directed to needy individuals from a pure heart of love. Their works will stand in opposition to the miracles of the False Prophet, who performs them before the world solely for the purpose of demonstrating supernatural power. Those who experience the miracles of God in their lives probably will not be deceived by the False Prophet, and therefore the kingdom of God will continue to increase. The sincere love for the common people emanating from Christ's knighted disciples will be clearly obvious to many when compared to Satan's disciples, who will resemble popular Hollywood performing stars seeking to enamor the masses.

The Image of Antichrist

The False Prophet will command the people to make an "image of the Antichrist," which will then be given breath and the ability to speak. When this image is complete, all the inhabitants of the world will be required to worship it. Those who refuse to worship this "speaking image" will be sought out and slain. This scenario is somewhat difficult to envision. Let's look at a couple of possibilities.

- Perhaps this may resemble a "golden image" like that erected by Nebuchadnezzar in ancient Babylon. He too required all persons to bow down and worship it or be put to death.[239] This image is in the likeness of the Antichrist, however. If the image of Antichrist is located in a particular geographic area, then it will require television-type technology to visibly manifest it around the world. If so, there will probably be a law requiring all to gather before a picture of this image and worship it at designated times throughout their daily routine.
- A second scenario could be that a new religious organization will be set up, using existing church facilities around the world, where people can gather and worship the Antichrist. This religious organization itself then will be the "speaking image." Envision this in a nation of Christianity: statues and pictures of Christ, together with any sign of a cross would all be replaced with this image of the Antichrist. All peoples would then be required to join and regularly worship in these churches. Imagine a world of false Christianity, believing

that the Antichrist is the true Jesus, and the Islamic people believing him to be the Mahdi. They would be united in worshiping their perception of god.

The Mark of the Beast = 666

The False Prophet will command that mankind receive the mark of the Beast in order to participate in the marketplace. The mark is the number of a man, and this number is 666. This verse probably receives more attention than any single verse in Scripture. The mark not only identifies those who worship the Antichrist, but it also appears as if this number will one day identify the man himself. Over the centuries, many have attempted to identify evil leaders in their day with this number, using Latin, Greek, and Hebrew alphabets, which also can be converted to designated numbers.[240]

As mentioned in an earlier chapter, numbers are frequently used to provide deeper understanding of certain passages in Scripture. In this passage, the number 6 is commonly understood to represent man, while the number 3 is representative of our Triune God. Therefore, 666 is man attempting to be God, though he can never reach the number 7, which represents perfection. However, I wouldn't recommend that we spend time trying to satisfy our curiosity by attempting to identify potential Antichrists. The title the man receives when he obtains worldwide authority probably will be a part of the number. It will be plain to the people of God when he arrives on the world scene as the sole leader.

The purpose for the mark is to control all of the world's commercial activity. In order to legally buy or sell in this anti-Christian kingdom, one must have this mark upon the forehead or the right hand. Who are the ones who receive the mark on their forehead, and who are the ones who receive it on their right hand? The forehead is the most exposed and conspicuous part of the body. Perhaps this will be reserved for the leaders in commerce and government so that they may be immediately recognized. If so, the mark on the right hand is for the common workers who are also committed to the Antichrist. This mark also will be beneficial for those among the body of Christ since its absence provides a visible means of identifying those who remain faithful to the Lord. The ongoing gospel message being proclaimed during this period most certainly will include warnings against receiving this mark of the Beast. Many will fall away, yet many will remain faithful unto death. They may not be able to buy or sell, but they will faithfully cling to the name of Jesus. Thus, in the midst of tribulation, Christians will be social outcasts in the world, but they will maintain, "The Lord almighty is our God, and Christ alone is our King." And they will not be ashamed.

FALSE TEACHERS ALIGN WITH THE WORLD

The contemporary church is flooded with false teachers who have avoided, and will continue to avoid, awkward confrontations with the political system over important biblical truths. It is much easier to speak the words people want to hear, for this gains them popularity among their followers, who will embrace them for supporting their lifestyles. This is parallel to the attitude of the Jewish people of the old dispensation when they were warned by God's prophets concerning the coming judgments of God. However, false religious teachers opposed this message of the prophets and preached peace and prosperity and the love of God, asserting that God would never allow His nation to be conquered. Thus, the people vanquished all thoughts of future captivity and continued on their merry way, buying and selling and mocking those messengers God had sent to warn them. What happened to the Jews in historical Babylon is the same thing that will happen to the spiritually lazy in Mystery Babylon. They will be captivated by the Beast because their hearts will be made drunk with the wine of materialism. These are people who will be churchgoers, neighbors, coworkers, and relatives who may acknowledge Christ, but in reality, they are trusting in money.

Paul was certainly including the Christian church of the Western world in his prophetic warnings concerning false teachings.

For the time is coming when people will not endure sound teaching, but having itching ears they will accumulate for themselves teachers to suit their own passions, and will turn

*away from listening to the truth and wander off into myths.
As for you, always be sober-minded, endure suffering, do the
work of an evangelist, fulfill your ministry.* (*2 Timothy 4:3-5*)

Remember this: Whatever people choose to believe, they
will somehow find a way to validate it as a truth, regardless of its
absurdity.[241]

SATAN'S TACTICS MANIFESTED IN THE
HEADS OF THE BEAST

Satan has employed two primary tactics in his zealous rage to
obliterate the kingdom of God from the earth.

First, he uses *an all-out frontal assault* with the intent of
completely annihilating God's people from the earth. This tactic
visibly reveals his deep hatred toward us. This has been historically
manifested time and again as God's people frequently have been in
danger of complete annihilation. Following is a brief examination
of how Satan has employed this frontal assault, using the first six
heads of the Beast to attack the kingdom of God. We can expect to
see these same methods used in the future.

- Brutal enslavement, which suggests that we can expect mass
  imprisonment in concentration camps.
- Women and children targeted for slaughter in order to create
  tremendous fear among the masses.
- Murder of the elderly and newborn babies for the purpose of
  controlling population growth.
- Brutal and humiliating torture. For example, the Assyrians
  captured many Israelite army leaders and lifted them up
  naked but alive on the heads of spears and paraded them in
  front of their people.
- Attempts to destroy all worship of God by destroying the
  physical churches; this is parallel to the destruction of
  Solomon's temple by the Babylonians.

- Destruction of all Christian Bibles, music, and worship under the threat of death. Antiochus Epiphanes of the Grecian Empire outlawed the worship of the God of Israel and declared that all Hebrew Scriptures were to be destroyed.

Second, Satan *entices God's people to voluntarily turn from the worship of the Lord to worshipping the "prince of this world."* This is the more preferable tactic of Satan, since he takes much greater pleasure in turning a man's heart than in killing him. He believes that this proves that he is more worthy of worship than the Lord. Here are some examples of what to expect.

- Satan enticed the Israelites with the Egyptian lifestyle. Instead of trusting the Lord during the hardships encountered in the wilderness, they grumbled and wanted to return to Egypt. This may parallel a great falling away during tribulation times.
- The influences of the Hellenistic culture, which encouraged self-seeking pleasures and immorality, threatened to wipe out the worship of God from the nation of Israel. Many of the youth of that day scorned the traditions of Israel and embraced the pleasures of the Greeks. This is very prevalent in today's Western culture, which emphasizes commercialism, sexual immorality, and entertainment as the epitome of an enviable lifestyle.
- The Roman Empire established a powerful but dark authority within Christianity that was designed to turn Christian worship away from Christ and to a human representative, a pope who is unknowingly controlled by the spirit of Satan. Expect liberal Christianity to be encouraged within the seventh kingdom as long as Jesus Christ is not the focus of worship. These false Christian churches, comprised of Roman Catholicism and liberal Protestantism, will support this anti-Christian kingdom and will be a major player in the betrayal of true believers who refuse to compromise their faith.

Christian soldiers, we must anticipate that similar tactics will be employed by the enemy with even greater power in the seventh kingdom ruled by the Antichrist.

A SEVEN-YEAR COVENANT

As we've seen in a prior chapter, Jesus Christ comes to confirm the true covenant between God, His Father, and all who embrace Him as their Lord. It is a covenant that ushers in everlasting righteousness and ends with the anointing of a most holy place.[242] However, there is also a covenant that will soon be established by Satan, who is intent on counterfeiting the true works of Jesus Christ. A future prince, who is shortly to come upon the worldly scene, will make a seven-year covenant with the secular nation of modern Israel. This covenant, or peace treaty, is made by Israel without the Lord and is described in Scripture as the "covenant with death," because it is made with the sons of darkness and will be confirmed by the Antichrist.[243]

However, after three and a half years, this dark covenant that was founded on lies will be broken by the Antichrist, who will then set up his own image in the Jerusalem temple as another counterfeit anointing of the most holy place. Perhaps the event that triggers the Antichrist's sudden claim to deity will be his miraculous recovery from a head wound. At any rate, the setting up of this satanic image in a newly built temple in Jerusalem will be the sign of the beginning of that great tribulation that will suddenly ensnare the world.[244] Therefore, it appears that Israel will soon begin to rebuild a physical temple to the Lord and then again start daily sacrifices like their ancestors under the old covenant.

Jesus confirmed His Father's covenant when He kept the law perfectly and then laid down His life at the cross for the sins of mankind. Thus, after three and a half years, Jesus Christ gave His own life as a perfect sacrifice and thereby did away with the need for the sacrificial system of the old covenant.[245] Antichrist appears to be counterfeiting the three-and-a-half-year ministry of Christ with his first three and a half years of uniting world government—afterwards, this will be followed by the mandatory worship of his image.

Perhaps it is when Israel is rebuilding their physical temple that the Lord will rebuild His temple made without hands in the Spirit, a temple in the hearts of His people. This may very well be the time of the anointing of the 144,000, who will represent the body of Christ in the second half of the seven-year covenant that ushers in everlasting righteousness.[246] This may also be the hour when men of wisdom will arise and their voices will be heard in the wilderness, declaring to the whole world, "Make straight the way of the Lord, for the day of the Lord is at hand."[247] These are chosen ones who have been prepared by God Himself. Until this time, they have been hidden away like David and his mighty men in the cave at Adullam. They have been prepared like Joseph in prison, where suffering and sorrow was experienced, until the day they are called to arise. They must first be purged with fire before they can be used at this glorious level.[248]

PURPOSE AND DIFFERENCES BETWEEN TRIBULATION AND THE WRATH OF GOD

Tribulation is a time of warfare between the forces of good and evil. It is God's judgment on the world's evil system. However, tribulation is also the attack of the world's system against the true believers of Jesus Christ. Good and evil cannot coexist. The characteristics of each become more prevalent during a time of conflict. As the battle intensifies, the people on both sides become more visible and neutrality begins to disappear. Tares among the church are continually exposed, as they fall away and side with the religiosity of the world. The armies of the world become larger and darker and more violent in their hatred against God and His people. At the same time, the Army of God becomes stronger and more radiant as they stand for the truth of God and His Spirit grows stronger and stronger among them.

Tribulation will increase in escalating stages, but so will the strengthening of the Lord's army. Within the church, there will be

increasing levels of purging the tares, purifying the people, evange-
lizing among the nations, and receiving power from on high. This
fierce pressure takes place because of God's love for mankind and
His desire to bring out of darkness into salvation every single soul
possible and to destroy every demonic stronghold that has held
the human race captive. Traditional or lukewarm Christianity will
collapse during the great tribulation.

The wrath of God is a military action on the part of the armies of
heaven to avenge and rescue God's people in the world. God's wrath
is directed solely against the forces of darkness. What restrains the
outpouring of God's wrath is the ability of His people to maintain
their stand and communicate their faith. There are many in the world
of darkness who will be called into the light. When this is complete
and God's message is shut down within His people, then the full
wrath of God will be poured out on the earth. Until then, many
warnings are poured out from heaven that tend to either draw people
to the Lord or to solidify their hatred toward Him.[249]

OUR LORD'S CALLING: "ENDURE AND REMAIN FAITHFUL" (Revelation 13:10)

Antichrist is not looking solely for political control of the world;
he is intent on receiving worship from every single individual who
lives on earth. The working of miracles and the requiring of image
worship, together with a marked body, are all designed to visibly
identify and unite the individual peoples among the nations in loyalty
to Antichrist as well as to one another. They are also intended to
help identify those persons who refuse to receive the mark of the
Antichrist or bow down to his image. These faithful believers will
be classified as enemies among the nations and a hindrance to world
peace.

The world system will make war against the people of God who
continue to witness during the reign of this Antichrist. These are
warriors who refuse to submit to his authority and maintain that it
is not Antichrist, but Christ, who is their King. They will be deeply

hated, and the world will wage a continuous war against them and eventually overcome them. These will be extremely hard and faith-challenging days of persecution, a time of "wearing out" the people of God. All Bibles and biblically related books will be outlawed, and the peoples will be required to turn them over to the authorities for burning. Those who refuse will be criminally charged and sentenced to imprisonment. Murderous executions, imprisonment in concentration camps, brutal torture, separation from family, and forbidding the purchase of food and water will all be commonly employed tactics of this evil kingdom. These are the days of persecution.

One may wonder why imprisonment of many of God's people is employed by the enemy instead of simply executing them. Imprisonment allows time for the enemy to break down the spirit of people for the purpose of allowing them to voluntarily turn away from the Lord and render allegiance to the Antichrist. Though deep in their heart they may still believe in the Lord, some will give up. Ultimately, their life in this world will mean more to them than their faith in Christ. Satan rejoices when people visibly turn away from almighty God and render allegiance to him, even if it is not from a pure heart. Turning people to him is more important than murdering them, for it means he has defeated what is most important to God— the steadfast faithfulness of His people. The one who has turned away from the Lord undoubtedly will be praised before the world as a newly enlightened hero. This will be a shameful experience.

Our Lord will provide a hiding place for us when the time of persecution arrives. Where is that hiding place?

- For the prophet Daniel, it was both in a king's palace and in a lions' den.
- For Shadrach, Meshach, and Abednego, it was in a fiery furnace.
- For Joseph, it was in an Egyptian prison.
- For David, it was in a cave out in the wilderness.
- For the apostle Paul, it was in prison or shipwrecked in the Mediterranean.
- For the spies sent by Joshua, it was in a harlot's house in Jericho.

- For Corrie Ten Boom, it was in a flea-infested barracks in a Nazi concentration camp.

They were all right where God wanted them, and not a hair on their heads perished. So our hiding place is wherever the center of the Lord's will is for us. The only thing we should fear is being out of God's will. We must trust in the Lord for our individual hiding places, for they will probably be different for every believer in the end times. Meanwhile, let us stand in the gap and prepare our brothers and sisters for the coming hour of trial.[250]

Although Christians will be physically overcome during this horrendous period of time, they are the ones who are victorious in this war. They have become outcasts from society, mocked by former neighbors, family members, and friends, imprisoned, and killed. This is the body of Christ, having an experience similar to what their Lord Jesus Christ endured two thousand years earlier. They are now glorious participants in His great victory. In the crucial test of faith, they have chosen to relinquish their lives rather than their faith in their God. This is true victory.

REJOICING IN THE MIDST OF PERSECUTION

*Blessed are those who are persecuted for righteousness' sake, for theirs is the kingdom of heaven. Blessed are you when others revile you and persecute you and utter all kinds of evil against you falsely on my account. Rejoice and be glad, for your reward is great in heaven, for so they persecuted the prophets who were before you. **Matthew 5:10-12***

*Indeed, all who desire to live a godly life in Christ Jesus will be persecuted. **2 Timothy 3:12***

*Count it all joy, my brothers, when you meet trials of various kinds, for you know that the testing of your faith produces steadfastness. And let steadfastness have its full effect, that you may be perfect and complete, lacking in nothing. **James 1:2-4***

*In this you rejoice, though now for a little while, if necessary, you have been grieved by various trials, so that the tested genuineness of your faith—more precious than gold that perishes though it is tested by fire—may be found to result in praise and glory and honor at the revelation of Jesus Christ. Though you have not seen him, you love him. Though you do not now see him, you believe in him and rejoice with joy that is inexpressible and filled with glory, obtaining the outcome of your faith, the salvation of your souls. **1 Peter 1:6-9***

A CHINESE SONG—"TO BE A MARTYR FOR THE LORD"

Many attend that big American church and hear that if you serve God, you will be healthy and prosperous. In China, it's the exact opposite. You may be healthy and prosperous before you are a Christian, but once you start serving God, seldom will you stay that way. Chinese Christians have learned to be committed in their faithfulness, even though they realize that they may be torn from their families and martyred. The following song has been very popular in the Chinese underground churches:[251]

From the time the early church appeared on the day of Pentecost,
> *The followers of the Lord all willingly sacrificed themselves.*
Tens of thousands have sacrificed their lives that the gospel might prosper.
> *As such they have obtained the crown of life.*
Those apostles who loved the Lord to the end
> *Willingly followed the Lord down the path of suffering.*
John was exiled to the lonely isle of Patmos.
> *Stephen was crushed to death with stones by the crowd.*
Matthew was cut to death in Persia by the people.
> *Mark died as his two legs were pulled apart by horses.*
Doctor Luke was cruelly hanged.
> *Peter, Philip, and Simon were crucified on the cross.*

Bartholomew was skinned alive by the heathen.
Thomas died in India as five horses pulled apart his body.
The apostle James was beheaded by King Herod.
Little James was cut up by a sharp saw.
James the brother of the Lord was stoned to death.
Judas was bound to a pillar and died by arrows.
Matthias had his head cut off in Jerusalem.
Paul was a martyr under Emperor Nero.

I am willing to take up the cross and go forward,
To follow the apostles down the road of sacrifice.
That tens of thousands of precious souls can be saved,
I am willing to leave all and be a martyr for the Lord.

To be a martyr for the Lord,
To be a martyr for the Lord,
I am willing to die gloriously for the Lord.

CHAPTER 11

MYSTERY BABYLON THE GREAT: CAPITAL OF WEALTH, PLEASURE, AND HARLOTRY
(Revelation 17—18)

As previously mentioned, the book of Revelation is not necessarily chronological. Frequently, a general vision is first recorded, and then later visions are given to provide additional detail. The events recorded in these two chapters concerning Mystery Babylon and the seven-headed beast actually occur prior to the reign of the Antichrist recorded in chapter 13. In fact, the one-world government that will be ruled by the Antichrist will come to "ultimate power" only after the destruction of Mystery Babylon. This is apparent from the crowns on the heads of the ten kings in Revelation 13. Yet, here in chapter 17, as the harlot woman continues to ride the beast, the ten kings have not yet received their royal power.

Now who this ungodly woman is, what she represents, and where she exists today is so important to God's chosen people that more has been recorded concerning her identity and purposes than has been recorded concerning the Antichrist. That is because she is capable of such great deception that everyone who follows her will be eternally lost. Even many people attending today's Christian churches have fallen in love with her.

Christians need to listen to the cry of our Commander in Chief:

Come out of her, my people, lest you take part in her sins, lest you share in her plagues; for her sins are heaped high as heaven, and God has remembered her iniquities. **(Revelation 18:4-5)**

Mystery Babylon will be burned up prior to the supreme reign of the Antichrist; perhaps she is the target of the "trumpet series," which destroys one-third of the earth. This is very important for our comprehension, as most teachers of Revelation simply warn Christians about receiving the mark of the Beast. Yet, before the time of the "mark," those who have not come out of Mystery Babylon will be burned up. One needs to understand who, what, and where she currently resides in the world if one plans to survive her destruction.

The identity of this woman, commonly referred to as Mystery Babylon, is of extreme practical importance for our present generation. Yet this continues to be one of the most controversial passages in the book of Revelation, and there have been numerous different interpretations concerning her identity over the last two thousand years. These interpretations have struggled with the fact that Mystery Babylon is pictured as both a woman and a city. However, in order for God's chosen people in our generation to refuse to have fellowship with her, they must be able to discern who and/or what she is during these times.

BABYLON—A CONTROLLING INFLUENCE OVER MIGHTY NATIONS

Now consider the manlike statue in Nebuchadnezzar's dream, which portrayed the different parts of the human body as representative of mighty world empires—empires that would arise and oppress the people of God prior to both the first and the second comings of the Lord Jesus Christ.[252] You may recall that the "head of gold" was representative of the Babylonian Empire. Now we always recognize a person by looking at the person's face, for it provides the identity for the entire body. The head consists of the eyes, the ears, and the brains, all of which develop the vision and guide the body in the direction the head desires to go. Therefore, the successive kingdoms that have risen to power after the fall of the Babylonian Empire are all part of Mystery Babylon. These are also the kingdoms of Satan, which would oppress the people of God in separate places over the centuries. These kingdoms first arose in the Middle East, where they warred against the nation of Israel, and now they have expanded westward as the Christian church has grown over the last two thousand years and moved westward. Babylon is the "head" that controls the affairs of the world and the authority that oppresses the people of God throughout all the ages since the beginning of time.[253]

BABYLON THE GREAT—IDENTIFYING THE CITY

After watching seven bowls of tremendous destruction poured out across the earth, John is summoned by one of the seven-bowl angels to witness the judgment "of the great prostitute who is seated on many waters." Earlier, John had seen a beautiful woman clothed with the sun who was the mother of all true believers. Now when he sees this harlot woman, he is truly astonished. Perhaps his astonishment is because this harlot woman has the same facial features as the woman who was symbolic of the true church. But instead by being clothed with the sun, this woman is adorned with clothing and jewelry symbolic of great riches and tremendous worldly beauty. She also appears to be celebrating, for she is intoxicated from drinking the blood of those martyred for Christ. Remarkably, she is astride the seven-headed beast, which apparently reveals that she is the one who steers the direction of the kingdom of the world.

This evil woman is further described as sitting on many waters, which represent many peoples and nations across the world. Furthermore, she also is referred to five different times as representative of the "great city." Just as the waters are symbolic of peoples and nations, this great city appears to be symbolic of the capital of these peoples and nations, the capital of a gigantic system for the pursuit of wealth and pleasure — Babylon.

Note the following parallel with another woman who is also symbolic of a great city.

Then came one of the seven angels who had the seven bowls full of the seven last plagues and spoke to me, saying, "Come, I will show you the Bride, the wife of the Lamb." And he carried me away in the Spirit to a great, high mountain, and showed me the holy city Jerusalem coming down out of heaven from God, having the glory of God, its radiance like a most rare jewel, like a jasper, clear as crystal. (Revelation 21:9-11)

New Jerusalem is symbolic of the bride of Christ, and Mystery Babylon is symbolic of a prostitute. These are two spiritual capital cities; one reigns within the kingdom of God, and the other controls the direction of the kingdom of the world. However, they also have physical locations. Babylon currently exists within the world, while New Jerusalem resides in heaven, awaiting its time to descend to the earth.

Now does the city commonly known as Mystery Babylon have a single geographical location? Well, yes and no! She is that city where the idolatry of commercialism, immorality, and hatred of God exists. She is worldwide, yet she is located more strongly in certain sections of the world. Consider where her primary location exists today.

The United States of America is also a nation seated on many waters, both physically and symbolically. Physically, she is bordered east, west, and south by the two greatest oceans, and by five great lakes in the north, and through her interior run mighty rivers. Symbolically, she rules many diverse peoples, for her population encompasses peoples from every land around the world: Europeans, Asians, Africans, Jews, Arabs, Hispanics, etc. People everywhere dream of a day when they can come to the great land of America. She is the pride of the whole earth, as well as being the focus of great jealousy from nations who envy her riches. America, a once great nation that exported the gospel of Jesus Christ throughout the earth, has turned from the Lord and now exports pollution among all nations with her adulterous lifestyle. The world watches scenes of lust and greed from Hollywood movies, buys American pornography, listens to the dark lyrics of popular American music, and thus idolizes the American culture composed of a materialistic and pleasure-seeking spirit. A nation that once proclaimed the righteousness and truth of God among the nations now pollutes the earth with her filth.[254] Our nation may or may not be the final location of Mystery Babylon, but in this generation, the spirit of the whore is most prominent in the great cities of America. There is no doubt among discerning Christians that our once proud and mighty nation is shortly heading for a great and terrible fall.

HISTORICAL ATTEMPTS TO IDENTIFY MYSTERY BABYLON

Recall that John sees this harlot woman sitting on the beast that has seven heads and ten horns. These seven heads are described as seven mountains and also as seven kings. Our early Christian fathers, who experienced the horrendous evils of Roman Catholicism through the dark ages, strongly believed that John was seeing a vision of the power of the Roman papacy represented by this harlot woman seated on seven mountains. They believed that these mountains were representative of the city of Rome, which is known for being built upon seven hills. However, mountains in Scripture are frequently symbolic of mighty empires.[255] Just as a mountain is visibly manifested above the normal surface of the earth, these ancient empires were the greatest among all the surrounding nations in the world. Thus, it appears that this mysterious Babylonian woman, who sits on the top of these symbolic mountains, is the primary controlling influence over all the great empires that have arisen over the centuries.

Certainly the Roman Catholic Church has been in bed with the kings of the earth through the centuries. She has partied with these kings and made both them and their respective nations drunk with the wine of her spiritual fornications. Her cup also is filled with the blood of saints, for she has been responsible for the murder of countless numbers of the Lord's sons and daughters through the centuries. The Catholic Church is very much of this world. Her popes have built a worldwide empire of property, wealth, and influence. They have fought with armies and navies in the name of Christ to build a huge kingdom that is very much of this world. And to amass their earthly empire, they have repeatedly engaged in spiritual fornication with emperors, kings, and princes. Claiming to be the bride of Christ, the Roman Catholic Church has been in bed with godless rulers down through history.[256] Because of her worldwide influence and wealth, every world leader will have to deal with the Catholic Church in order to attain and maintain political power. Therefore, many renowned theologians believe that this harlot woman is representative of the Roman Catholic Church throughout the New Testament age.

Still others believe this harlot is not only representative of Roman Catholicism but also includes the false Protestant churches that claim to be the bride of Jesus Christ. They too have departed to climb into bed with the commercial and political leaders of the world. Although she continues to claim that she is rightfully married to the Lord, she is really the counterfeit church pretending to be the true bride of Christ.

Finally, many have written that Mystery Babylon is representative of the great world cities of today, such as New York, Paris, Chicago, Rome, London, Los Angeles, and Hollywood. These are cities in supposedly Christian nations that have exported evil across the globe. Thus, they see her as the city-prostitute who commits fornication with all the nations of the earth and reigns from a city that is the center of worldwide commerce and industry. However, can we really equate "Babylon the great" with any single city or geographical area? Perhaps! First, let's look deeper into some symbolic truths represented by both the woman and the beast.

BABYLON—UNITING POLITICS, COMMERCIALISM, AND RELIGION

The city of Babylon embraces different public activities that align themselves with one another for a sole purpose; they each want to achieve power and wealth through their own efforts. Every mighty world empire has embraced the following three sources of power within society. These are the ones who will mourn the destruction of the woman, Mystery Babylon.

The "kings of the earth" represent the political and military arena. (18:9)
The "merchants of the earth" represent the commercial arena. (18:11)
The "unfaithful woman" represents the religious arena. (17:5-6)

The uniting of these three elements of society represents a gigantic humanistic system in pursuit of wealth, pleasure, and eternal life. The focus of the citizens of Babylon is to achieve more and more earthly riches and comforts without the hand of God. Babylonian laws are continually passed to accommodate their worldly pursuits. These are laws contrary to the laws of God, for they are laws designed to appeal to mankind's desire to be their own gods.

THE WOMAN = COMMERCIALISM AND RELIGIOUS POWER

Now commerce is certainly a legitimate pursuit. Every honest worker has a connection to commerce. The Bible mandates that we work and engage in legitimate business in order to provide for our families.[257] However, while commerce is a legitimate pursuit of profit, *commercialism* is an attitude of the heart that can grow into the religion of money worship. Commercialism is the love of money and luxury that seeps into our psyches, hardening our hearts to needy people and distracting our minds from the priorities of God's kingdom.[258]

The great world of commercialism has become virtually a religion to countless millions of people; its leaders, who are the captains of industry, are practically the rulers of the world. The world of commercialism is tangible and visible, but the animating spirit behind it all is the love of "money." Money is the god that many worship in our day, for a person's true god is that to which he consecrates his life. Money is the greatest of all the idols in our generation. It is the greatest rival of God for the affections and devotions of man.[259]

The harlot woman appears to be in control of worldly governments because of her great riches and her millions of followers, who continually seek comfortable answers for their lives. These followers of the woman are in pursuit of worldly riches and comforts, but they are also seeking assurance that their happiness will continue in the eternal realm after their death. Both "religion," for its millions of followers, and "commercialism," for its wealth, are extremely powerful and generally control the affairs of public life. Therefore, "politicians" have to climb into bed with the whore in order to gain the support of the people that will allow them to succeed in rulership over the various kingdoms of the world.

All the injustices that are committed in the commercial and religious segments of society are symbolized by this harlot woman. Her cup is full of the abominations of an evil, worldly kingdom that has persecuted the true people of God since the beginning of time. Babylon is the capital city of all humanism, which seeks the unifying and salvation of mankind through his own works. Her merchants are the great ones of the earth, whereas Christ, whose followers have no place in this world, has commanded His people to take the lowest place in it.

THE BEAST = POLITICAL AND MILITARY POWER

This seven-headed beast that is being guided by the harlot woman is the same as the one that will eventually establish that final world empire and murder the two witnesses in the streets of Jerusalem.[260] This beast is representative of the anti-Christian world power from a political and military point of view. It is the attempt of Satan to establish his own kingdom, using the agencies of power that have been instituted in the world. Both political and military powers were initially established by God to help bring social justice and order to the world. However, they have been continually abused by greedy kings and politicians to bring about social chaos and disorder in order to attain power and control over the peoples and wealth of the world.

Now in Revelation 17 and 18, we are presented with a brief historic survey of the development of mighty world powers, as well as a preview of their final defeat and descent into hell. The seven heads represent six stages of development of various kingdoms that existed in the past, plus the coming kingdom of the Antichrist repre-sented by the seventh head. The ten horns represent ten powerful kings who will rule during the final manifestation of the seventh kingdom. They will unite and establish their final anti-Christian kingdom with the Antichrist as the supreme world ruler. This future realization of the kingdom of Antichrist shall come into being through a united confederation of nations rather than through mili-tary conquest. Thus, the seventh head is representative of a league of nations that will anoint the Antichrist as the ruling authority over the final world empire. They will be viciously dedicated to wiping out the people of Christ from the face of the earth in order to provide more blood for their rich and beautiful whore.

The eighth beast is obviously distinct from the other seven. He is the Antichrist, not simply another human ruler. Daniel describes him as another horn among the ten, with eyes like a man and a mouth speaking great things. He is even greater than his companions. He blasphemes almighty God and makes war with the followers of Christ. He also overthrows three of the ten horns in his rise to supreme power.[261] He is not a human ruler through whom the power of evil finds expression; he is that evil power itself. He appears to be Satan incarnate.

However, before this eighth beast, the Antichrist, can come into supreme worldwide power, he must control all the commerce and religions of the world. Thus, he must overthrow the woman who symbolizes that great and immoral city of Babylon. This overthrow of Mystery Babylon will take place in a single day without any advance warning. The world will be in tremendous shock and grief as their idols are suddenly swept away and replaced by a single man. This will be a quick and powerful attack on the areas in which the harlot exercises the greatest control—that place where all the merchants of the earth were in bed with her.

THE WOMAN LOVES THE BEAST—THE BEAST HATES THE WOMAN

The woman is committed to the beast, for it is because of its legislative and military powers that she is enriched. However, unknown to the woman, the beast is not committed to her but is using her to gain power in the world governments. The Antichrist will suddenly attain supreme power by burning the city of Babylon and taking control over all of her commercial and religious activities. This sudden attack appears to be nuclear, for it is described as being a great fire with rising smoke that is seen from far off.

Behold, I am against you, O proud one, declares the Lord God of hosts, for your day has come, the time when I will punish you. The proud one shall stumble and fall, with none to raise him up, and I will kindle a fire in his cities, and it will devour all that is around him. (Jeremiah 50:31-32)

Following the destruction of Mystery Babylon, the final kingdom will be committed to bring all three sources of power under the complete control of the Antichrist.

Commercialism will continue to exist for those embracing the "mark of the Beast." But free enterprise among the merchants of the earth will disappear. "No one can buy or sell unless they have the mark of the beast!" In order for this to happen, all economies of the world must merge into one. And for that to occur, the present economies must crumble in order to induce the people of the world to accept the new system. This new world money system will be the lifeblood of the beast government of Antichrist.

Religion will continue to exist for those worshipping the "image of the Beast." But freedom to worship other gods will disappear. Yet a remnant of God's chosen people, previously identified as the 144,000, will not take the mark of the Beast and will not bow down to his image. They will continue to be a strong and powerful light in the midst of this darkest period in the history of mankind.

THE BABYLONIAN WHORE AND FALSE CHRISTIANITY

In Scripture a woman is frequently symbolic of God's chosen people. Time and again His people are represented as a bride who has pledged by covenant to be faithful to Him. In the Old Testament, Israel is the wife of Yahweh, while in the New Testament; the church is the bride of Christ. Also, in the book of Ezekiel, we see the nation of Israel being identified as the wife of the Lord. She was immensely blessed by her Husband but later went whoring after other gods. She also sacrificed her children to these gods, much like today's abortionists.[262] Hosea presents a similar picture. Thus, it is apparent in Scripture that a spiritual harlot is one who claims to be faithful to her Husband yet runs after the gods of other religions. The true church is the spiritual bride of Christ. But the counterfeit church claims to be the true church, and outwardly she may look like the church; but she really embraces the worldly lifestyle. She enjoys the favor of the world, as they bless her with precious jewels and gold. She becomes great and powerful, but she is nothing but a harlot. She fornicates with those who dwell on the earth and laughs at the need for atonement by the blood of Christ. She invents a Christianity of her own, which may not deny Christ as a god but will trample on the need for His redemptive blood. She secretly whores with all that opposes the Lord and His people. Her churches are filled with false teachings that are designed to support her adulterous lifestyle and provide assurance that she is loved by God.

The preaching of "tolerance" is a doctrine promoted by the enemy to effectively weaken the truth of the biblical gospel. There is a fast-growing movement within our nation to ridicule people for being "intolerant" in their Christian beliefs. For example, if Christians proclaim that Jesus Christ is the one and only way to eternal life, they will be maligned as bigots and fanatics, as judgmental and unloving, and therefore a hindrance to the establishment of a peaceful society. The "tolerance" doctrines assume that man is basically good, even if at various times in life people may need counseling help. Tolerance will be communicated around the world as the ultimate expression of love. Eventually it will become unlawful to share the true gospel message with people, because that would be considered offensive. This religious prostitute will side with those governmental authorities that insist that the church must be "tolerant" of those who believe that there are many ways to eternal life. She will help blend Christianity with other faiths and continue to dilute the true gospel of Jesus Christ.

Gradually, she will reveal her character more clearly until a great apostasy takes place. Eventually the false church will openly separate from those who are faithful to the Lord Jesus Christ. Denominations will come to an end; all will unite under a single purpose: the reconstruction of the world. The gospel of Christ will be trampled underfoot by those who insist that they are the true representatives of God. Protestantism will openly join with Catholicism in embracing all religions worldwide. Thus, the woman known as Mystery Babylon is also representative of the apostate church in the present, as well as in past generations. The following sections will provide an overview of why I believe the United States of America is the primary site of Mystery Babylon today.

AMERICA AND ISRAEL — BOTH NATIONS FOUNDED UNDER GOD

America and Israel are the only nations ever founded from the beginning upon the purposes of almighty God. Israel was God's nation under the old covenant. The Western world, which was relatively unknown in biblical times, represents the world of Christianity under the new covenant, and certainly America has been the most influential nation in the promotion of Christianity throughout the world. The Lord obviously has called America as a representative of the new covenant; and over the last four centuries, she has greatly influenced most of the nations of the world with the gospel truths of Jesus Christ. Godly leaders built this country under the biblical principles of justice, truth, and religious freedom. These founding fathers were Europeans seeking freedom from persecution within the countries of Western Europe. They were the early pilgrims who pursued and honored the Lord. Our present-day heritage of freedom, peace, and prosperity is the fruit of our forefathers' obedience to and love for, the Lord Jesus Christ and His heavenly Father.

Today, America has become a whoring nation that worships the gods of money and immoral pleasures. The United States of America is a nation gone terribly astray. Over the last four decades, we have seen a tremendous decadence rise up and control a once Christian culture. For example:

- Prayer and Bible study are no longer permitted in our schools, although our college campuses are floating in New Age and Far Eastern mysticism.
- Abortion clinics have butchered tens of millions of babies over the last thirty years, and now our government funds abortion clinics around the world.
- Violent youth gangs and desperate drug addicts make many city streets unsafe.
- The pop music industry is dominated by drug-using rock stars who have become cult leaders for our youth. Their songs glorify rebellion against parents, drug abuse, sexual promiscuity, violence, murder, and Satanism. Many of our children know every lyric and sing along with every word.
- Violent and demonic TV, movies, and video games, along with drugs, have spawned a dangerous belief system among American youths in the twenty-first century. Today's youth culture is not unlike the young disciples of Adolph Hitler in the early thirties who were adamant worshippers of their new charismatic leader.

- Sin is running rampant, yet the church is strangely silent and in fact, has lost its influence concerning a righteous direction for our nation and has turned to a watered-down proclamation of the true gospel message.

AMERICA—IN THE WORLD'S SPOTLIGHT

Many say that America is not mentioned in Scripture, and therefore the destiny of our nation is unknown to our generation. It certainly is not specifically mentioned, but why would it be? The Bible was completed two thousand years ago, and the discovery of the Western world would not take place for another thousand years. The Lord does not specifically mention geographical regions of the world before their discovery. Mankind has received a mandate to go out and discover it for themselves, and having done that, more and more clarity emerges from the prophetic scriptures. Jesus commanded His people to take the gospel of the kingdom into all the nations. What country has made the greatest impact upon the growth of Christianity worldwide?

When Jesus teaches on events that precede His second coming, He warns of false teachers who will lead many astray and of many in the church who will betray others. Think about it! What other country has such a large Christian population that will fall away and betray many of His people? America is the greatest representative of Christianity since the last page of the Bible was written. However, the American church also is flooded with false teachers who speak the words people want to hear, for this is what allows them to grow in popularity among those who want to continue in their worldly lifestyles. Paul certainly was speaking to these popular American churches who are led by false teachers.

For the time is coming when people will not endure sound teaching, but having itching ears they will accumulate for themselves teachers to suit their own passions, and will turn away from listening to the truth and wander off into myths.

227

As for you, always be sober-minded, endure suffering, do the work of an evangelist, fulfill your ministry. (2 Timothy 4:3-5)

This is similar to the attitude of the Jews, when they were warned by God's prophets concerning the coming invasion by the Babylonian army. In the days of Jeremiah, false teachers among the Jews continued to preach peace and prosperity and insist that the love of God would never allow them to be invaded by the heathen Babylonians. The people listened to these comforting teachings and continued on their merry way, buying and selling until, suddenly, terrible destruction fell upon them and destroyed them as a nation.

Today, in most American churches, the leaders who claim to know His Word fail to recognize that the hour of judgment is at hand. Many of these churches are filled to overflowing to hear their pillow prophets teach a gospel of prosperity and easy believism. These are churches that support their congregations in the idolatrous worship of commercialism, while the few voices declaring the impending judgment of God are ignored. Like the Judeans in the days of Daniel and Jeremiah, Americans today are hardened in sin, embracing the popular but false gospel of peace. The majority of the American church is oblivious to what the Lord is about to do within our country in this generation. Everything is about to change. You will not recognize this nation in the very near future.

Several commentators have taught that ancient Babylon or ancient Rome will again arise in the latter days and that these chapters refer to a yet future city. If that is true, then the second coming of our Lord is in the distant future. However, if we are presently on the verge of the Day of the Lord, as many of us believe, then the United States is the only nation that possesses the characteristics of Mystery Babylon to the level reflected in the book of Revelation.

AMERICA—BIBLICAL DOCTRINES
REPLACED BY IDOLATRY

The great prosperity experienced in this nation has lulled God's people to follow a cross-less, painless gospel that accommodates selfishness and laziness within Christians. The thoughts and intents of the heart remain unchallenged.

Lukewarm congregations avoid the preaching of the cross and the discipline of the Lord. This message exposes a person's carnal and hypocritical nature, and that is not popular with many church attendees. So the pulpit becomes virtually silent on the most powerful life-changing truths of the gospel. The church today has a "Christian welfare mentality" that caters to the wounded, giving out large doses of feel-good teachings that perpetuate self-absorption and empowers the ego of the listeners. Christians are misled to jump into the resurrected life by a shortcut that bypasses the continuing work of the cross in the believer's life. The teaching that Christ did everything for us and that we don't have to suffer death to our carnal self is a deadly doctrine leading millions down the wrong path and to the wrong destiny.

The blindness existing within the church is horrendous. While individual churches continue to compete with one another for more people and more money, they remain virtually silent concerning the sin that is rapidly overtaking our nation. A country that was founded on Christian principles has now chosen to throw off our Christian heritage and embrace the principles of Sodom and Gomorrah. We are a country where millions of babies continue to be slaughtered, where the presence of our Lord is not welcome in governmental and educational facilities, where immoral sexual relations and pornography are now uncontrollable, and where same-sex marriages are beginning to be welcomed. It's getting worse and worse, and many believers within the church undoubtedly will continue in their comfortable blindness until the time comes when the American society turns its hatred toward the Lord into a violent persecution of His church. When that time arrives, and it is rapidly approaching, there will be widespread fear and panic followed by a great falling away.

Sin and lawlessness have replaced righteousness and justice in our once great and mighty land. America has fallen into the same trap as ancient Israel. Power and riches has led a nation of God into a great apostasy. Instead of teaching people how to "think and grow rich," these churches should be encouraging one another to pursue the Lord and His holiness. With their teaching and preaching of materialism, *these churches are doing a better job of paving the way for the rise of the Antichrist than preparing for the return of Christ.*

AMERICA — WHERE IDOLATRY THRIVES

In America, the voice of demons sounds quite pleasant. They are heard on television, in the newspapers, in theatres, in our classrooms, and even in many of our churches. They are voices that continually speak to us about living a happy and successful life, but in reality they conceal the truth that leads to true eternal happiness. Materialism, entertainment, pleasure seeking, celebrity worship, abnormal sexual relationships, obsession with shopping and eating — these are our idols. We worship those things that provide physical and emotional pleasure, and we worship all those people who contribute to our individual pleasures. Our religion is all about "meism"; we are our own god. These are the worshippers of Mrs. Mystery Babylon, that adulterous whore who pretends to be the bride of Christ.

Even though America has existed only for some three hundred plus years, it is probably the greatest and most prosperous nation in the New Testament era. The age of technology all started with America. Technological equipment and toys have spawned tremendous worldwide commercialism over the past thirty years. America also has had the greatest controlling impact on the commercial sector of the world's culture for several decades leading up to these last days. The world may hate America, but it certainly yearns for its lifestyle. Like Babylon, which was represented by the golden head in Nebuchadnezzar's dream, America certainly appears to be the home of the harlot woman, who is the guiding source of the beast in this era. We are a nation in love with money and toys. The modern temples and altars where we worship are our shopping malls and TV game shows. We bow down to the gods of pleasure, materialism, and money.

The following verse describes the world's social system in the last days. Doesn't this sound like the common lifestyle of today's America?

But understand this, <u>that in the last days</u> there will come times of difficulty. For people will be lovers of self, lovers of money, proud, arrogant, abusive, disobedient to their parents, ungrateful, unholy, heartless, unappeasable, slanderous, without self-control, brutal, not loving good, treacherous, reckless, swollen with conceit, lovers of pleasure rather than lovers of God, having the appearance of godliness, but denying its power. Avoid such people. 2 Timothy 3:1-5

Is modern America, together with those great historical empires, represented by Mystery Babylon who rides and steers the beast? Probably! At any rate, there can be no doubt that our country loves to fornicate with the lady who rides the beast. And we must be aware that if the rise of the Antichrist is coming within our generation, then obviously America will be the last of the nations represented by this harlot woman. If so, she will soon burn in a single day. That does not mean that the entire population of America will be destroyed, but our nation will no longer exist as a worldwide power. This will be a time of tremendous destruction and grief among Americans, which will open many hearts to the gospel message proclaimed by those warriors in the Army of God.

COMING TO AMERICA:
CHRISTIAN PERSECUTION AND SPIRITUAL REVIVAL

Many Christian leaders have been teaching that God is preparing a great wave of revival that will allow the restructuring of society, restore all things, and establish the kingdom of God on earth, thus reclaiming the earth so that Christ can return. Of course, this is not what He taught concerning His return. A terrible persecution will precede His coming, and it will cause a great falling away and a separation between false Christians and those who are truly faithful to the Lord. This will be the foundation for the coming, true move of God, a terrifying and glorious move of God that will bring the true gospel of Christ to the forefront of humanity.

The great tribulation will produce a final harvest of souls and a revival that will awaken many sincere Christians who have been put to sleep by their teachers. This move of God cannot be purchased, video produced, or manufactured like some movements over the last twenty years, for this move will be accompanied by judgment and persecution. The leaders of this movement will pay the price, like the first disciples, who challenged the falseness that had infiltrated the true church. These leaders will guard the sheep and speak forth in the power of God. There is a showdown coming between true leadership and those false teachers who will attempt to oppose the true movement of God.[264]

For the American believer, it is hard to imagine that Christian persecution could happen in our country, much less to begin to prepare for it. Yet it is coming, and it will shortly be commonplace for both Jews and Christians to face imprisonment and death in these last days. It may be even more severe in America than in other nations, for here is where the enemy will concentrate his efforts to stamp out the name of Christ from the Christian church. The political system, the courts, and the media will continue to promote their anti-God agendas. I recommend reading Romans 1:18-31 to see what happens to mankind when they trade the truths of God for lies. This is America in Scripture.[265]

The great majority of Christian teachers in America completely miss the point that the Lord makes in the following passage regarding events at the end of the age.

> *Then they will deliver you up to tribulation and put you to death, and you will be hated by all nations for my name's sake. And then many will fall away and betray one another and hate one another. And many false prophets will arise and lead many astray. And because lawlessness will be increased, the love of many will grow cold. But the one who endures to the end will be saved. And this gospel of the kingdom will be proclaimed throughout the whole world as a testimony to all nations, and then the end will come.* (**Matthew 24:9-14**)

Jesus Christ, our Commander in Chief is warning His people that in the midst of intense worldwide persecution, masses of "Christian pretenders" will betray one another to government-led persecutors.

A generation of American Christians are watching the early birth pains, convinced by their teachers that the next major event will be the rapture of the church or a sudden, peaceful return of Christ; yet what is actually before us is intense persecution. One day soon, the American church will awaken and realize that they have been deceived by those in church leadership whom they trusted but did not warn them concerning persecution that was coming upon the church. Therefore, most Americans are neither emotionally nor spiritually prepared for the sudden and intense persecution that is shortly before us. Nominal professing Christians will stumble and fall under the threat of persecution and will deny their faith. They will also betray those who were once their friends who continue to stand strong in the Lord. This will happen in America. What other country has such a large Christian population that will "fall away?" Certainly not China, for the Christians there are committed. America is the greatest representative of Christianity in all of history. It is here that these tragedies will occur.

Also, whole American churches that embrace the visions of their forerunners in Sardis and Laodicea will unite against the true believers in the Lord Jesus Christ. They want their churches to visibly continue, so they will continue to embrace the universal doctrines of religion that are acceptable to the kingdom of the world. These are beliefs that will deny the need for man's redemption from sin and mock those who proclaim that Jesus Christ is the eternal Son of God and the only way to eternal life. We know from history that these harlot churches will rejoice when true believers are imprisoned and killed for the gospel of Jesus Christ. They will join with the whore on top of the seven-headed beast in order to continue sharing in her riches and beauty and to retain their popular position in American society. These are the tares that detest the blood of our Lord Jesus but have an unquenchable lust for the blood of His martyrs. They are a part of the religious nature of Mystery Babylon.

Don't be fooled by the smooth words of these false teachers. They will tell you that all it takes to be a Christian is to do certain good things and abstain from certain bad ones. Over the centuries, these teachers have deceived many into believing that they are true Christians. We need to ask ourselves the following questions:

- Am I bearing the fruit of Jesus? What would my family say? What would my coworkers say? What would others outside my church say?
- Am I willing to risk people's disapproval of me in my workplace?
- Am I willing to risk all my popularity with family and friends?
- Am I willing to give up my freedom and even my life if it comes to that?

Perhaps you need to pray the following prayer from a seeking heart:

It is hard for me to believe in you, Jesus. Yet I do believe what is written. It has the ring of truth. You are the One I have run from. You are what I have longed for all of these years. Maybe I never believed even when I thought I did. You're the King, not me. I'm tired of trying to run my life. I'm not qualified. I've messed up everything. I do believe now that Jesus is the Christ, the Son of God. I ask for the life you promised. I ask for your Holy Spirit inside me. Please wash me from my sins. Please fill the hole in my heart, Jesus. Please be to me what I've always longed for. I can't make it on my own. I need You. [266]

CHRISTIAN WARRIORS ENDURING HARDSHIPS

In the coming days, true believers in Jesus Christ will be challenged from every direction. Every believer who commits to an all-out relationship with our Lord will come under spiritual oppression, various afflictions, and persecution. We may initially struggle in our trials because discipline and suffering is foreign to us, but as we continue to endure, we will recognize how meaningful the discipline of the Lord really is. Our hearts will continually grow deeper in our love and commitment to Him. At times it may seem unbearable when some friends and even family members become spiteful toward us.

Enduring the scorn and persecution from the world joins us in a partnership with Christ as we share in His sufferings in this life. Suffering with Christ produces a strong heart bond in our relationship with Him and with one another as we follow Him down the same path that He walked. In order to better comprehend this, consider the following. Marines in combat or boot camp who experience really tough trials together eventually grow in strength and closeness with one another. Marines will put their own lives on the line for their fellow marines. Yet a heart that experiences the hardships that Christ also experienced produces a much greater bond than what Marines share with each other. For a deep spiritual love for one another begins to grow which will throw off all the cares of this world and focus only upon the kingdom of God.

Listen to Paul speaking to his disciple, Timothy.

Share in suffering as a good soldier of Christ Jesus. No soldier gets entangled in civilian pursuits, since his aim is to please the one who enlisted him.
(2 Timothy 2:3-4)

Endure suffering, son! You are a soldier in the Lord's army. You have been trained to undergo hardship on the spiritual battlefield.

Satan undoubtedly will attack many with, "This is too hard. It's not fair. God has forsaken me." Be aware that when these thoughts begin to surface that you are a soldier in the Army of God under attack. Stand fast. Evil disguised as decency, together with a lukewarm Christian community, may be strong weapons the enemy will use against you. They will attack your faith and attempt to get you to make compromises so that life won't be so hard. This will be tough when loved ones embrace you and try to get you to compromise your faith just a little bit by saying, "God will understand." Fight this! Your steadfastness is of tremendous importance to both you and your loved ones who are considering small compromises.

Day and night, God's intercessors have cried out to the Lord that His kingdom will come and righteous judgment will occur on the earth. Yet our Lord tarries. Though He is at work every moment of every day, it is not always as we wish or in ways that are visible to us. He is on the throne of justice; so we may wonder just how long justice can be postponed. Yet we must remember that He is also on the throne of grace. This grace is intended not only for those being persecuted but also for the persecutors. If postponement of justice for one more day results in bringing one more person into the kingdom of Christ, then so be it. We must remember, for the Lord a thousand years is like a single day. If a million years from now we were to ask ourselves whether our momentary suffering during our earthly life was an acceptable exchange for eternal glory, how would we answer?

When considering these hard but wonderful truths, I am reminded of the Roman centurion who was in charge of the crucifixion of Christ. Listen to him.

When the centurion and those who were with him, keeping watch over Jesus, saw the earthquake and what took place, they were filled with awe and said, "Truly this was the Son of God!" (Matthew 27:54)

I wouldn't be surprised if this Roman centurion and some of his men, who led the military unit assigned to crucify our Lord, will reign with us in glory. Such is the long-suffering of Him who sits on the throne of grace.

Soldiers, consider this: Being imprisoned is not so bad, for prisoners are not as distracted as those on the outside, and therefore the message of the gospel can be more powerful in a prison environment. They do not put hope in their plans for worldly success, and they think about the end of life more than those on the outside. Tell them about Jesus, and they are much more eager to hear. "If the Son sets you free, you are free indeed." That is real freedom. One man stands inside a prison and is free. Another man stands outside a prison in luxurious living and is in bondage.[267]

My brothers and sisters in Christ, also remember this well: we are alive this day because Jesus has a mission for us that is yet to be fulfilled. When we die, that will be a sign that He wishes us to do something else. Eternal missions await each of us. We must move forward in our assignments each and every day of our short lives in this world. Our deepest motivation must be to hear Him tell us face to face,

Well done, good and faithful servant. You have been faithful over a little; I will set you over much. Enter into the joy of your master.' (Matthew 25:21)

COME OUT OF HER, MY PEOPLE

The call to come out of Babylon is first heard in the prophecy of Isaiah, and it is heard seven times in all, the last being in this chapter of Revelation.[268] This call implies that the way is open for people to depart from her. The Lord brought His people out of Egypt with a strong hand. This is different with respect to being delivered from Babylon; for here He simply opens the way, and only those who come out are considered His true people.[269] This call to come out of her doesn't mean that we are to physically leave our homes; unless, of course, He calls us to physically relocate. It is a call to depart from the idolatrous pleasures of the world and turn to serving in the army of our Lord Jesus Christ throughout our lifetime.

Who are the Christians who are in Mystery Babylon? If you are in a church that compromises the following foundational truths, come out now!

- Mankind is a natural-born sinner who cannot enter the kingdom of God unless this sin has been washed away by the shed blood of Jesus Christ.
- Jesus Christ is God's Son who came to earth to pay the penalty of death for all those who believe on His Name.

- Jesus Christ is truly divine and existed from all eternity as the Son of God. He is the Word of God that was present when creation was spoken into being.
- Jesus Christ is the one and only way to eternal salvation. There is no other way.
- One must be truly "born again" in order to enter into the kingdom of God.

False teachers who occupy many of the pulpits in our churches may not admit to their unbelief in the above truths concerning our Lord and His Word. Many of these "silent teachers" of today's churches embrace the doctrine of "open theology" — which limits the divine attributes of God by believing that He is not omniscient, omnipotent, or omnipresent. They may remain silent in order to maintain their attendance numbers. However, if their message does not regularly embrace the above truths, it is a warning sign; come out now!

Here are some additional false teachings we need to be aware of.

- Compromising the truth of the Bible's inerrancy, claiming it is simply a book written by men that contains some truths but also false beliefs. Come out now!
- Teaches that "tolerance" is the ultimate expression of true love for others, that man is basically good, and that we must be tolerant of those who profess different beliefs in God. Come out now!
- Teaches that the God of Abraham, Isaac, and Jacob is the same God as Allah, whom the Muslims worship and that the gods of Buddhism and Hinduism are the same as the God of Christianity; they just have different names depending on one's culture. Come out now!
- Teaches that financial prosperity is available to each of us if we will only begin to tithe our limited resources to their individual ministries and that our personal pleasure and financial security is how we measure success in this life. Come out now!

- If you are among those who are more impressed with your blessings than with our Lord, who gave those blessings, if financial prosperity has priority in your life, if your comforts have replaced the cross in your life, and if entertainment has replaced evangelism in the workplace, then come out now!
- If you are in a church that is persecuting Christians who will not deny their faith in Jesus, you are in Mystery Babylon. Come out now!

These are some of the idolatrous doctrines of Mystery Babylon, and the true people of God must run from these lies that are intended to compromise our faith in God and bring about a great smile on the face of Satan.

There is a day coming when Christians will need to make a definite decision as to whom they will serve. Just as the prophet Elijah spoke to the Israelite on Mount Carmel:

How long will you go limping between two different opinions? If the Lord is God, follow him; but if Baal, then follow him. (1 Kings 18:21)

The present-day application of this demand might be:

- If the Christ of Scripture is the true Savior, then surrender to Him. But if the false Christ being commonly preached in many pulpits is your savior, then go ahead and follow him.
- One who demands the denying of self and another who allows the gratifying of self cannot both be right.
- One who insists on separation from the world and another who permits you to enjoy its friendship cannot both be right.
- One who came to bring division among the people and another who came to unite the world cannot both be right.

God will not accept a divided heart; He will have all or none. He will permit no compromise.[270] Come out now!

CHAPTER 12

THE LAST HARVEST FOLLOWED BY DESTRUCTION
(Revelation 14—15; 16:1-9)

DARK STORIES ARE ALWAYS FOLLOWED BY THE LIGHT

The entire book of Revelation is the prophetic unveiling of the great war between the kingdom of God and the kingdom of the World for possession of the entire earth. Over and over, readers are presented with several important contrasts between the kingdoms of light and darkness. For example, in chapter 12 we are presented with contrasts between Jesus Christ and Satan, between the woman and the dragon, and between the church in the wilderness and the world in the cities. Throughout the book of Revelation, a story on the dark side is always followed by a story of light. Here are some additional examples.

- Chapter 6 reveals the opening of the sixth seal, releasing a dark and terrible scenario in which all of heaven and earth are shaken and climaxing with the question, "Who can stand?" Then in chapter 7, we see the Lord answering this question by commanding the sealing of 144,000 who will be protected in the midst of great tribulation for the purpose of ministering to the peoples who are confused, scared, and suffering.

- This is followed by the trumpet series, resulting in the destruction of one-third of the natural earth as well as the death of one-third of mankind. Just when one would think that the time of the end is here, we see a mighty Angel come down to earth, indicating that these events that have occurred in the world are under the control of almighty God. He has a purpose for His people during this period of great tribulation that requires our preparedness, for destructive times are about to intensify on the earth.

- Next we see the Antichrist reigning with all power and authority throughout the civilized world. Almost everybody worships this "beast," believing that he is their great hope in life. The people of God are outlaws in his kingdom and are not allowed to buy clothes to wear or food to eat. It is a picture of Satan and Antichrist at the peak of their power, together with a picture of great tribulation for the uncompromising believers in Jesus as the Son of God. Just when this war between the two kingdoms appears to be lost, we see in chapter 14 the great power that opposes this worldly kingdom and its king. We see that glorious spiritual power that will bring salvation and eternal joy to those who stand for the kingdom of God and the great King in the midst of the darkness of the world, a mighty King who will soon destroy this dark worldly kingdom that seems so indestructible.

"BLESSINGS AND WARNINGS" SUMMARIZED IN SEVEN MAJOR EVENTS

Between the devastations of the seven trumpets and the seven bowls of wrath yet to be poured out on the earth, there appears to be another series of "sevens." Chapter 14 presents the reader with a group of seven victorious visions that briefly summarize the events during the final proclamation of the gospel of the kingdom of God throughout the earth. These blessings and warnings culminate with the downfall of the kingdom of this world.[271]

ONE: THE LAMB AND HIS 144,000
TOGETHER ON MOUNT ZION
(Revelation 14:1-5)

In the midst of great evil in the world, the Lamb of God stands on Mount Zion, together with His 144,000 disciples who are the ministers of His light throughout the period of dark tribulations in the latter days. Chapter 13 described the state of the world under the reign of Antichrist, which, from a natural and visible point of view, certainly would appear as if this unholy trinity is completely victorious in their mission to destroy the kingdom of God. However, in chapter 14 the true reality of these events is depicted from our Lord's perspective; for as our eyes are opened to the spiritual realm, we see the people of God safe and secure in the presence of their Lord just before the worldly kingdom of Antichrist is about to be destroyed.

The world demanded that all professing Christians commit spiritual adultery and worship the Antichrist or they would be expelled from the earth. And a great number of professing believers listened to the demands from the world and turned from the Lord.

*Therefore God gave them up in the lusts of their hearts to impurity, to the dishonoring of their bodies among themselves, because they exchanged the truth about God for a lie and worshiped and served the creature rather than the Creator, who is blessed forever! Amen. (**Romans 1:24-25**)*

However, the 144,000 who are standing with the Lord on Mount Zion are the ones who maintain their spiritual virginity in the midst of great pressures and temptations. Their love for the Lamb of God who sacrificed His life for His people was of much greater value than their own lives. These are the warriors in the kingdom of God who continue to hear the voice of their Commander in Chief.

If anyone would come after me, let him deny himself and take up his cross and follow me. For whoever would save his life will lose it, but whoever loses his life for my sake and the gospel's will save it. <u>For what does it profit a man to gain the whole world and forfeit his life?</u> For what can a man give in return for his life? <u>For whoever is ashamed of me and of my words in this adulterous and sinful generation, of him will the Son of Man also be ashamed when he comes in the glory of his Father</u> with the holy angels. (Mark 8:34-38)

These are those who follow Christ in all of His ways while on earth. They are His disciples. Many will be sealed prior to the judgments, yet many more will enter the kingdom as they hear and believe the gospel message of the 144,000 and stand for Him in the midst of persecutions. Being "sealed" implies protection from the judgments of God that fall upon the earth so that they may proclaim the everlasting gospel during the great tribulation, right up to the end of their lives or until the coming of their Lord. This may or may not lead to martyrdom, but a significant number of those who enter the great tribulation certainly will experience martyrdom. Unlike pagan Christendom, which "exchanged the truth of God for a lie," they make no compromise with the heretical demands of the anti-Christian government. Thus the great question for the people of God is not whether they will undergo great sufferings for the cause of Christ but whether they will remain faithful in the midst of tribulation.

A truth that is not commonly taught in the contemporary church is that there is a distinction among the saints in eternal life. All will be "perfectly" blessed, but all do not reach the same state of glory. God has prepared some of His people to do great things; namely, to fight the kingdom of darkness as mighty warriors. They have been prepared to do more than others, and they will suffer more than others. These are the leaders in His army who, if they remain faithful to their calling, will have a leadership position in the eternal kingdom. Just as He prepared men like David, Elijah, Isaiah, and Paul for special works, and they also suffered more than many others of God's people, so shall it be during the coming period known as the great tribulation.[272] I believe these will include the 144,000 chosen warriors who will openly and boldly proclaim the gospel of Christ with great signs and wonders in the midst of the trumpet series and the first three and a half years of rulership by the Antichrist.

Consider this: Many may have been called to this leadership role, yet they did not forsake their lives and thus did not achieve their full calling. They certainly are among the saints of God, but they did not attain to the leadership role that God had prepared them for. Many of us wrestle with this calling while living in the midst of our blessed comforts. Those who have been called know it deep down inside, yet many are continually excusing their laziness by believing they will start tomorrow. However, tomorrow never seems to come. We need to fight these comforting temptations that impede our calling to make the Lord a priority in our lives. Every one of us faces these temptations toward apathy, as it is an ongoing attack from the enemy. Today we must continually resist and prepare, for the Day of the Lord is shortly before us. Warriors, we must continue to seek the individual destinies He is calling us to and preparing us for!

TWO: THE ANGEL AND THE EVERLASTING GOSPEL
(Revelation 14:6-7)

This section of Scripture does not mean that in the end times angels will proclaim the gospel of Jesus Christ in order to sound the final warning. That is an absurd conclusion some have made, believing that the church has been raptured and that angels are the only ones available to warn the people remaining on earth. The reality is that, like many of the visions in the book of Revelation, this is also symbolic. Here is a picture of a final great evangelistic work of God's people, proclaiming the gospel of the kingdom throughout the earth. It is a last call to repentance!

This angelic vision symbolizes the well-known truth that before the time of the end, the gospel message will be proclaimed to all peoples of different languages residing in every nation throughout the world. This is the mission of the 144,000 who have been anointed on Mount Zion and dispatched by their Commander in Chief into all the nations across the globe. Thus, these verses depict the final proclamation of the gospel to the world. Mankind shall be well acquainted with the gospel message of Jesus Christ before the final judgments fall on the earth. Those who scorn the message will be without excuse when they stand before the judgment seat of almighty God. Certainly many people will respond and be brought into everlasting life, but the great majority of the world will blaspheme this message and persecute those who proclaim it. Finally, this gospel message not only will be a calling to mankind to repent and give glory to God, but it also will contain the prophetic warning that final judgments are soon coming to the world. Therefore, this vision of a gospel-proclaiming angel is symbolic of a short season of vigorous and rapid evangelism across the earth. It is an evangelistic mission that will go out in a power never before seen in the world, the power of Jesus Christ manifested within His body of 144,000. The time is coming when Jesus words will be realized:

> *Truly, truly, I say to you, whoever believes in me will also do the works that I do; and greater works than these will he do, because I am going to the Father. Whatever you ask in my name, this I will do, that the Father may be glorified in the Son. If you ask me anything in my name, I will do it. (John 14:12-14)*

Just imagine being a true disciple of Jesus Christ during this time. The earth has experienced great chaos at this point. Some parts of the world have been completely decimated. From out of this chaos, Antichrist has setup his kingdom. Many who have formerly professed belief in Jesus Christ have fallen away and turned to follow the Antichrist. God and His truths are denied by the devoted citizens of this dark kingdom. The sacrifice of Christ is laughed at, and His shed blood has been continually trampled underfoot. Satan and his anointed earthly king shall be the objects of worldwide worship. On every street corner and in every store, you meet with the image of the Beast; his words and his pictures are everywhere, and the people must continually bow down before them or they certainly will be reported to and apprehended by militia forces assigned to seek out and arrest uncompromising Christians. Everywhere you meet with people bearing the visible sign of the Beast on their foreheads and/or their right hands. As one who has refused to take this mark of the Beast, you will not be able to buy nor sell; and you will be continually pushed to the wall. There appears to be no refuge from this darkness, and the suffering is awful. This is a world of tribulation and the blasphemy against God's name appears to go unnoticed from the heavenlies.[273]

Now what questions will be arising in the minds of many Christians? Why does God allow all of this? How long shall the glory of His name be trampled underfoot? How long shall the persecution of His people go unpunished? Doubt will begin to creep into even the most faithful of God's people. It is probable that many of His people will believe that they are the only faithful ones who remain, and they will cry out like Elijah of old, "It is enough O Lord, take away my life. For I've been jealous for my Lord and your people that have not forsaken your name. They have been killed and now I am the only one left." And the Lord responds, "Arise for you have a gospel to proclaim for there are yet 144,000 who have not bowed their knees to the Antichrist."[274]

This is a probable scene into which the final proclamation of the eternal gospel will come. It appears as if Christianity has all but disappeared from the earth. You may feel alone, but He will never leave your side.[275] In the world they will say, "Antichrist has made all things. Who is like unto the Beast, and who can war with him?" But over against this claim, the people of the Lord cry out, "Fear God and give Him glory, for the hour of His judgment has come, and worship Him who made heaven and earth." "For the hour of His judgment has come" clearly indicates that this final message precedes the sounding of the seventh trumpet, which launches the final series of bowls of wrath being poured out upon the earth, a time when the gospel message will no longer be heard.

THREE: THE FALL OF BABYLON
(Revelation 14:8)

This announcement of the judgment of almighty God upon this capital of world secularism is so important to mankind that great detail of her fall has been provided throughout the Scriptures. Since the Garden of Eden, Babylon has been the seat of the power of darkness that has opposed all the works of our Lord in order to draw the hearts of mankind away from Him. There is no greater wrong done to our Lord than to set the affections of our hearts upon other objects. Remember the greatest commandment that He has given to us:

You shall love the Lord your God with all your heart and with all your soul and with all your mind and with all your strength. (*Mark 12:30*)

Babylon possesses that spirit of godlessness that continually lures the hearts of mankind away from their loving Creator. Her allurement is so powerful that she seduces hearts by the fascinating attractiveness of worldly delights, which build that great lie in individual lives that "It's all about me." The people of God have been persecuted continually by Babylonian governments, yet many more of God's people have been enamored and drawn away from the Lord by Babylon's alluring promises. Babylon is a kingdom that makes nations drunk by the wine of her fornication. Being drunk with wine is a depiction of a helpless and shameful condition brought about by excessive drinking. By drinking Babylon's "wine," the worshippers of the Beast shall receive the wrath of God as a burning fire within their souls. This is a spiritual torment that is everlasting, for never shall the worshippers of the Beast receive even one glimpse of God's love. Here upon the earth they receive the things of the world, and God allows His light to shine upon both the wicked and the good alike, but eternal agony awaits all those who choose to follow Satan and the Antichrist. These are Babylonian patriots who loved the excesses offered by the world.

The Lord's call to come out of Babylon appears to be directed to those who have professed faith in Christ—yet continue to revel in the midst of the attractions of the world. Among these are also those religious-minded folks and their feel-good, but false gospel, which claims that there are many ways to eternal life and that a God of love would never relegate anybody to eternal destruction. This gives many great comforts and a green light to continue to drink to excess on the beautiful materialism of Babylon. This is the final warning to come out from her for she is about to be destroyed. Come out now!

FOUR: WARNING AGAINST WORSHIPPING THE BEAST
(Revelation 14:9-11)

Among the strongest of emotions that will bind many in allegiance to the Antichrist is "patriotism." This is a blind and fanatical love for some earthly kingdom. It has been a strong bond in countries such as America and also in Nazi Germany, countries in which allegiance was not forced but taught from their youth. The image of the Beast will be worshipped much like Americans pledge allegiance to the flag.

The fearful punishment that awaits those who worship the beast is twofold.

They will drink the wine of the wrath of God.
They shall suffer the fiery punishment of hell.

The first judgment falls upon them while yet alive in this world and will be experienced when the seven bowls are poured out throughout the earth. The second occurs in the world to come. It is a warning that there is a much worse fate for taking the mark, for the punishment of those who accept the "mark of the Beast" is eternal.

Our Lord, in His merciful and long-suffering love for mankind, patiently warns people concerning the consequences of rendering allegiance to Antichrist. This warning is not a threat but is the last call from our Lord to leave Babylon and embrace His eternal love.

FIVE: BLESSED ARE THOSE WHO DIE IN THE LORD FROM NOW ON
(Revelation 14:12-13)

"Here is a call for endurance of the saints" is evidently a warning that is expressed in the strongest of terms. Every deceptive and cruel power with which Satan will anoint his Antichrist will be brought into play during this last stage of human affairs in order to draw away the affections of mankind from the Lord and unto the Beast. Remember the instruction given to His people in the midst of the world of Antichrist:

If anyone is to be taken captive, to captivity he goes; if anyone is to be slain with the sword, with the sword must he be slain. <u>Here is a call for the endurance and faith of the saints</u>. (Revelation 13:10)

This call for endurance tells us that in the midst of persecution and suffering that God's people are to remain calm and submissive. They do not try to gain control of things by force. Even though they cannot buy or sell, they do not use weapons to obtain what they want. Their suffering will not persuade them to deny their God. Even though the smallest of compromise might gain them favor and keep them out of prison and feed them, they will refuse to compromise. How will they bear this suffering? They know their captors will not escape from eternal destruction and that they themselves will receive an eternal crown of glory for their steadfast righteousness. They trust and embrace these words from the Lord:

And I heard a voice from heaven saying, "Write this: Blessed are the dead who die in the Lord from now on." "Blessed indeed," says the Spirit, "that they may rest from their labors, for their deeds follow them!" (Revelation 14:13)

Now not all are equally strong among the people of God. Not all are equally fit to testify and bear the brunt of the battle. It is not because they themselves are less faithful or that those who are stronger are so as a result of any power of their own. They have been prepared for a different mission. Yet the works of all who do not compromise their faith in the Lord will follow them, and all will be eternally rewarded. This does not mean that all attain to the same state of glory. There is a distinction. All those whom God prepared to do more work than others and to suffer more than others may thank the Lord for this great privilege, for their works shall also follow them into the new creation.[276]

The Word is clear; faithfulness to Christ may result in martyrdom, but those who persevere are the true victors in the battle between the two kingdoms. This stands in sharp contrast to those professing Christian apostates who will deny their faith and to the pagans, who have never accepted it.

SIX: THE HARVEST OF THE EARTH
(Revelation 14:14-16)

This section of the vision appears to be the fulfillment of Jesus' parable concerning the weeds in the field that were allowed to grow in the midst of the good seeds.[277] The "field" is representative of the world, while the "good seeds" are the people of God's kingdom in the midst of the world. The "weeds" are the people of Satan, who has sown them in the midst of the good seeds. Now the time has come when they will be separated by angelic reapers, who will gather the weeds together to be burned with fire.[278]

Jesus Christ, the Commander in Chief, is the one who supervises the reaping. The actual reapers are the angels. This is the fulfillment of Jesus' words:

And he will send out his angels with a loud trumpet call, and they will gather his elect from the four winds, from one end of heaven to the other. (Matthew 24:31)

The harvest definitely will be gathered but not until it is fully ripe, and only almighty God knows this hour. Here we see an angel who comes out from before the presence of the Father and announces to the Son of God that the reaping is to begin. This means that everyone who will come into the eternal kingdom of God has now come in.

Some believe that the gathering of the wheat may well be the removal of God's people from the earth prior to the wrath of God, which brings the reign of the Antichrist to an end. Yet there will be a remnant of His saints who are alive at His coming.[279] However, it is probable that His people who are alive at this time will be separated from those places where God's wrath will fall. For example:

- Noah was separated into an ark prior to the flood.
- Israel was separated and protected when plagues fell upon Egypt.
- Lot was moved prior to the destruction of Sodom and Gomorrah.

Jesus also spoke of this time when He said,

Then two men will be in the field; one will be taken and one left. Two women will be grinding at the mill; one will be taken and one left. Therefore, stay awake, for you do not know on what day your Lord is coming. (Matthew 24:40-42)

When the remnant people of God have been separated to places of safety, the destruction of the wicked, symbolized by the harvest of the grapes, may proceed. Thus, it appears that there will be a short period of time during which there are no more Christians living in the midst of the world, for they have been set apart until they behold the coming of the King of Kings. At this point in time, the preaching of the gospel message for the present age will have been completed.

SEVEN: GOD'S WRATH FALLING UPON THE WORLD OF EVIL
(Revelation 14:17-20)

Here we see an angel coming out from the presence of the altar that lies before the throne of God. Underneath this altar is where the martyrs of Christ have been calling out for vengeance against the enemies of the Lord. But the Lord had told them to wait until the number of all their fellow servants who were yet to be martyred was complete. History must first run its course.

- The gospel must first be preached to all nations to allow all of mankind the opportunity to repent and turn to the Lord.
- The kingdom of the Antichrist must be fully manifested so there is no gray area between good and evil.
- The wickedness of the earth must be full, and the remnant of the Lord separated from the worshippers of the Beast.

When that time arrives, the vengeance of almighty God will fall upon all the dark nations of the earth. It will begin with the pouring out of the first five bowls of wrath, resulting in tremendous devastation and suffering throughout the earth. This suffering will not bring repentance, but it will visibly reveal the evil hearts of mankind as they continue to blaspheme the Lord. With the sixth bowl, we witness a gathering together of all the kings of the earth and their dark armies at Armageddon. Unknown to them, this is really the winepress of God's wrath, which will be manifested with the pouring out of the seventh bowl. Here the governing forces of this dark world will be trodden down in God's winepress, resulting in the squashing of millions and millions of those who embraced the Antichrist as their messiah. These are the great and mighty kings of the world who have gathered together with all of their loyal followers for the purpose of wiping out all of the Lord's beloved people from the face of the earth once and for all. The smashing of these kings and their armies will be so great that their blood will run four feet deep over a course of approximately184 miles. But before this occurs, this hateful army that has gathered together at Armageddon will slaughter millions of Jewish inhabitants in the nation of Israel. The following chapter provides a descriptive scenario of this last great battle.

These seven bowls, called the "wrath of God," are His holiness falling upon the world of sin. The divine work of His kingdom people made great and wonderful changes within this world throughout history, but they could not overcome the darkness, which continued to grow stronger and stronger. Now God the Father and His Son will release their holiness from heaven against this darkness and utterly destroy this world of sin. First, comes great worldwide destruction, but it will soon be followed by a great cleansing that will restore the earth to the days of the Garden of Eden.

HEAVEN CELEBRATES WHILE THE WORLD BLASPHEMES (Revelation 15)

From the perspective of the saints and angels of God residing in heaven, a "great and amazing" event is about to occur. A few years earlier the sounding of the trumpet judgments resulted in great devastation around the world, yet the kingdom of God continued to be proclaimed in the midst of these chaotic events by His mighty warriors known as the 144,000. This resulted in the awakening of great multitudes of people among all the nations who repented and entered into the gates of the kingdom. Now it is time for the wrath of God to be poured out upon those who refused His word and instead continued to render allegiance to their chosen messiah, the Antichrist, the anointed son of Satan. At God's chosen time, these legions of darkness will be allowed to silence the gospel of Jesus Christ, and the 144,000 will join their martyred brothers and sisters under the altar in heaven. This is a time when the number of all those who are to be martyred for Christ is complete. This then launches the final outpouring of the wrath of almighty God over the kingdom of the World, whose citizens have always despised the Lord and His people. Now their tremendous hatred of the Lord will be manifested in shouted blasphemies in the midst of their sufferings.

The victorious army of those martyred for their testimony stands together in heaven on a sea of glass mingled with fire. During their lifetime on earth, they passed through fiery trials from the enemy until the time came for their martyrdom. Now they stand in victory amidst the fires of heaven, which, like Nebuchadnezzar's fiery furnace, will not harm the children of God but will totally destroy His enemies.[280] Among this victorious army are those who refused to worship the Antichrist even though they could neither buy nor sell nor live in the midst of that society without offering such worship. They were outcasts—many imprisoned and tortured, many betrayed by friends and loved ones, many terribly executed for their faith. They were tested to the extreme, yet they continued to call upon the Lord for their strength. They fought the fiercest of all battles, but they were continuously sustained by their faith in the Lord Jesus, whom they knew would one day come as the victorious King of Kings. Now they stood by the sea of glass mingled with fire, singing the song of great victory before the throne of God. Yes, this is a time of special privilege for the Army of God, who fought the greatest and most challenging of all battles. They stood up against Satan and his king, the Antichrist, in the midst of the greatest tribulation this world had ever known.

I recently listened to series a of CDs concerning end-time events from a nationally popular pastor who provided some fine insights. Yet, he is a believing rapturist, and when he talked about the 144,000 that will be God's worldwide evangelists, he was adamant when he told his audience, "You do not want to be among the 144,000; you do not want to be among the 144,000." What was his reasoning? They will go through fiery tribulations, and you need to be among those who simply "fly away" to heaven. Ugh! This was a very gifted speaker, but when it comes to warfare he is obviously a pacifist. Hopefully, when the tribulation hits this country, he will be able to overcome his disappointment and minister in the midst of warfare without fear for his own life.

Warriors for Christ, consider the following: Are not soldiers of war the recipients of greater honors when they fight in the thickest of the battle? Should not a soldier of the kingdom of Christ receive great honors for being in the thickest of the fight against the powerful armies of the Antichrist and showing he fears nothing, even though he is hated by all men? To belong to the chosen forces of Christ in the world at the time of Antichrist shall be the greatest honor conceivable. Undoubtedly there will be a special place of privilege in both the new heaven and the new earth for such ones.

*Blessed are you when others revile you and persecute you
and utter all kinds of evil against you falsely on my account.
Rejoice and be glad, for your reward is great in heaven, for
so they persecuted the prophets who were before you.*
(Matthew 5:11-12)

But is this multitude limited only to those warriors who
fought during the great tribulation? Certainly not! The spirit of
the Antichrist has been in the world fighting against the armies of
God in all historical dispensations. Warriors of God have fought
this same battle throughout all the ages, even though it rages most
severely during this era of the end-times, anti-Christian kingdom.
Abraham fought this battle. Moses fought this battle. David fought
this battle. All the witnesses and prophets of the Old Testament era
fought this same battle. All the witnesses and martyrs of the New
Testament era also fought this same battle. But the battle becomes
most severe at the time of the final reign of the Antichrist. Therefore,
it is certainly true that all who have remained faithful, from Abel to
the very last witness in the kingdom of God on earth, shall stand by
the fiery sea of glass singing their song of Moses and of the Lamb.
The combining of these two songs embraces both the Old Testament
and New Testament eras as one kingdom. Old and new dispensations shall be one; there is no break, no difference between them in
glory.

This scene of mighty warriors who have conquered the Beast
and its image should remind us of the children of Israel standing
on the edge of the Red Sea, looking back over those waters that
had just consumed their Egyptian enemies. The greatest and most
powerful army in the world of that age had just been completely
annihilated because they were attempting to slaughter a nation that
God had raised up to manifest His glory throughout the world. At
this point Moses and the Israelite people began to sing the "song
of Moses" to the Lord, glorifying Him and giving thanks for this
miraculous deliverance from their enemies.[281] The heavenly "sea of
glass" is a reminder of the Red Sea, which delivered the Israelites
and destroyed their enemies. It is also a reminder of the great flood,
which delivered Noah and his family and destroyed the enemies of

God. These were waters whereby the Lord provided salvation for His people and destruction of their enemies. Fires and waters both save and destroy, depending on which side of the battlefield one has chosen to fight. What a glorious prelude to the destruction that is about to rain down upon the kingdom of Satan and his followers. The physical earth, which also has been worshipped over the centuries, is now about to experience tremendous destruction, along with the inhabitants of this end-times generation.[282]

Warriors for Christ, we too may learn to sing this song of Moses and the Lamb while still in this world. We are in the midst of the battle, which will grow fiercer and fiercer, yet we can continue to sing this song, remembering that one day we will be standing with all our brothers and sisters in Christ alongside this fiery sea of glass, singing and watching the destruction of all wickedness in the kingdom of the world.

THE FINAL JUDGMENTS OF OUR LORD BEGIN
(Revelation 16:1-9)

This final series of plagues that will be poured out upon all of mankind parallels the trumpet judgments that previously tormented the inhabitants of the earth. However, unlike the trumpet judgments, which affected only one-third of the earth and still allowed an opportunity for millions to awaken and embrace the Lord through the testimony of the witnesses of Jesus Christ; these seven bowl judgments will devastate the world at a time when the testimony of Christ has been silenced. This is the time of the final battle in a war that has raged since the fall of mankind in Eden.

It is the time the martyrs under the altar in the heavenly temple are waiting for.

They cried out with a loud voice, "O Sovereign Lord, holy and true, how long before you will judge and avenge our blood on those who dwell on the earth?" (**Revelation 6:10**)

It is the time our sovereign Lord fulfills the promise He made to them.

Rest a little longer until the number of their fellow servants and their brothers should be complete, who were to be killed as they themselves had been.
(Revelation 6:11)

It is the time for the righteous judgment of God to be poured out across the earth.

Since indeed God considers it just to repay with affliction those who afflict you,
(2 Thessalonians 1:6)

First Bowl of God's Wrath Poured Out—On the Earth

Harmful and painful sores will break out upon everybody who bears the "mark of the Beast." This will be very nasty as Job, a servant of God, can testify. Recall that Satan attacked Job, the beloved of God, with boils all over his body.[283] Now Satan's worshippers are suffering a similar fate but without any hope of being healed. Perhaps these sores will be seen as a worldwide plague. Certainly these suffering people will be crying out to their god, the Antichrist, for miraculous healing.

But, it won't happen!

Second Bowl of God's Wrath Poured Out—On the Seas

All the oceans around the world will become like the "blood of a corpse." Obviously, all sea life will die. Now there can be no question in the minds of all the inhabitants of the earth that this is more than just a passing plague. God is raining judgment down upon the earth. Again, they will turn to their Antichrist and call upon him to heal the seas with his miraculous power.

But, it won't happen!

Third Bowl of God's Wrath Poured Out—On Rivers and Springs

All the fresh waters, from streams, lakes, and rivers across the earth, will turn into blood. All the promised comforts and necessities of life are being taken away. Listen to the response from God's angel, who is placed in charge of the waters on the earth.

They have shed the blood of saints and prophets, and you have given them blood to drink. It is what they deserve! (Revelation 16:6)

These bowls of wrath poured out upon the earth are not about vengeance. The judgments of God are not vengeful. They are an expression of His righteous nature and His intense hatred of sin. Listen to the response to these judgments from out of the altar, where the souls of the martyrs reside and also where the prayers of the saints rise up before the throne of our almighty God.

And I heard the altar saying, "Yes, Lord God the Almighty, true and just are your judgments!" (Revelation 16:7)

Contrary to this viewpoint within the kingdom of God, imagine the fear and confusion in the kingdom of the world as suffering and frightened people cry out, "Antichrist, our god, where are you? Remember your promises. Don't you care? Please, help us."

But, it won't happen!

Fourth Bowl of God's Wrath Poured Out—On the Sun

Here the wrath of God is poured out upon the sun, resulting in tremendous scorching heat falling upon a populace that is covered with painful boils and having only bloody waters to drink. Yet, even in their unimaginable suffering, they will continue to curse almighty God and look to their Antichrist for their deliverance from God's wrath. "O, our beloved Antichrist, please stop this. We've suffered enough. Remember your promises to take care of us."

But, it won't happen!

CHAPTER 13

THE RETURN OF THE KING
(Revelation 16:10-21; 19:11-21)

AN OVERVIEW OF THE FIRST FOUR
BOWLS OF WRATH

At the time of the outpouring of these bowls of wrath, Antichrist has established a universal kingdom, uniting all the nations of the world under his authority. From a worldly point of view, the kingdom of Antichrist will be the perfect kingdom that patriotic sinners have always dreamed about. The nations will have pledged allegiance to Antichrist and his global agenda, and the people will be overjoyed at having silenced the gospel testimony of Jesus Christ and His followers. Now they can live life any way they want, as long as they continue to worship the image of the Beast. Sorcery, idolatry, pornography, adultery, homosexuality, abortion rights, child sacrifice, and pedophile acts, will all be acceptable and commonplace. Everything that despises and opposes the commandments of our Lord will be embraced. Antichrist is their messiah and also their eternal hope. Yes, all the civilized nations of the world will enthrone the Antichrist as their hope for eternal security and happiness. They will admire him, worship him, and bow down and acknowledge him as the greatest of all kings. He will have control over the entire civilized world, and his followers will love, trust, and embrace him as their god. The small, surviving remnants throughout the earth that refuse to obey him will become social outcasts and probably forced into hiding while being provided for by the Lord.[284] Many of these will be end-times prayer warriors who are obediently calling for the return of the King.

It is at this point in time that almighty God will come to demonstrate His omnipotent sovereignty. Our Lord now decrees that through these bowl judgments all those who worship the Beast will not be able to buy or sell, for He is taking it all away from them. The crops, the rain, the food, the water, the medicines, the wealth of the earth—it all disappears. Just as Antichrist had done to God's people, so now God does to the people of Antichrist. As the first four bowls of wrath are poured out, the world will continue their hateful blasphemies of God and put their faith for deliverance in their Antichrist. Now it is time to demonstrate the impotence of Antichrist before the world.

FIFTH BOWL OF GOD'S WRATH POURED OUT—ON THE THRONE OF THE BEAST

When the fifth bowl is poured out, a great darkness descends over the Antichrist's throne and spreads throughout his entire kingdom. All of his followers begin to gnaw their tongues in tremendous pain. It is difficult to imagine the effect of this supernatural darkness; but it will certainly intensify the distress of the previous four plagues. Following on the heels of a "scorching sun," this darkness will probably cause a tremendous freezing across his kingdom. Yet, even in the extreme distress that has been launched upon the world of mankind, his people will continue to blaspheme almighty God. Their anger demonstrates that they certainly do not doubt the existence of God, but their hard and rebellious hearts hate Him more and more as bowls of wrath continue to fall upon the earth.

These unstoppable plagues undoubtedly will diminish the glory of the Antichrist; and his supernatural power and authority certainly will begin to be questioned. Up to this point, his people have dedicated both their earthly and eternal lives into his care; but now they will begin to doubt his divinity. These are the same people who had previously declared,

Who is like the beast, and who can fight against it? (Revelation 13:4)

Jesus Christ, our Commander in Chief says, "I can!"

SIXTH BOWL OF GOD'S WRATH POURED OUT—ON THE EUPHRATES RIVER

During this period of painful darkness, which obliterates the glory of Antichrist in the world, the intensity of hatred toward almighty God will reach a boiling point unlike at any period in the history of the world. Many Christians have been taught to believe that the Lord will gradually gain complete victory over the kingdom of the world without a great upheaval. However, the end of this age shall not be a time of peace but of a tremendously bloody war in which armies from all the nations of the earth will gather together with the mission of completely destroying the nation of Israel from the face of the earth. The land of Israel, where the kingdom of God was physically established four thousand years ago, has been chosen to be the location of the final battle between the kingdom of God and the dark armies of Satan's kingdom. That time has now arrived, and our Lord is challenging all of His enemies from around the world to gather together at a location in northern Israel known in the Bible as Armageddon.

The sixth bowl poured out upon the earth releases the demonic forces that will allow a gathering of these armies, which are motivated by their tremendous hatred of the Lord. The first event to take place is the drying up of the Euphrates River. After looking at the devastating consequences of the first five bowls, one may wonder what is so significant about the drying up of this river. After all, the Euphrates River, though it is very wide and deep and now flowing with bloody waters for nearly two thousand miles, should not be a major hindrance to modern armies' intent on attacking the nation of

Israel. However, the Euphrates has been very significant throughout the history of the Middle Eastern countries. This river always has been the eastern boundary line between Israel and the heathen nations. From a spiritual sense, it is symbolic of the boundary line between God's people and their enemies.[285] The drying up of this river appears to symbolize an invitation from the Lord, calling all the heathen armies to a battlefield located in the land where He has historically manifested His power and glory to His people and their enemies.

The second event that arouses the armies around the world to align together against the kingdom of God are unclean spirits that proceed out of the mouths of the unholy trinity; that is, Satan, Antichrist, and the False Prophet. This is a powerful spiritual event that will infect millions and millions of kings, religious leaders, generals, and their armed soldiers worldwide with a demonic spirit that will replace any semblance of morality with a deep hatred for, and desire to rape and murder, all those who live in the nation of Israel. The "kings from the east" appear to be representative of the pagan nations of the Eastern world that have never played a major role in the history of civilization. They are the nations with the greatest populations: China, Japan, India, Indonesia, Pakistan, and others. Yet, the majority of these peoples are poor, uneducated, and blindly follow the religious leaders and their wealthy, but corrupt governments. They are worshippers of the gods of Buddhism, Hinduism, and Islam, who have persecuted the Christians in the midst of their countries for centuries. Their armies will surely include millions of foot soldiers who will march across the dried-up riverbed of the Euphrates. They will organize and unite with the forces of Antichrist from the Western and Middle Eastern countries on the plains of Megiddo, commonly referred to as Armageddon.

Armageddon is a Hebrew word that refers to a place known as Mount Megiddo, which overlooks a great valley located about fifty-five miles north of Jerusalem. The Megiddo valley, which also may be viewed from Mount Carmel, is a magnificent sight that captures the imagination of all who visit there. As one stands alongside this great plain, it is easy to envision a gathering of millions of enemy soldiers readying for a great battle against the city of Jerusalem.

Now Armageddon is merely the gathering place for the world's armies, not the site of the last great battle. It is the place where they will organize and develop their strategies for the destruction of all of Israel, beginning with the city of Jerusalem. The real battle will take place in the Valley of Jehoshaphat, otherwise known as the Kidron Valley, which lies between Jerusalem and the Mount of Olives.[286]

In the midst of this demonic gathering, our Commander in Chief again alerts His people residing in Israel to remain vigilant and not be fearful or deceived by this tremendous darkness that appears to be unstoppable in its mission to finally annihilate the kingdom of God.

Behold, I am coming like a thief! Blessed is the one who stays awake, keeping his garments on, that he may not go about naked and be seen exposed!
(Revelation 16:15)

SATAN'S FINAL MISSION STRATEGIES—AN OVERVIEW

Satan knows that his time is short, as he too recognizes the signs that precede the return of Jesus Christ and His mighty army. He knows that he needs to prevent this return of Christ, or He must overwhelm and defeat Him with an earthly and demonic army prepared to engage Him when He sets foot on the Mount of Olives. This is no secret; Satan understands what is shortly ahead, and he needs to defeat the purposes of God and His Son in order to set his throne above that of God and to avoid his eternal destruction.[287]

The historic tactic used to accomplish Satan's purposes has always been *deception*. He has deceived mankind into believing that the tremendous potential that resides within each of us can be more fully realized by living life under our own guidance rather than under God's. Thus, he convinces the majority of mankind that they have no need for God and that they can be their own gods, doing whatever is pleasing to them, even if it is harmful to others. However, in order to truly experience the abundant life, they must remove all those who are not deceived and are totally committed to almighty God and to

His Son, Jesus Christ. Satan does this by convincing world govern-ments, together with false religions, that God's people are the only obstacle that keeps them from achieving their worldly goals, and so they must be either converted to the world's belief system or killed. If he could prevent all of mankind from reflecting God's glory upon the earth, then Satan himself would be the recipient of worship and glory throughout the earth. Thus, he could claim that he is now in control of all those initially created in the "image of God," for they have been reborn into the "image of Satan."

However, the time for these tactics of deception has passed. It is now time for a frontal assault on the beloved land of Israel and its inhabitants who have refused to render allegiance to the Antichrist. This was the "Promised Land" created by our Lord to manifest His glory throughout the world, and now it has been chosen to be the final battlefield between the spiritual forces of God and Satan, as well as the physical forces of Jesus Christ and the Antichrist. The powers of good and evil are about to meet head on, and the victor will receive eternal rule over the earth and be glorified in the heavenlies.

FROM ARMAGEDDON TO JERUSALEM

Now comes the launching of the final great battle of this age between the evil kingdom of the world and the holy kingdom of God, a confrontation that has been building for six thousand years. Very little detail depicting this final battle is provided in Revelation; however, some of the Old Testament prophets, especially Zechariah and Joel, provide additional insights that assist in picturing this end-time event. Let's begin.

Satan gathers together his legions of "human-orcs" for the mission of bringing final defeat to the purposes of the Lord for mankind, which will allow him to grab the reins of control over the entire world. These massive armies are representative of the hatred that has expressed itself throughout human history in hostility toward, and persecution of, the people of God. Those who have seen the movie trilogy *The Lord of the Rings* certainly recognize the deep evil that is manifested in the terrible appearance of the "orcs," which comprise the army of a dark lord. They have a visible murderous and gnawing hatred for those who oppose the reign of their lord over the entire earth. They growl, slobber, and gnaw their teeth while awaiting orders to launch a murderous attack on their enemies. The term "human-orcs" is meant to convey a picture of the inner hearts of these end-times forces that will run to the war when called forth by the demons of Satan, Antichrist, and the False Prophet. This unholy trinity obviously believes that they are the ones initiating this final war against the kingdom of God. However, it is really our Lord who, in His timing, has planned this gathering together of His enemies from out of every tribe and nation.

> *I will gather all the nations and bring them down to the Valley of Jehoshaphat. And I will enter into judgment with them there, on behalf of my people and my heritage Israel, because they have scattered them among the nations and have divided up my land, and have cast lots for my people, and have traded a boy for a prostitute, and have sold a girl for wine and have drunk it. (Joel 3:2-3)*

The time has now come:

- To bring about both an external and spiritual cleansing to the land of Israel by purging the nation of its secular idolatry and manifesting the power and the glory of almighty God unto all the nations of the world.
- To remove the powers of darkness from within the nations across the earth and bring them into the valley of God's judgment, where they will be violently destroyed. Those people who remain in all the nations will then have the opportunity to receive and worship the Lord during the coming millennial reign of Jesus Christ.[288]
- To manifest the power and glory of the Son of God as the Lion of Judah, when He comes to bring sudden and total destruction to the enemies of His people and to establish His reign over the nations of the earth.

Now when these massive armies composed of soldiers from around the entire world have organized and coordinated their plans for conquering the land and eliminating the Israelites from the face of the earth, they will begin their march toward Jerusalem, destroying all the peoples and ravaging the land that lies before them. Envision the innumerable orcs in the *Lord of the Rings*.

Fire devours before them, and behind them a flame burns. The land is like the Garden of Eden before them, but behind them a desolate wilderness, and nothing escapes them. (Joel 2:3)

As this murderous orc army arrives in Jerusalem, they will ravage and rape.

For I will gather all the nations against Jerusalem to battle, and the city shall be taken and the houses plundered and the women raped. Half of the city shall go out into exile, but the rest of the people shall not be cut off from the city. (Zechariah 14:2)

THE WARRIOR REMNANT OF ISRAEL

Now, the Israel Defense Forces, as well as many of the Israelites who have refused to pledge allegiance to the Antichrist, have no intent to surrender to this evil army, even though they may be outnumbered by as many as 1,000 to 1. Perhaps they have not yet recognized Jesus as their Messiah, but, to their credit many among them have steadfastly refused to take the "mark of the Beast" and to "worship his image."

However, the tremendous numbers of the enemy will still inflict much pain and death in the city of Jerusalem, for two-thirds of the inhabitants of Israel will be killed.

*In the whole land, declares the Lord, two thirds shall be cut off and perish, and one third shall be left alive. (**Zechariah 13:8**)*

These will be the secular lovers of the Babylonian lifestyle, together with the Pharisaic-type of religious leaders who have voluntarily received the "mark of the beast."

*All the sinners of my people shall die by the sword, who say, "Disaster shall not overtake or meet us." (**Amos 9:10**)*

However, for the heroic one-third remnant of God's chosen people who battle against these forces of evil, the hand of the Lord will be strong upon them.

*And I will put this third into the fire, and refine them as one refines silver, and test them as gold is tested. They will call upon my name, and I will answer them. I will say, "They are my people"; And they will say, "The Lord is my God." (**Zechariah 13:9**)*

These are certainly the ones the Lord will protect and anoint them with the "strength of David" in the midst of the battle.

*And the Lord will give salvation to the tents of Judah first, that the glory of the house of David and the glory of the inhabitants of Jerusalem may not surpass that of Judah. On that day the Lord will protect the inhabitants of Jerusalem, so that the feeblest among them on that day shall be like David, and the house of David shall be like God, like the angel of the Lord, going before them. And on that day I will seek to destroy all the nations that come against Jerusalem. (**Zechariah 12:7-9**)*

The Old Testament prophets clearly reveal the contrast between the Israelite peoples who truly belong to Him and those pretenders who do not. The following passages may help clarify who the *two-*

thirds are who are killed in this final battle and the *one-third who survive* and eventually escape from the enemy through the Valley of the Lord.

> *Therefore thus says the Lord God: "Behold, **my servants shall eat**, but you shall be hungry; behold, **my servants shall drink**, but you shall be thirsty; behold, **my servants shall rejoice**, but you shall be put to shame; behold, **my servants shall sing for gladness of heart**, but you shall cry out for pain of heart and shall wail for breaking of spirit. You shall leave your name to my chosen for a curse, and the Lord God will put you to death, **but his servants he will call by another name**. (Isaiah 65:13-15)*

> *But you who forsake the Lord, who forget my holy mountain, who set a table for Fortune and fill cups of mixed wine for Destiny, I will destine you to the sword, and all of you shall bow down to the slaughter, because, when I called, you did not answer; when I spoke, you did not listen, but you did what was evil in my eyes and chose what I did not delight in." (Isaiah 65:11)*

His chosen people who will be called by another name include this one-third remnant among the Jews who remained faithful in their hearts to the God of Abraham, Isaac, and Jacob.

> *And it shall come to pass that everyone who calls on the name of the Lord shall be saved. For in Mount Zion and in Jerusalem there shall be those who escape, as the Lord has said, and among the survivors shall be those whom the Lord calls. (Joel 2:32)*

SEVENTH BOWL OF GOD'S WRATH POURED OUT — INTO THE ATMOSPHERE

As the battle continues, the seventh bowl is poured out into the air. Lightning and thunder are manifested worldwide, followed by an unimaginably great earthquake that shakes the entire planet. Yet the nations continue to fight and rage in great despair for their beloved world. Cities fall, mountains and islands disappear; and great hailstones weighing approximately one hundred pounds each fall upon the masses of people. This plague of hailstones will kill tens of thousands, causing a tremendous fear to arise among the ranks of the enemy. They become insanely scared, and like the orcs in the *Lord of the Rings,* they are at each other's throats, slaughtering their own comrades, for a great panic grips them.

And on that day a great panic from the Lord shall fall on them, so that each will seize the hand of another, and the hand of the one will be raised against the hand of the other. (Zechariah 14:13)

These one-hundred-pound hailstones that are poured out onto the heads of the enemy also may be directed against the "principalities and powers of the air" since this seventh bowl is poured out into the air, the air being the abode of armies of evil powers and spirits.[289] Historically, hailstones have been a part of the arsenal of weapons used by our Lord against His adversaries, resulting in mammoth destruction and death.[290] Thus the seventh bowl being poured out into the air appears to represent destruction of the demonic forces of Satan, as well as of the earth. One can imagine that these great hailstones may be the result of demonic casualties falling out of the air.

Suddenly a voice is heard from the temple of God: "It is finished." This was the same voice that spoke those exact words some two thousand years earlier when His work was completed on the cross.[291] Now the judgments of God that have been poured out on the earth are complete. The time of His second coming is being readied. The total redemptive purposes of God will now be consummated, both for salvation and for judgment.[292] Immediately, the Lord brings about a great earthquake in the midst of the battle and causes the Mount of Olives to split in two, allowing His faithful remnant to escape and separate themselves from the enemy who is about to be destroyed.

> *On that day his feet shall stand on the Mount of Olives that lies before Jerusalem on the east, and the Mount of Olives shall be split in two from east to west by a very wide valley, so that one half of the Mount shall move northward, and the other half southward. And you shall flee to the valley of my mountains, for the valley of the mountains shall reach to Azal. And you shall flee as you fled from the earthquake in the days of Uzziah king of Judah. <u>Then the Lord my God will come, and all the holy ones with him</u>. (Zechariah 14:4-5)*

This earthquake will be beyond man's comprehension. Isaiah presents us with an eye-opening description.

> *The earth is utterly broken, the earth is split apart, the earth is violently shaken. The earth staggers like a drunken man; it sways like a hut; its transgression lies heavy upon it, and it falls, and will not rise again. On that day the Lord will punish the host of heaven, in heaven, and the kings of the earth, on the earth. They will be gathered together as prisoners in a pit; they will be shut up in a prison, and after many days they will be punished. (Isaiah 24:19-22)*

Up to this point in time, our Commander in Chief has employed three major weapons in this Great War against His enemies.

- Seven bowls of God's wrath being poured out on the earth, into the seas, into fresh waters, on the sun, on the throne of the beast, into the Euphrates River, and finally, into the atmosphere above the earth.
- Sending a spirit of fear and madness into the midst of the enemy forces, causing them to fight among themselves. This is the same "sword of the Lord" that was used against

His enemies when Gideon and his three-hundred-man army came against the huge army of Midian.[293]

- Equipping warriors among the Jewish people with a heart of David, so that they become like "a blazing pot in the midst of wood and a flaming torch among sheaves."[294]

In summary, the armies of the Antichrist are experiencing unexpected resistance to their plans for conquest of the kingdom of God, for they have suffered tremendous loss of life to this point. Yet, millions of this enemy still remains alive, and their hatred is raging. They have just slaughtered two-thirds of the Israelites and are intent on pursuing the remaining third that has escaped through the valley of the Mount of Olives, which has split in two. This scenario parallels the pursuit of the Israelites by the Egyptian armies through the Red Sea. There He parted the sea for His people and then destroyed their pursuers, here He parts the Mount of Olives for His people and is about to destroy their pursuers. It is now time for the fourth and most powerful weapon in the arsenal of God to be revealed; a weapon that will completely annihilate the kings of the world and their armies. "Look up, the Lion of Judah is coming with His mighty army!"

> Behold, _he is coming with the clouds, and every eye will see him_, even those who pierced him, and all tribes of the earth will wail on account of him. Even so. Amen. "I am the Alpha and the Omega," says the Lord God, "_who is and who was and who is to come_, the Almighty." *(Revelation 1:7-8)*

THE COMING OF THE KING OF KINGS
(Revelation 19:11-21)

Many in the church of today believe that Jesus was a pacifist who preached, "Make love, not war." This is a popular belief among the average churchgoing Americans, even though it is contrary to Jesus' own assertion.

> *Do not think that I have come to bring peace to the earth. I*
> *have not come to bring peace, but a sword. . . . And whoever*
> *does not take his cross and follow me is not worthy of me.*
> *Whoever finds his life will lose it, and whoever loses his life*
> *for my sake will find it.* **(Matthew 10:34; 38-39)**

In truth, our Commander in Chief calls His warrior leaders to "make war, because we love." Throughout the New Testament, He calls us time and again to the frontlines of the battlefield. He doesn't tell us that we won't be wounded or even killed; but He does tell us that He will walk alongside of us through the "valley of the shadow of death," assuring us that we will not be killed until our assigned mission is complete. This age is a time of warfare, and peace will never be a true reality in this world until every single enemy of the Lord, both the fallen angels and sinful man, have been thrown into the lake of fire.

At His second coming, Jesus Christ rides down from heaven on a stallion of war rather than a donkey of peace. He is followed by a mighty army, and His weapon is a great sword proceeding from His mouth, which will slaughter thousands of kings, generals, and mighty men among His enemies. This graphic portrayal of Jesus Christ as a mass killer comes as a shock to respectable worshippers used to seeing Him gazing benignly from stained-glass windows, or to those who love to portray Him over and over again as a little baby in a manger. How sweet! He will never be that again.

Has Jesus changed since His first coming? It is not His character or personality that have changed but His mission. His first coming was to "seek and save what was lost"—not to condemn, but to save.[295] He was still the Warrior who challenged the false religions of Israel that were leading His people astray. But He came to give mankind the opportunity to be separated from their sins before all sin has to be destroyed. Now His second coming is for the opposite purpose: to destroy rather than to save, to punish sin rather than to pardon it.[296]

Let us visualize this second coming of our Commander in Chief.

The Rider on a White Horse

The last time Jesus came to Jerusalem, He came riding on a donkey, a beast of burden, for He was about to suffer an agonizing death for those who had been and would be called into the kingdom of God. He was the King entering Jerusalem, but then His kingdom was not of this world. Now He comes as a victorious warrior King to fight and destroy His enemies, who have killed millions of His people over the last six thousand years.

He Is Called "Faithful and True"

Since the days of Abraham, the people of the Lord have been looking for His coming to establish the kingdom of God upon the earth. Century after century elapsed, and generation after generation passed away. Dark and troublesome times continually engulfed His people, and yet He did not come. Over time, many of His people who initially awaited His coming fell away and worshipped other gods and even persecuted those who remained faithful to the Lord. This included the Israelites of the old dispensation, as well as the church of this dispensation. Yet He did not come. Why? Because the number of His people who have been chosen to enter the eternal kingdom was not yet complete. At the time of His coming as the warrior King, it is complete. He is called the Faithful One to His people of faith.

He is also called "True," for He is the true Messiah in distinction from all the powers that have ever opposed Him. Antichrist claimed that he was the promised Messiah, but he was simply the last of many wannabes. Jesus Christ is the true Prophet, the true King, the true Word of God, and the true Son of God whom the prophets of the Old Testament and the apostles of the New Testament have told us about.

His Eyes Are Like a "Flame of Fire"

The eyes of Jesus Christ penetrate into the darkness, and the deepest corners of iniquity are completely visible to Him. Nothing remains hidden from the King when He comes for judgment.[297] He is gloriously focused on bringing righteous judgment to the world.

There Are Many Crowns upon His Head

On His head John sees many "crowns," which are symbolic of all of the victories our Lord has won in the historic battles against the forces of Satan. These multiple crowns also leave no doubt that Jesus Christ is the King of Kings who has come to set up His eternal kingdom upon this earth.

He Is Clothed with a Robe Dipped in Blood

Past victories in the kingdom also have been very bloody, as evidenced in both the old and new dispensations. Yes, He is our beloved Lamb of God who sacrificed His life so that His people may have eternal life. But He is also our beloved Lion of Judah, who has continued to walk with His people through the "valley of the shadow of death" for the past six thousand years. This blood is spiritually symbolic of all those in the body of Christ who also laid down their lives for the glory of the Lord.

He Has a Name Written that No One Knows but Himself

This appears to be a name given to Him by His Father, a name that exalts Him above every name in heaven and on earth. He also says to His conquering people that He will give them a white stone with their name written upon it—that no one knows except the one who receives it.[298] These names appear to be known only to the Father and His Son, so when we hear them throughout our eternal lifetime, we will know that He is calling us to His presence.

He Has Other Names

He is known to Himself and to His Father by His hidden name; He is known to the churches as the Faithful and True and as the Word of God; He is known to the world as King of Kings and Lord of Lords.[299]

Armies in Heaven Arrayed in White Linen Follow Him on White Horses

These armies are probably composed of both His holy angels who continually fought against Satan and his traitorous demons and those saints who stood alongside the sea of fiery glass, singing the Song of Moses and the Song of the Lamb.[300] Their numbers also will increase when those of the Lord's people who are alive on the earth at this time will be "caught up in the air" where they will join with their fellow soldiers on their return to the earth.[301] They wear robes of white linen, which are representative of their holiness before God, who gives them their robes.[302] They do not have armor or swords, for they are not entering into the midst of the battle. They are present so that their Lord will be glorified among them, for they are God's witnesses to an event that His people have been anticipating for centuries.[303]

He Treads the Winepress of God the Almighty, Putting His enemies under His Feet

Jesus is the Commander in Chief who treads the winepress of the wrath of God.[304] The gathering of the grapes for the winepress takes place at Armageddon, while the crushing takes place in this final battle. God's generals have crushed the necks of their enemies in the past.

And when they brought those kings out to Joshua, Joshua summoned all the men of Israel and said to the chiefs of the men of war who had gone with him, "Come near; put your feet on the necks of these kings." Then they came near and

275

put their feet on their necks. And Joshua said to them, "Do not be afraid or dismayed; be strong and courageous. For thus the Lord will do to all your enemies against whom you fight." (*Joshua 10:24-25*)

This is also the time that David spoke of.

David himself, in the Holy Spirit, declared, "'The Lord said to my Lord, Sit at my right hand, until I put your enemies under your feet." (*Mark 12:36*)

From His Mouth Comes a Sharp Sword

This sword is symbolic of the Word of God, which proceeds from the mouth of Jesus Christ in tremendous power against His enemies. The same omnipotent Word that "spoke" all of creation into being will now destroy these last armies of all those who worshipped the creation yet hated the Creator.

Now when the armies of Antichrist see the coming of the King of Kings, they will gather together to make war against Him and against His holy army of angels and saints coming down from heaven. But they have no chance against them, for immediately, like a mighty sword in the midst of great combat, the "Word" is shouted against the armies of Antichrist.

This shall be the plague with which the Lord will strike all the peoples that wage war against Jerusalem: their flesh will rot while they are still standing on their feet, their eyes will rot in their sockets, and their tongues will rot in their mouths. (*Zechariah 14:12*)

The Lord's enemies are completely consumed by the Word of His mouth, that same powerful Word that created the heavens and the earth.[305] The Army of Christ is witness to this great victory over the millions of human-orcs who were once committed to completely slaughtering the people of God on the face of the earth. Now they see the flesh of their enemies melting from their bodies.

Calling the "Birds of the Air" to the Battlefield

The birds of the air are summoned by the voice of an angel to share in the victory by eating the flesh of those who have been struck down by the Word of God. To give one's flesh to the birds of the atmosphere is expressive of the most complete defeat and shameful subjection of the enemy conceivable.[306] In the past, the enemy has humiliated the dead bodies of God's people by allowing the birds and the beasts to feed upon them.[307] Likewise, Goliath threatened this same humiliation to young David, yet David responded by telling him that it was he and his entire army that would be killed and whose bodies would be given to the birds of the air.[308]

The Lake of Fire Receives Its First Victims

Antichrist and the False Prophet are the first two who are thrown alive into the lake of fire. The Antichrist's army has been totally slain and their flesh eaten by the birds of the air. Yet their souls will suffer in hell while awaiting the final Day of Judgment, at which time they will follow their "beloved" Antichrist into the lake of fire, which burns with sulfur. This is a lake that is probably composed of the same sulfurous fire that the Lord rained down on the cities of Sodom and Gomorrah.[309] This is a torturous lake that is not only intensely hot but also has a foul, putrid smell as well. The Antichrist and the False Prophet are its first inhabitants. Later, Satan himself, together with Death, Hades, and all of sinful mankind will join them in this place of torment.

The Victorious Descending of the Messiah to the Mount of Olives

As Jesus descends, His feet will touch down on the Mount of Olives. The one-third remnant of the Jewish people who survived the great war will come before Him on the Mount of Olives. Then when they recognize that their promised Messiah is truly Jesus Christ who was proclaimed by the Christian church, they will deeply mourn and weep.

And I will pour out on the house of David and the inhabitants of Jerusalem a spirit of grace and pleas for mercy, so that, <u>when they look on me, on him whom they have pierced, they shall mourn for him, as one mourns for an only child,</u> and weep bitterly over him, as one weeps over a firstborn. **(Zechariah 12:10)**

Then the Lord Jesus will completely cleanse His beloved Jewish people who refused to take the mark of the Beast or to worship the image of the beast.

On that day there shall be a fountain opened for the house of David and the inhabitants of Jerusalem, to cleanse them from sin and uncleanness. **(Zechariah 13:1)**

These are the ones who cried out for His coming, for Jesus had previously told the Jewish people,

For I tell you, you will not see me again, until you say, "Blessed is he who comes in the name of the Lord." **(Matthew 23:39)**

To summarize, the second coming is an all-out military attack by the armies of heaven against the rebellious angels and against the armies of the nations. The Lord Jesus will shout at the head of His armies; He is leading the attack. Can you hear it? There is such passion in it, such anger, and such power. Surely the mountains will shake, the dead will be raised, and the enemies of God will flee from before Him. Surely the seas will roar and the trees of the field will clap their hands. Let us tremble before Him, for the King is coming. He is coming to judge the earth in righteousness. His shout is like the roar of a lion. Jesus is at one and the same time a sacrificial Lamb and a roaring Lion. He who died on the cross as a suffering Servant is the same one who's coming back as a conquering King.[310]

For the Lord himself will descend from heaven with <u>a cry of command</u>, with the voice of an archangel, and with the sound of the trumpet of God. And the dead in Christ will rise first. **(1 Thessalonians 4:16)**

CHAPTER 14

THE KINGDOM OF GOD REIGNING UPON THE EARTH
(Revelation 20—22)

M any in the church have a problem understanding the reign of the kingdom of God during the millennial age, which precedes the coming of the new heaven and new earth. They have been taught that there is no actual future physical kingdom and that the words in Revelation 20 are simply "spiritual." That is, Satan already has been bound since the resurrection of Jesus and we are currently living in the millennial age. If this is true, then there is certainly no ongoing spiritual warfare; it already has been won for us. However, one only has to look at two thousand years of continuing persecution and rampant false teachings within the church in order to understand that this is another deceptive teaching designed to put Christians to sleep while the real war is raging across the world. These "spiritual teachings" of the millennial period first surfaced with the influence of Greek Platonism on the church around the fourth century. They were popularized by Augustine (AD 350–430) and later taught and embraced by the early Roman Catholic Church, which then insisted that any teachings of a physical reign of Christ were heretical.[311] Thus, this has been a spiritually weakening teaching that has been passed down through the ages to this day. My personal experience tells me that most Christians who adhere to views known as amillennial or postmillennial are among those who fail to discern the times for this present generation; they do not see a time of great tribulation and judgment coming upon the Christian church and our nation.

Contrary to those "spiritualized" teachings, the majority of the ancient church understood the millennial period to be an earthly, physical reign of the Lord Jesus Christ and His saints that follows the defeat of the Antichrist and precedes the Day of Judgment and the coming of the new heaven and earth.[312] This is known as "historic (or classical) premillennialism" and was embraced by our most prominent early church fathers, such as Ignatius, Polycarp, Irenaeus, Justin Martyr, and Tertullian. Other respected theologians, such as Sir Isaac Newton, Charles Spurgeon, George Eldon Ladd, Merrill Tenney, Carl Henry, and Francis Schaeffer, also taught the truths of historic premillennialism.[313] They understood Revelation 20 in its plain, simple sense. That is, many saints will be raised at the beginning of this thousand-year period and a second resurrection will occur at the end. A suggestion to my readers: "Read Revelation 19 and 20 without listening to anyone else."

REMOVAL OF SATAN FROM THE EARTH
(Revelation 20:1-3)

Before a millennial kingdom can be established, the deceiver of the nations must be removed. At this time, the human armies of Satan have been completely annihilated. His two human cohorts, Antichrist and the False Prophet, have been thrown into the lake of fire. Now an angel from God has been dispatched from heaven with the authority to remove Satan himself from the earth so that he cannot deceive the nations during the coming millennial reign of Christ. How will Satan be removed from the earth? This mighty angelic representative of almighty God will seize Satan and bind him with a great chain that will not be removed for a thousand years. He will then be thrown into a deep, bottomless pit. When Satan has been cast down, the angel will shut and lock the door to the pit, which no one can open until the proper time. Additionally, it appears that the demonic angels who were the dark agents of Satan for six thousand years also are imprisoned at this time.

> *God did not spare angels when they sinned, but cast them*
> *into hell and committed them to chains of gloomy darkness*
> *to be kept until the judgment (2 Peter 2:4)*

However, Satan's confinement is temporary. At the end of the millennial period, he will again be released to go out among the nations to recruit an army for the final showdown between the kingdom of the world and the kingdom of God.

THE MILLENNIAL AGE—THE SEVENTH DAY OF REST

The millennial age will precede the coming of the new heaven and the new earth and will be a time when the earth is being "restored" for both God and man's eternal dominion. Think of it like this: The time from Adam to Noah was a downward transition of the world away from paradise in the Garden of Eden. The time of the millennium to the new heaven and earth is an upward transition to a paradise restored. Thus, the millennium appears to be a one-thousand-year transition between the life that we now have and the Garden of Eden-type paradise that comes with the new heaven and new earth.[314]

We recall that the earth was created in six days, and on the seventh day God rested from all of His works. We have learned that these numbers are symbolic of many truths revealed in the Bible. For example, six days of labor must be followed by a day of rest known as the Sabbath. Also, the number six is symbolic of man, while the number seven symbolizes perfection and completion. Additionally, when the apostle Peter described events that must take place before the end of the age, he declared that a single day with the Lord is as a thousand years to mankind. This prophecy of Peter's also points out that as the earth once perished through a great flood, so will it also perish through a great fire that is yet coming. Following the flood there was a dawning of a new age; and, likewise, after the fires of the Armageddon war, there also dawns a new age known as the millennium.[315]

There certainly appears to be a parallel between the six days of creation and the first six thousand years of human history. These "sixes" may be described as a period of "labor" — six days of labor for the Creator and six thousand years of labor for mankind. The seventh one-thousand-year period, known as the millennium, represents the Sabbath day of rest when equating the seven thousand years of mankind's history to the seven days of creation. One of our very early church fathers, Polycarp, was discipled by his close friend, the apostle John. Obviously Polycarp would have received tremendous insights from the man who experienced and recorded the book of Revelation. Polycarp was later martyred, but before his death, he also taught others concerning the end of time. One of his well-known disciples was Irenaeus, who wrote a book called *Against Heresies.* In this book, Irenaeus says the following:

As God views 1,000 years as a day and He created the earth in 6 days and rested on the 7th, so shall the earth last for 6,000 years and rest under the reign of Christ for the last 1,000 years."

Here was a man who was taught by a friend of John's, stating that Jesus Christ would return to reign on earth for one thousand years, which would represent a period of rest from six thousand years of sinful, rebellious living in the world. Also, we should take note that the time frame revealed in the Bible puts us very close to the completion of six thousand years since the time of creation.

THE PURPOSE OF THE MILLENNIUM

Paul provides some clear insights into the purpose of this one-thousand-year millennial period.

For as in Adam all die, so also in Christ shall all be made alive. But each in his own order: Christ the firstfruits, then at his coming those who belong to Christ. Then comes the end, when he delivers the kingdom to God the Father after

destroying every rule and every authority and power. For he must reign until he has put all his enemies under his feet. The last enemy to be destroyed is death.
(1 Corinthians 15:22-26)

The Son of God must reign until he puts all of His enemies under His feet. During His millennial rule, all evil will eventually be exposed and destroyed forever. Until that time, death still exists, even though it has limited powers during the millennium. The millennium is also a time when Jesus Christ is vindicated before the nation of Israel and the world that persecuted Him. At the end of the millennium, death will be the last enemy destroyed, and then the kingdom is made ready for the Son to deliver it over to His Father. Thus, the millennial age is a time for the rulership of Jesus, while the following age of the new heaven and new earth will be under the rulership of God the Father. Jesus, as the last Adam, brings back obedience and fellowship to the Father, even as the first Adam broke that fellowship by disobedience.[316]

TWO RESURRECTIONS
(Revelation 20:4-6)

Two resurrections are mentioned in these verses, one at the beginning of the millennial reign and one at the end. The first resurrection appears to be a select group of saints who lost their lives for their testimony of Jesus but will live and reign with Him on this earth for a thousand years. This group certainly consists of those who have been martyred for the gospel of Christ through the centuries, but it is probable that it is also for those who surrendered their lives totally for the kingdom, even though they were not physically martyred. Additionally, this resurrection will include those who are alive at His coming and will be caught up into the air to join His holy army as they descend to the earth. These are also those who refused to worship the Beast and did not receive his mark on their foreheads and hands. These are the strongest and most mature warriors in the army of God. They will be the leaders in His kingdom, helping prepare the world for the final stage of paradise.

The remainder of the human race will be part of the second resurrection. The first resurrection is for a chosen group of the righteous only. The second resurrection is for the rest of the righteous and for the wicked. The righteous ones of the second resurrection will be joyfully waiting in heaven during the millennial reign of Jesus and then descend with the heavenly Jerusalem at the end of the millennium. Then all those who are the bride of Christ will be united forever. It is not my purpose to analyze who are the representatives of the righteous in the first and second resurrections. Yet, it should be our goal to make it to the first resurrection. If it means being physically martyred, so be it. If it means total dedication as if spiritually martyred, so be it.[317]

Listen to Paul's hope for a better resurrection.

. . . that I may know him and the power of his resurrection, and may share his sufferings, becoming like him in his death, that by any means possible I may attain the resurrection from the dead. **(Philippians 3:10-11)**

Paul obviously did not doubt his salvation. What he desired was to attain a higher level of resurrection and be part of the first resurrection.

The same principle applied to other heroes of the faith.

Others were tortured, not accepting their release, so that they might obtain a better resurrection. **(Hebrews 11:35) (NASB)**

MILLENNIAL REIGN BEGINS—45 DAYS AFTER BOWL JUDGMENTS?

The following end-times prophecy in Daniel has been the subject of much speculation over the centuries. Perhaps the understanding of the coming millennial age might provide some insights into the blessings inherent within this prophecy.

And from the time that the regular burnt offering is taken away and the abomination that makes desolate is set up, there shall be 1,290 days. <u>Blessed is he who waits and arrives at the 1,335 days</u>. But go your way till the end. And you shall rest and shall stand in your allotted place at the end of the days.
(Daniel 12:11-13)

Since Antichrist is to reign for 1,260 days from the time the abomination of desolation is set up in the temple mount, it would seem as if the additional 30 days represent the period of the "bowl judgments." Thus, it seems as if the 1,290 days mark the end of these bowl judgments. If true, then the reign of Christ appears to begin on day 1,335, which is 45 days after the completion of the bowl judgments.[318] These 45 days may be a time when the earth is being prepared for the millennial kingdom and the first resurrection of those saints who will reign with Him takes place. This certainly would explain the blessedness associated with the 1,335 days.

RESURRECTED BODIES OF THE SAINTS

In order to get an idea of what our resurrected bodies will be like, we can look at Jesus' appearance when He walked the earth following His resurrection. He suddenly appears and disappears. Thus during the millennium the natural people on earth will live in different locations and travel by normal means, while the resurrected people will be free to move into different locations as they are led by the Spirit of God. Like the resurrected Jesus, His resurrected saints also will walk, talk, and eat with those in their natural bodies. They will have physical bodies, which can be touched like those in the natural and perform physical functions, but they will be bodies that have great supernatural capabilities. Thus, the resurrected saints will be real people in real bodies—bodies that are incorruptible and eternally free from sin. These will be resurrected bodies of immortality with infinitely greater capabilities than the old physical bodies of this world, which have been corrupted by sin.

NONRESURRECTED PEOPLES IN THE MILLENNIUM

Within the nations around the world will be innumerable peoples who survived the "bowls of wrath" and were not among the armed forces that gathered at Armageddon and were subsequently killed. These are men, women, and children, both young and old, from all races and cultures who, in their natural bodies, are confused, scared, and wondering what is going to happen next. These will constitute the first generation of human beings living in the millennial kingdom. Prior to this time, the gospel of the kingdom will have been preached throughout the nations, but many may not have heard it or perhaps did not believe. However, after witnessing the Lord's almighty power poured out across the earth, their understanding will have grown and there will no longer be any question in their minds that the God of the Christians is truly God. Many will have suffered tremendous grief at the loss of loved ones during this period, and others undoubtedly are stricken with sickness from the plagues; but a tremendous cleansing of the earth is about to begin. They may not be quickly accepting of Jesus Christ, since initially they will be in a state of shock and confusion, for the world is completely different from what they have known and been taught from birth. But they will undoubtedly listen to the teachings that are about to go forth to the nations.

These are people in various stages of maturity. There will be babies, children, fathers and mothers, aunts and uncles, and grandparents. There may be some whose hearts will never be aligned with God and will eventually be standing on the left side of the judgment seat. Those who die during this period will become part of the second resurrection, at which time they will receive either eternal life or damnation.

Many questions are in all Christian minds concerning people whom we believe have never had the opportunity to hear the gospel message during their lifetime. These would be peoples living in distant countries in both the old and new dispensations who never had opportunity to hear the truths of the Lord and respond. Ancient peoples in far countries, children who die at a young age, babies that have been aborted: these are examples of human lives that certainly never had the opportunity to know the Lord. Perhaps this millennial period is a time for those people to be resurrected into their natural bodies and experience life under the reign of Christ. Perhaps these are people who comprise much of the natural population during those times. I know this is speculative, but I believe it to be quite probable.

THE MILLENNIAL AGE—A TIME OF RESTORATION

The thousand-year, millennial, period is a time designated by the Lord to bring about a restoration of all things. This will be a day-to-day restoring of the world to that condition that existed in the Garden of Eden, a perfect world that our Lord calls "very good." It will be a time when Jesus Christ, who reigns and oversees this restoration process, will put all of His enemies under His feet, and mankind will walk in the fullness of Jesus Christ as sons and daughters of our almighty Lord. The earth, which has been groaning for six thousand years, will again rejoice over the righteous reign of the children of God.

> *The creation itself will be set free from its bondage to decay and obtain the freedom of the glory of the children of God. For we know that the whole creation has been groaning together in the pains of childbirth until now. And not only the creation, but we ourselves, who have the firstfruits of the Spirit, groan inwardly as we wait eagerly for adoption as sons, the redemption of our bodies.*
> *(Romans 8:21-23)*

The death and resurrection of Jesus Christ provided the means for the human race to be restored to our Father's design for us.

> *Repent, then, and turn to God, so that your sins may be wiped out, that times of refreshing may come from the Lord, and that he may send the Christ, who has been appointed for you—even Jesus. He must remain in heaven until the time*

comes for God to restore everything, as he promised long
ago through his holy prophets. (Acts 3:19-21) (NIV)

Much of the detail concerning this restoration process is found in the prophetic books of the Old Testament. Some examples follow.

The Earth's Dead Waters Will Be Restored

A large river of fresh water will flow out of the Lord's millennial temple in Jerusalem so deep that one can swim in it. It flows through the eastern part of the land and into the sea, where it will change the seas into fresh water. These seas will again be populated with living creatures and every kind of fish.[319]

The Animal Kingdom Will Be Restored to the Splendor of the Garden of Eden

The wolf shall dwell with the lamb, and the leopard shall
lie down with the young goat, and the calf and the lion and
the fattened calf together; and a little child shall lead them.
The cow and the bear shall graze; their young shall lie down
together; and the lion shall eat straw like the ox.[320]

The Earth Will Again Yield Tremendous Fruit for the Beloved People of the Creator

"Behold, the days are coming," declares the Lord, "when the
plowman shall overtake the reaper and the treader of grapes
him who sows the seed; the mountains shall drip sweet wine,
and all the hills shall flow with it."[321]

Humans and Animals Will Be United in Love for One Another

The infant will play near the hole of the cobra, and the young
child put his hand into the viper's nest. They will neither
harm nor destroy on all my holy mountain, for the earth will

be full of the knowledge of the Lord as the waters cover the sea.[322]

Length of Life Will Be as in the Pre-Flood Era

Never again will there be in it an infant who lives but a few days, or an old man who does not live out his years; he who dies at a hundred will be thought a mere youth; he who fails to reach a hundred will be considered accursed.[323]

There Will No Slavery Among Mankind—Each Will Reap the Fruit of Their Own Labors

They shall not build and another inhabit; they shall not plant and another eat; for like the days of a tree shall the days of my people be, and my chosen shall long enjoy the work of their hands.[324]

These millennial peoples certainly will live long and healthy lives, but all will eventually be subjected to death since they have not yet been resurrected. This will be a period similar to that era between the Garden of Eden and the great flood.

Finally, there is a remarkable parallel between the restoration of the earth during the millennial age and the sanctification process of "born-again" Christians. In both cases, the spiritual regeneration precedes the physical. That is, the earth requires the presence of Christ in order for it to be "born again" and begin the process of physical restoration to its original state. Also, Christians require the "born-again" experience of the Holy Spirit before we can undergo the maturing process of restoration to our original state.[325] Pretty interesting!

RESURRECTED SAINTS—THEIR MILLENNIAL MISSION

As previously mentioned, when Jesus was resurrected and appeared before various groups of people, He interacted socially with those who lived in human bodies. He talked with them, ate with them, and cooked for them; they all fellowshipped together, much like they did before His death.[326] There was even a group of Old Testament saints whom Christ brought forth from Hades. They entered Jerusalem in their resurrected bodies and appeared before many believers in the city.[327]

The resurrected saints of the millennial kingdom are going to interact with the peoples of all the nations from a heart of deep, passionate love—a heart of Jesus! The resurrected believers will be governing authorities, evangelists, teachers, and advisors to the nations. They will be in positions of authority at various levels, depending on each person's gifts and proven record of dependability.[328] The more faithful one is during our present natural life determines the degree of leadership authority that will be given in the life to come. Jesus will be the King ruling from His temple in the capital city of Jerusalem.

Those who sit upon the thrones are probably martyrs who were victims of unrighteous judgments in the courtrooms of the world. What an encouragement it is to those hearing the death sentence pronounced on them by earthly judges to know that one day they will be sitting on thrones. Their experiences of injustice in court will strengthen their ambition to be absolutely fair when they come to judge others.[329]

Some of the resurrected saints will be in the King's cabinet, overseeing various areas of government such as the departments of agriculture, commerce, or transportation. Some will be governors over provinces, and some will be mayors over cities. Others will be in charge of leading worship in the temple. Still others will take the message of Jesus out to the peoples worldwide. Jesus will be teaching from the city of Jerusalem, and His evangelists and teachers will be taking His message to the nations around the world. Some teachings will include in-depth lessons on nature in the millennial world—about fish, birds, animals, and vegetation. However, teachings concerning the kingdom of God that is among them will have the greatest impact. These teachings will cause many people to say,

*"Come, let us go up to the mountain of the Lord, to the house
of the God of Jacob, that he may teach us his ways and that
we may walk in his paths." For out of Zion shall go the law
and the word of the Lord from Jerusalem. He shall judge
between the nations, and shall decide disputes for many
peoples; and they shall beat their swords into plowshares,
and their spears into pruning hooks; nation shall not lift up
sword against nation, neither shall they learn war anymore.
(Isaiah 2:3-4)*

THE MILLENNIAL GOVERNMENT

Unlike the original government established in the United States,
the government ruling over the kingdom of God will not be democratic. It will be a glorious monarchy with Jesus Christ, the King
of Kings, ruling from His throne in the capital city of Jerusalem.
His position of authority is not chosen by popular vote but by the
divine choice of almighty God, our Father. The Bible informs us
that both Christ and His chosen leaders will rule over the world with
a "rod of iron." This is indicative of strong and uncompromising
rulership that will establish laws based upon the foundational truths
of righteousness and holiness. The character of our Lord will be the
ruling character in the lives of His sons and daughters who will live
eternally under His kingship. This will be a glorious and righteous
government that all of His conquering people will love to be a part
of.

God's boundary lines for the nations, which have been usurped
by man, may again be reestablished by this government.

*And he made from one man every nation of mankind to live on
all the face of the earth, having determined allotted periods
and the boundaries of their dwelling place. (Acts 17:26)*

Most likely people groups will be broken down into seventy
nations, which is the number of the sons of God.

*When the Most High gave to the nations their inheritance, when <u>he divided mankind, he fixed the borders of the peoples according to the number of the sons of God.</u> (**Deuteronomy 32:8**)*

*<u>All the descendants of Jacob were seventy persons</u>. (**Exodus 1:5**)*

Nevertheless, during the millennial reign of this government, there will be many who will rather pursue the lusts of their hearts rather than the ways of the Lord. Though they will outwardly obey the laws of the kingdom, within their hearts they are hoping that a time will come when they can throw off the shackles of God's righteous laws and pursue their individual destinies. These are those whom our Lord describes as

*the cowardly, the faithless, the detestable, as for murderers, the sexually immoral, sorcerers, idolaters, and all liars, their portion will be in the lake that burns with fire and sulfur, which is the second death." (**Revelation 21:8**)*

SATAN RELEASED AND THE LAST WORLD WAR

During the millennium, the earth is restored, peace reigns, and inhabitants of the nations live with great joyous freedom. And it is even going to get better. However, before that time, the true people of God must be separated from those who would rather make their own laws and live life anyway they please. Yes, they are still in the world, but their hearts have not been visibly exposed.

Although the Lord Jesus Christ visibly and physically reigns over mankind during the millennium, when the deceiver is set free from his prison at the end of that period, he will find the hearts of many will still be responsive to his seductions. This makes it plain that the ultimate root of sin is not found in poverty or inadequate social conditions but in the rebelliousness of the human heart and its hatred for our Lord. The millennial age and the subsequent rebellion of men will prove that people cannot blame their sinfulness on their environment or unfortunate circumstances.[330] Our Lord always has given mankind time to exercise their own free will and thereby choose their destiny. Then he allows circumstances to evolve whereby the intentions of the heart are visibly manifested. People are given the final opportunity to choose sides. In the end, they will have no excuse beyond the sinfulness of their own rebellious heart when they stand before the judgment seat of our righteous and almighty God.

When Satan is released, he will be allowed to move among the nations and tempt people to turn from the Lord, exactly like he tempted Adam and Eve in the garden. The rest of the imprisoned demonic hoards undoubtedly will be released with him and will be employed to deceive and rally mankind to rebel against the kingdom of God. In the end, Satan and his demonic allies build an army so numerous that "their number is like the sand of the sea."

Recall that there appear to be three major battles between the forces of light and darkness described in end-times prophecy.

- The battle of nations from Magog that comes against Israel. As mentioned in a previous chapter, I believe this to be the sixth-seal event described in Ezekiel 38-39.
- The second battle is that known as Armageddon and described both in Revelation 19 and Old Testament prophecies. This comes at the end of the six-thousand-year age of mankind and is followed by the second coming of Jesus, our Messiah, to establish a one-thousand-year, millennial, reign.
- The third battle is the final attempt by Satan and his followers to defeat the purposes of God at the end of the millennial reign of Christ. Here the enemies of God will be quickly consumed by fire. This will be followed by a day of final judgment.

This last attempt to attack and seize Jerusalem, now the capital of the world, fails completely. In fact, the battle is never joined by the people of God on earth. The kingdom of God no longer has need for armies, a Joint Chief of Staff, or a Secretary of Defense. Our

Father in heaven sends down fire upon these enemy forces as they surround the city of Jerusalem, and they are completely consumed. The final Great War between the forces of light and darkness is also the shortest ever. The entire army of Satan is killed without the loss of a single human life among those in the kingdom of God. This great climax will occur on the old earth before the new earth appears so that the entire world will witness the final victory of good over evil.

Many of us probably wonder why Satan would arise to lead this final rebellion. Does he not expect his defeat? Does he expect his last bid for earthly sovereignty to succeed? Is he self-deluded, as well as the deceiver of nations? Does he really think he is stronger than God's people and, therefore, God Himself? Or, knowing his fate is sealed, does he seek to take as many as he can to share in his ruin in a last fit of frustrated rage? We may never know![331] However, we do know that the heart of Satan certainly epitomizes the depths of arrogant pride that refuses to recognize the righteousness of God even in the face of eternal judgment.

HADES OR SHEOL—A TEMPORARY ABODE

Hades, in the New Testament, is the "temporary" holding place for the spirits of unrighteous men and women who have died in their sins. It is not their eternal destiny but a place where they will experience continual unrest and torment until the coming of that day when they will be resurrected to stand before the judgment seat of almighty God. *Sheol* in the Old Testament is the equivalent of *Hades;* however, prior to the resurrection of Jesus Christ, Sheol was the holding place for both the righteous and the unrighteous. It was composed of two entirely separate compartments that may be referred to as paradise for the righteous and torments for the unrighteous. These two compartments are visibly described in the parable of the rich man and Lazarus.[332]

When Jesus laid down His life on the cross, he first descended into Hades, or Sheol, and released the righteous ones, whose spirits had been awaiting His coming. Then the spirits of the righteous in

Christ arose and accompanied Him into heaven, although some of them appeared to many of the inhabitants of Jerusalem before they ascended into heaven.[333] The spirits of our faithful brethren of the Old Testament dispensation could not go directly to heaven until their sins had been completely cleansed by the shed blood of Jesus at the cross; thus they had to wait in Hades. But now, all who die in Christ will ascend directly to heaven and stand with all their brethren in the holy presence of our glorious Lord. The spirits of the unrighteous dead will remain in Hades until the end of the millennial reign of Christ and His chosen saints. At that time they will be resurrected to stand before the judgment seat of almighty God, who will then determine their eternal destiny.

"ETERNALLY CONDEMNED" OR "ETERNALLY TORMENTED"?

It is understandable that all of mankind, both believers and unbelievers, have difficulty with the doctrine of eternal punishment. We all shrink from this teaching, for none of us dare visualize how eternal punishment might be experienced by someone we know and love. Yet the Bible does not ignore this teaching, and neither can we. The reality of the fiery torments of hell should spur all of us to continually communicate this truth with great zeal and urgency.[335]

How long will the unrighteous be tormented in the lake of fire? Traditional teachings stick to the view that hell is a place of eternal, conscious torment. That is, a person who is sentenced to hell is doomed to be painfully tormented forever and ever. Wow! Does the Bible "clearly" teach this? Many respected theologians certainly believe so. However, there are others who do not believe that sinners are eternally tortured but that after completing their allotted period of torturous punishment, their souls disintegrate into what they perceive as the "second death." This is called the "conditionalist view." It sees sinners as being punished for a period of time before ceasing to exist. This is opposed to the "traditionalist view," which see sinners as suffering eternal punishment.[336] "Eternally condemned" means that sinners do suffer for a period of time in the lake of fire, but eventually their soul disintegrates into nothingness; however, the memory of their tormenting punishment is never forgotten. At times, the Bible certainly does appear to say the souls of sinners suffer eternally, while in other places it is evident that there are varying degrees of suffering—some suffer more than others. Does that mean some places are hotter than others, or do some suffer longer than others? What the conditionalist view does is magnify:

- The justice of God—each doomed sinner receives precisely what he or she deserves and nothing else.
- The mercy of God— even the worse sinner finally perishes forever.
- The holiness of God— His wrath is real, but it is measured with exact precision in keeping with His own character.[337]

For, readers who want more information on the conditional view as opposed to the traditional view, I would recommend reading Dr. David Reagan's *Lamplighter* publication dated March-April 2006 entitled, "The Reality of Hell." This article is quite an eye-opener for those who have heard only the traditional teachings of eternal suffering in hell. Personally, I tend to lean toward the conditionalist view, although I do remain open-minded to either teaching. There is so much that lies beyond our comprehension, and I find all mysteries of the future to be very exciting and am looking forward to the adventures of discovery awaiting each of us in God's glorious kingdom.

LAKE OF FIRE—THE PERMANENT ABODE OF THE UNGODLY

When the word *hell* is mentioned in the Bible, it frequently refers to the fire into which the unrighteous are thrown and where they will be eternally punished. Thus, hell appears to be synonymous with the lake of fire. It is described in various sections of the Bible as a place of darkness, sadness, fiery torment, disgrace, and everlasting contempt. The lake of fire is said to burn with sulfur, a yellow substance that burns readily in the air. It is found in its natural state in volcanic areas. A lake of burning sulfur would not only be intensely hot, but it would be stinking and rotten as well. This is a place devoid of the presence of God. However, it is a place that will always be remembered, for even the sons and daughters of the Lord will have opportunity to look upon the dead bodies of those who perished in the lake of fire. This scene will be an eternal witness to the righteousness and holiness of our Lord.

> *And they shall go out and look on the dead bodies of the men who have rebelled against me. <u>For their worm shall not die, their fire shall not be quenched,</u> and they shall be an abhorrence to all flesh. Isaiah 66:24*

That their "worm shall not die" may simply refer to the eternal memory of their suffering or perhaps even to the residue of their dead souls, like a skeleton is the residue of dead bodies. At any rate, we are told that we will witness the eternal destruction of our earthly enemies, who once tried to eternally destroy each of us. This will be a visible, eternal reminder of the righteousness of the wrath of God against the enemies of all our brothers and sisters who once suffered under their cruel tyranny.

Death is the last enemy to be defeated. Death lost much of its power when Jesus was raised from the dead, and it will lose even more throughout the millennial period. Death only has power over sinners, and many of the inhabitants of the millennial kingdom are His resurrected sons and daughters. It appears that both Death and Hades, who will be thrown into the lake of fire following the Day of Judgment, are actually powerful fallen angels who are cohorts of Satan. Death appears as the evil angel who is the rider on the pale horse and Hades as another evil angel who follows right behind him.[338] These are probably the two most powerful angels under the rulership of Satan in the demonic realm. They will all join the Antichrist and the false prophet in this horrendous, putrid, and tormenting lake of fire.

The lake of fire is an eternal demonstration of the wrath of God. God's power and glory can be demonstrated both in blessing and in punishment. We have a positive motivation not to fall into sin: the goodness of God. We also have a negative reason not to sin: the severity of God. The eternal witness of the lake of fire is a perfect deterrent to protect us from sin.

Note then the kindness and the severity of God: severity toward those who have fallen, but God's kindness to you, provided you continue in his kindness. Otherwise you too will be cut off. **Romans 11:22**

THE DAY OF JUDGMENT
(Revelation 20:11-15)

Many Christians really don't believe that they will be standing before the judgment seat of our Lord on this glorious day that takes place prior to the coming of the new heaven and new earth. They feel deep in their hearts that there really is no need for judgment since the destiny of a person already has been determined by the time of his or her death. However, the purpose of this final judgment is more than just announcing each person's future destiny before all of creation. To begin, let's briefly examine three points that will provide us with a more complete understanding of the purpose of this coming day of God's judgment.[339]

- The day of judgment will display the perfect sovereignty and glory of God in the determination of each person's destiny; that is, will they live eternally with the Lord in the new heaven and new earth, or will they be consigned to a "second death" in the lake of fire? All will truly understand God's omniscient (all-knowing) and omnipresent (always present) nature. That is, He knows our every thought and the true motives behind our every action, for His eyes not only have been upon us outwardly but also see into our minds and hearts during every second of our entire lives. Nothing that has ever taken place in the actions, minds, and hearts of each man and woman is hidden from the omniscient and omnipresent God of all creation. And as the true heart of each person becomes visible to all, then all will come to understand His righteousness, which determines man's eternal destiny.

- A second purpose is to reveal the degree of reward as well as the degree of punishment each person shall receive. Some rewards are greater than others, and some punishments are more severe than others. The degrees of reward or punishment are related to the lives that people have lived, and they will be revealed to the world when the "books" are opened before the throne.

- The third purpose is to execute God's judgment on each person before the entire universe. Are they truly sons and daughters of God who will live together with Him in the new heaven and new earth; or will they be cast into the lake of fire from which they will never leave?

This is a universal judgment over all of mankind, a judgment passed upon the wicked and the righteous at the same time. All will be judged, and this judgment will bring both varying degrees of rewards to His people, as well as varying degrees of punishments to His enemies.[340] From this judgment, there shall be no appeal; it is everlasting.

JUDGMENT DAY—WHO WILL BE THE JUDGE?

Who is the mighty Judge on the great white throne? The Bible clearly reveals that all will appear before the judgment seat of Jesus Christ. However, it also appears that the one who sits on the great white throne, from whose presence both the heavens and earth flee away, is almighty God, the Father of our Lord Jesus Christ. A number of Bible passages ascribe judgment to God the Father. Yet, it is also very clear in the Bible that God the Father judges the world in and through His Son. Jesus Christ is God in human form, and He is the

Father's representative to the entire world. The Father's authority has been given to His Son.

The Father judges no one, but has given all judgment to the Son, that all may honor the Son, just as they honor the Father. Whoever does not honor the Son does not honor the Father who sent him. (John 5:22-23)

They show that the work of the law is written on their hearts, while their conscience also bears witness, and their conflicting thoughts accuse or even excuse them on that day when, according to my gospel, God judges the secrets of men by Christ Jesus. (Romans 2:15-16)

However, when the entire creation appears before the throne on the great day of judgment, it is unquestionable that the Father will personally be present sitting on the great white throne. Therefore, we shall all stand before the Father and His Son, who also sits on His throne at the right hand of the Father; and in the Son's hands will be the Book of Life.[341]

This will be the day when we hear the following words of Jesus spoken in finality before each and every person.

So everyone who acknowledges me before men, I also will acknowledge before my Father who is in heaven, but whoever denies me before men, I also will deny before my Father who is in heaven. (Matthew 10:32-33)

JUDGMENT DAY—WHO WILL BE JUDGED?

Who will stand before the great white throne in judgment? All of mankind, from Adam to the very last person who ever lived, shall appear before the final judgment seat. Cain and Abel, Moses and Pharaoh, Elijah and Jezebel, David and Goliath, John the Baptist and Herod, Paul and Nero, Martin Luther and all the Catholic popes, Charles Spurgeon and Karl Marx, Hitler and Corrie Ten Boom,

Stalin, Mao, and the millions of Christians they slaughtered, the Clintons and the Reagans, Hollywood celebrities and the homeless, great and small, kings and slaves, rich and poor, young and old—all will appear before the judgment seat of almighty God. Bodies of the dead that were never retrieved, such as those of suicide bombers, those lost at sea, those devoured by beasts, and those who have been dead for thousands of years, all will be resurrected, and their bodies and souls will be reunited.

Following this final resurrection, mankind will appear one-by-one before the throne; the books will be opened, and the thoughts and deeds of every living being will be disclosed to every generation throughout the history of mankind. Obviously, this day of judgment is not a literal twenty-four-hour day but will last until every single being has stood before the throne and their moment-to-moment lives are unfolded before all. Then as judgment is pronounced on each person, they will either go to stand with the righteous at the right hand of God or with the unrighteous on the left.

> *When the Son of Man comes in his glory, and all the angels with him, then he will sit on his glorious throne. Before him will be gathered all the nations, and he will separate people one from another as a shepherd separates the sheep from the goats. And he will place the sheep on his right, but the goats on the left. <u>Then the King will say to those on his</u>* **<u>right</u>**<u>, "Come, you who are blessed by my Father, inherit the kingdom prepared for you from the foundation of the world."</u>
> *(Matthew 25:31-34)*

> <u>*Then he will say to those on his* **left***, "Depart from me, you cursed, into the eternal fire prepared for the devil and his angels."*</u> *(Matthew 25:41)*

And finally, this also may be the day when some of the saints of God will be seated on thrones, for it is they who will judge the angels.[342] And indeed the rebellious angels that aligned with Satan against the Lord also will be judged.

And the angels who did not stay within their own position of authority, but left their proper dwelling, he has kept in eternal chains under gloomy darkness until the judgment of the great day. (Jude 6)

Every soul that ever lived will gather together before the great white throne to witness judgments and to be judged. Then all will come to understand the righteousness of God's judgments in the lives of every human being.

JUDGMENT ACCORDING TO "WORKS"

All the works of men must be revealed in their true ethical character. All of our works in their proper light shall be exposed before God, before the world, and before ourselves. The reason is that God must be justified when He judges. He has always declared righteous judgments throughout history, no matter whether mankind agreed or disagreed with the consequences of His judgments. This day of judgment is at the end of an age when the thoughts and intents of every heart are exposed and the righteousness of almighty God cannot be disputed by either His people or His enemies. Many times throughout our lives, we see evil people getting away with rape, murder, and all kinds of evil, and we wonder why God does not immediately pour out His wrath upon these people. But on this day, every mouth will be stopped, and all shall acknowledge the perfect justice of God in both His righteousness and His timing. No one shall be dissatisfied with His judgments. Satan and his demonic world, as well as God's people and heaven's angels, will have to acknowledge that God's judgments are perfectly righteous.[343] Although believers have nothing to fear from the judgment, the realization that they will have to give an account for everything they have said, thought, and done should be a continuing incentive to fight against sin.

What will be the standard by which people will be judged? The standard is the revealed will of God in each of our lives, but it is not the same for all. Some have received fuller revelation of the will of God than others.[344] Those who have received a greater revelation of

God's will also have greater responsibilities. All of mankind, even those who are ignorant of the Bible, have had the laws of God written on their hearts. This is often referred to as our conscience.[345] What is very clear in the book of Romans is that people will be judged on the basis of the light that they had, and not on the basis of revelation that they did not receive. The reason the Bible teaches that the final judgment will be according to works, even though salvation cannot be earned by works, is the intimate connection between faith and works. Faith will always reveal itself in works; good works are the visible evidence of true faith. If the faith is genuine, the works will be present.[346] For those who profess belief in Jesus Christ but take advantage of His great love and forgiveness in order to maintain their worldly lifestyle, Paul has a warning.

> *Or <u>do you presume on the riches of his kindness and forbearance and patience</u>, not knowing that <u>God's kindness is meant to lead you to repentance</u>? But because of your hard and impenitent heart <u>you are storing up wrath for yourself</u> on the day of wrath when God's righteous judgment will be revealed. (**Romans 2:4-5**)*

THE "BOOKS OF WORKS" AND THE "BOOK OF LIFE"

As previously mentioned, all believers shall stand before the great white throne on judgment day, and we shall see our sins as they have never fully been seen before. We shall one day understand that even our best works were defiled by sin and, therefore, we have no hope for eternal life based upon our perception of "good works." However, there is another book, and it is probably held in the hands of Jesus Christ, sitting at the right side of His Father. This is the Book of Life, which contains the names of all His chosen ones who are redeemed by the blood of their Lord and Savior. Following the exposure of their works, the Book of Life will then be opened to determine if their names are recorded. If so, then their sins are removed from the presence of God as far as the "east is from the west."[347] All of our transgressions are removed from before Him, and then we will be clothed in white and will stand on His right side. The opening of this Book of Life has a negative significance for the wicked but a positive significance for the righteous. The great and final decision in judgment shall be whether or not one's name is written in the Book of Life![348]

However, not all those whose names appear in the Book of Life are alike. They all will be individually judged as righteous, but their works will determine the degree of rewards that each will receive.[349] It is neither unbiblical nor selfish to be motivated by rewards in the world to come. It *is* wrong to be motivated by the honor of man rather than the honor of God or to be motivated by the carnal rewards of this life rather than the eternal rewards of the world to come. But behavioral science teaches that rewards encourage behavior and punishments discourage. The concept of reward and punishment comes from God, and the degree of rewards seems to determine our individual proximity to Jesus in the kingdom. While everyone in the world will have access to meet Jesus, not everyone will have the same proximity to Him on a day-to-day basis. There will be assigned seating at events in the kingdom of God.[350] As citizens of the kingdom, we will have general access to meet with the King. However, only those on His immediate staff can meet with Him every day. Also, those with higher positions in the government can easily obtain an appointment with Him. The degree of one's accessibility to Jesus is considered a great reward in the kingdom of God.[351]

In the sense of being condemned, the true believer in Jesus is not "judged." However, there is another meaning to the word *judge* that does not refer to damnation or salvation but to reward and punishment. In this sense every believer will be judged.

For we must all appear before the judgment seat of Christ, so that each one may receive what is due for what he has done in the body, whether good or evil.
(2 Corinthians 5:10)

It also appears as if there may be punishments among those who receive eternal life. Any sin that has been repented of is washed away by the blood of Jesus. Yet any sin that is not repented of will be punished. I'm not speaking of losing salvation here but of losing rewards; by punishment, I do not mean damnation but chastisement. If Christians are leading a hidden, carnal life, it will be revealed.[352] The following passage certainly appears to speak to believers who allowed unrepentant sin to remain in their lives.

And that servant who knew his master's will but did not get ready or act according to his will, will receive a severe beating. But the one who did not know, and did what deserved a beating, will receive a light beating. Everyone to whom much was given, of him much will be required, and from him to whom they entrusted much, they will demand the more. **(Luke 12:47-48)**

The significance of the Day of Judgment may be summarized in the following four observations[353]

- The history of the world is not an endless succession of meaningless cycles but a movement toward a goal that follows the Day of Judgment.
- This day reveals to all that salvation and eternal blessedness is dependent on one's relationship to Jesus Christ.
- This day underscores man's accountability for his life and the opportunities that God has provided to allow one to accept or reject His holy authority over life.
- This day is the final and decisive conquest of all evil and the great revelation of the victory of the Lamb who was slain.

The Day of Judgment will reveal beyond the shadow of a doubt that at the end of this day, the will of God for this age will be perfectly complete.

THE NEW HEAVEN AND NEW EARTH
(Revelation 21:1-8)

Cataclysmic events will bring horrendous destruction over the present world. Great earthquakes, nuclear fires, multiple plagues, and hailstones raining down from heaven will cause tremendous devastation among all life on land, air, and water. The millennial age will be a period of cleansing and restoration of both life and nature to conditions that existed in the Garden of Eden. However, like Adam and Eve, sin will still exist deep in the hearts of numerous peoples around the world. Therefore, Satan and his legions are released in order to visibly manifest this rebellious, self-seeking nature. Subsequently, there is the final destruction of sinful man followed by the great Day of Judgment.

Judgment is now complete; the time has arrived that all of the people of God have been yearning for since the fall of Adam. A new heaven and new earth suddenly appears and together they shall be the eternal home of God our Father, the Lord Jesus Christ, the angels of God, and all the overcoming saints, who are God's eternal sons and daughters. Wow! This will be infinitely more glorious than the Garden of Eden. There, it was God walking with man, whom He created in His image. Here, it is our glorious Father and His sons and daughters who have been truly "born again" by the blood of the conquering Lamb of God. This is a picture of a great and glorious family who will live together forever and ever in the kingdom of God, which will reign over the entire universe.

However, a new heaven and new earth does not mean that the present heavens and earth have been completely annihilated and replaced. From the very beginning, God promised man nothing less than the earth itself as his proper habitation and inheritance. When man sinned, his dominion over the earth was not taken away, but the earth over which he now ruled was placed under a curse.[354] At present, the world is a battlefield full of strife and sorrow, for the plan of God has not yet been consummated. The new heaven and new earth is a "restoration" of the old, not a "creation" of a new. Consider the following four points.[355]

- Here the word *new* is the Greek word *kainos,* which communicates that it is new in nature and quality as opposed to a new creation. If it were "new" in origin, then the Greek word *neos* would have been used. This is a *kainos* heaven and *kainos* earth that is revealed in these passages.
- The book of Romans informs us that this present creation is eagerly awaiting the revealing of the sons of God so that it may be free from its bondage of decay and death.[356] All of creation awaits the coming restoration.
- If God had to annihilate the present cosmos because it has been so corrupted by sin, then Satan would appear to have won a great victory by obliterating the works of God's original creation. Instead, God will renew this very earth from the results of Satan's evil endeavors.[357]
- Finally, consider our very selves. Our resurrected bodies are not a new creation; we are reborn into new bodies in which sin can no longer enter. We will not be a totally new set of human beings but people of God who formerly lived lives upon the earth. Unrighteousness will never again be found in us, and, likewise, unrighteousness existing in the old creation can never enter the restored creation.

The new earth will still be as much earth as the new us will still be us. The earthly beauty that we now see won't be lost but will become even more beautiful following the restoration of the heaven and the earth. All of the old earth that matters will be drawn into heaven to be part of the new earth. Our mind-set changes when we grasp that everything we love about the old earth will be ours on the new earth—either in one form or another. God is no more done with the earth than He's done with us.[358]

THE NEW JERUSALEM
(Revelation 21:9-26)

The new heaven and new earth will need a capital city from which God the Father and the Son will govern the cosmos. This city is a place where they will dwell with their sons and daughters, as well as the beloved angels who have been guardians of God's people throughout the age of man. It is a city that was being prepared for His people when Jesus first ascended to heaven over two thousand years ago.

In my Father's house are many rooms. If it were not so, would
I have told you that I go to prepare a place for you? And if
I go and prepare a place for you, I will come again and will
take you to myself, that where I am you may be also.
(John 14:2-3)

John now sees this capital city descending upon the new earth. This is the New Jerusalem, the promised restoration of the beloved city of God. The presence of our Lord within the city is no longer confined to a section of the old temple known as the Holy of Holies, for the glory of God radiates like crystal throughout the entire city as it descends to the new earth. The city also is described as the bride of Christ, which indicates that all of His sons and daughters are within its walls as it descends to the new earth. It is likely that all those whose names were found in Jesus' Book of Life are gathered together following judgment day in preparation for their descent to the new earth.

The beauty of this city is far beyond our most greatest imaginations. Its construction consists of the most precious jewels and metals known to man. It is a city of pure gold, transparent as glass, with foundations adorned with every kind of jewel and with gates composed of a single pearl. Each of the twelve gates is inscribed with the names of the twelve tribes of the sons of Israel, and the twelve foundations under the walls of the city are inscribed with the names of the twelve apostles of the Lord Jesus. Thus, all His sons and daughters, from both the old and new dispensations have entered through the gates and live within these walls surrounding the city of New Jerusalem. This is a city that is approximately 1,400 miles in length and in width, with walls 216 feet high. For an American, this is the distance from the Canadian border to Mexico and from the Appalachian Mountains to the California border. The River of Life flows out from the throne of God throughout the city and perhaps through the gates into the world beyond. Trees of Life, which were denied to Adam following his fall, now grow on both sides of this river and are continually accessible to all of God's people. There will never again be any need for sun or moon, for the glory of the Lord provides a great and glorious light forever. It is quite an amazing picture!

HEAVEN: BORING OR EXCITING?

From the beginning, heaven has been dominant in the thoughts and lives of God's people worldwide. Even the nonbelieving populace tries to imagine what life will be like in the eternal realm. Unfortunately, most of these thoughts envision the afterlife as simply a spiritual world devoid of any physical environment. This deception crept into the church around the third century with the rise of Gnosticism. One of numerous false teachings of the Gnostics was that both the physical earth and the human body are basically evil, while the spirit world is supposedly good. Thus, the afterlife was depicted as being only a spiritual environment where the "saved" flitted around from cloud to cloud, carrying their harps and singing hymns forever and ever. Failure to understand the goodness of God's creation has blinded countless people from seeing heaven as a place of tremendous pleasure and enjoyment. Instead, they think that for heaven to be "spiritual," it must be drab and unappealing. How could anybody look forward to spending eternity in such an environment, let alone teach it to congregations? Sadly, countless evangelical Christians believe this thin concept of salvation as simply the saving of souls without bodies and without the earth and the rest of God's creation.

The heaven that Jesus described is not some ethereal realm of disembodied spirits. Such a place could never be home for us, because human beings were not created for a nonmaterial existence. Human beings are by nature physical as well as spiritual. Our home that we love is the place that God made for us—earth. We were made from the earth and for the earth. Earth is our home.[359] The coming of the new heaven and new earth is a real event that will visibly combine both the physical and spiritual together forever. The presence of our Lord is in heaven, but at the end of the age, when all evil has been cast away, God will unite the heavens and the earth under the headship of Jesus Christ, and His people will have access to His presence forever.[360]

The great majority of people will admit that they believe in both heaven and hell, yet most have little knowledge concerning the form of afterlife that awaits them in either of these realms. People sometimes say, "I'd rather have a good time in hell than be bored out of my mind in heaven." Many imagine hell as a place where they will hang around and shoot pool and joke with friends. Well, that could happen on the new earth but not in hell. Hell is a place of torment and isolation, where friendship and good times don't exist. Hell will be painfully boring. Everything good, enjoyable, refreshing, fascinating, and interesting originates with God. Outside of God's presence, there is no joy. On the new earth, our Lord will give us renewed minds and marvelously constructed bodies, full of energy and vision. All of our individual giftings and all that we love in this present life will be greatly enhanced on the new earth. Those that are gifted in art, music, farming, construction, accounting, writing, etc. will not abandon these gifts; they will be greatly enhanced and used in their assigned work on the new earth and in other areas of the universe. Those things that one enjoys most in this life will continue to be pursued with endless discoveries that will bring ever increasing satisfaction and enjoyment. The God who created us for good works will not abandon His purposes when He resurrects us to inhabit the new earth. We'll set goals, devise plans, and share ideas. Our best workday on earth, when everything turns out better than we planned, is just a small foretaste of the joy our work will bring us on the new earth. There will never be a moment of boredom among God's people on the new earth.[361]

Deep in our hearts, we all desire a resurrected life on a resurrected earth instead of a disembodied existence in a spiritual realm. We desire it precisely because it is God's plan for us to be raised to a new life on the new earth. It is our Lord who created us to desire what we were made for. He designed us to live on earth and to desire the earthly life.[362]

LIFE ON THE NEW HEAVEN AND NEW EARTH

The incarnation of Jesus Christ brought heaven down to earth. The coming new earth will be God's permanent dwelling place and will be as pure and holy as heaven has ever been. When we deny that the world is our home, we set ourselves up for hypocrisy. For we may pretend to disdain the world while sitting in church, but when we get in the car, we turn on our favorite music and head home to barbeque with friends, watch a ball game, play golf, ride bikes, work in the garden, or curl up with a good cup of coffee and a good book. We do these things, not because we are sinners, but because we are people. We will still be people when we die and go to heaven. This shouldn't be a disappointing reality, for it's God's plan. He made us who we are, except for the sin part, which has nothing to do with friends, eating, sports, gardening, enjoying coffee, or reading.[363]

God's greatest gift to us is "Himself." His presence brings about great joy and is fully satisfying, while His absence brings thirst and longing. One can easily see the joylessness in the unbelieving world. Joylessness is present even among the wealthiest people on earth. Kings, politicians, and celebrities who are worshipped by masses of followers are empty and lonely in their private lives and therefore seek for personal joy in the world of sexual immorality, alcohol, and drugs. Nobody will ever find true joy until they seek the presence of the Lord, who will then open His arms and embrace them.

Curiosity is an inherent part of our character that is also a gift from God. It allows us to daydream, imagine, and speculate about matters in life. This has led to numerous great discoveries in our lives. Curiosity about heaven frequently surfaces as family and friends gather together to socialize. They ask questions such as these.

What will our bodies be like? Will we eat and drink on the new earth? What will we know and learn? What will our daily lives be like? Will we desire relationship with anyone except God? Will animals inhabit the new earth? What about our pets? Will there be art, entertainment, and sports? Will we design new technology? What will be the mode of travel? Will we explore the stars and planets in the universe? Whom will we meet, and what will we experience together? Will we be with our family and friends?[364]

The finest book I have read that addresses these questions and many others is Randy Alcorn's *Heaven*. This is an exceptional work that addresses our curiosities and provides a solid biblical foundation for the author's insightful answers to many questions concerning life in the new heaven and new earth. It also has a study guide that can be used for groups desiring more information on heaven. The more we understand about the truths of heaven, the greater the impact we will have on our neighbors, friends, and fellow employees who may or may not be believers. It will motivate us to talk much more about the great joys that await His people on the new earth.

We will one day pass from this earth to the present heaven through death, but eventually we'll be back to live forever on the restored earth. Yes, we are pilgrims in this life, not because our home will never be on earth, but because our ultimate home isn't on the present earth, which is still under the curse. It was always the plan of our Lord for physical human beings to live on a physical earth; and when sin entered the world of man, God didn't abandon His plan but chose to become a man on this same earth. Why? So that His people would experience His glory forever and that the Lord Himself could enjoy the company of men and women in the world that He made for us.[365]

"BEHOLD, I AM COMING SOON!"
(Revelation 22:7; 12; 20)

Jesus is coming, and He has told us how He will come. He will come accompanied by wars, plagues, famines, persecutions, and sufferings and in a generation when knowledge will greatly increase. And the closer His coming gets, the more intense the power of

His enemies will be asserted. Yes, He is coming very soon, but to understand just how rapidly Jesus is coming, we need to consider what must take place before His actual physical coming. Herman Hoeksema, in his book *Behold, He Cometh,* uses an illustration from the Second World War to explain preparations needed prior to the actual coming.

> *When Germany pressed the Allies and pressed them hard, they were for a time in desperate straits. And longingly they looked for the coming of the Americans. The Americans said, "We are coming, and we are coming quickly." But many months elapsed before they actually did come. To the Allies in their desperate condition it seemed a long time before they actually came. Yet, did not the Americans come quickly? Surely, they did; and they came as fast as possible for them to come. But think what was implied in their coming. Many, many things had to be prepared before they could come. An army had to be drafted and trained. Money had to be raised. The army had to be equipped. The material, clothing and ammunition and weapons, had to be manufactured. Ships had to be built. In view of all this, it was absolutely true that they were coming quickly. The same may be applied to the coming of our Lord Jesus Christ. From our point of view it may seem a long time. But look! The children of God must be gathered. The whole church gathered from all nations must be filled: not one of the elect may be lacking.*[366]

All these things, especially over the last decade, are developing right before our very eyes. We see Him coming! The church in the very first century, as well as the church in every age, including our generation, finds itself caught up in a struggle between the kingdom of this world and the kingdom of God. This book of prophecy known as Revelation was written not only to provide essential information for the last generation but also to encourage the church in all generations to maintain their steadfast loyalty in the midst of demonic pressures and persecutions.

We may not know the exact timing of His return, and it will be unexpected to many, for He comes as "a thief in the night." However, for His people who are not in darkness but remain awake, His coming will not be unexpected.[367] Also, there are many followers of Christ today who are awake and like the "sons of Issachar" are discerning that the time of His coming is shortly before us, most probably in this generation.[368]

THE BOOK OF REVELATION MUST REMAIN OPEN TO BOTH KINGDOMS
(Revelation 22:10-11)

The words of the book of Revelation must never be sealed; they must be communicated by the church in the midst of the world. When this is done, the result will be twofold: there will be those who are saved and those who are hardened. Even among evangelicals, there are those who will have nothing to do with it. They like to say that things will all "pan out" in the end. This is a very dangerous mind-set that may lead them to being like the five virgins who were unprepared for the bridegroom's coming and reacted too late to enter into the marriage feast.[369] It wasn't their unbelief that kept them out; it was their apathetic attitude toward preparedness for his coming.

When this book is opened and expounded, it will strengthen the faith and hope of the people of God. However, there will be many who will have nothing to do with it. They will mock and belittle those who proclaim it. They will say, "You are a dreaming, hateful pessimist who is scaring people." It will also arouse opposition among the unbelievers whose hope lies only in the future of this present world, for this prophetic book leaves no hope for their vain dreams. Those who proclaim the end-time prophecies will one day be considered a threat to the national security of our country. What then? Should we keep the book closed because of a threatening and hateful opposition? No! Instead, we are to

315

Let the evildoer still do evil, and the filthy still be filthy, and the righteous still do right, and the holy still be holy.
Revelation 22:11

This book will draw the lines. It will strengthen and emphasize the great difference between the true people of God and the world. It will make the world more conscious of the great difference between its ideal and those of the people of God. And it will also make His people more conscious of the same fact. And for this latter reason, the book must not remain closed but must be open so that all can hear and read it and this twofold effect may be achieved.[370]

Stand fast, Christian warriors; the truths in this prophetic book need to be openly proclaimed to this generation of both believers and nonbelievers.

A FINAL WARNING
(Revelation 22:18-19)

There is also a responsibility connected with the reading and the hearing of the book of Revelation. The warning in these verses does not apply to the imperfect understanding of believers who read and teach this book. After all, these words are prophetic and therefore there are inherent difficulties in its interpretation. All who teach this book must clearly understand our fallibility when it comes to interpreting prophecy. No one person is going to have absolute understanding; each of us is just one member of the body of Christ, and we all need to seek truths from others who have different callings and giftings.

No, this "warning" refers to a conscious attitude of unbelief in what is recorded in this book. It is addressed to those who are acquainted with its contents but who would change the message of this book to suit their own purposes so that the kingdom of the world is confused with the kingdom of God. They do it by adding or detracting from it, so that the light of the truth of this prophecy is dimmed. Particularly *they deny the truth of a physical coming of Jesus Christ* by "spiritualizing" these words or by denying the "inerrancy" of these truths. Those who do this must be aware of the punishment that awaits; that is, they will be deprived of their part in the Book of Life.[371]

BLESSED IS THE ONE WHO . . . !"

My brothers and sisters in the Lord, note the following seven beatitudes in the book of Revelation. I would urge you all to memorize them until they are so deeply embedded in your hearts that not even the most severe of challenges could cause you to waver from the path of life or waver from your missional calling in the midst of great tribulation.

SEVEN BEATITUDES IN THE BOOK OF REVELATION

Blessed is the one who reads aloud the words of this prophecy, and blessed are those who hear, and who keep what is written in it, for the time is near. **Revelation 1:3**

Blessed are the dead who die in the Lord from now on. "Blessed indeed," says the Spirit, "that they may rest from their labors, for their deeds follow them!" **Revelation 14:13**

Behold, I am coming like a thief! Blessed is the one who stays awake, keeping his garments on, that he may not go about naked and be seen exposed! **Revelation 16:15**

Blessed are those who are invited to the marriage supper of the Lamb. . . . These are the true words of God. **Revelation 19:9**

Blessed and holy is the one who shares in the first resurrection! Over such the second death has no power, but they will be priests of God and of Christ, and they will reign with him for a thousand years. **Revelation 20:6**

*And behold, I am coming soon. <u>Blessed</u> is the one who keeps the words of the prophecy of this book. **Revelation 22:7***

*<u>Blessed</u> are those who wash their robes, so that they may have the right to the tree of life and that they may enter the city by the gates. **Revelation 22:14***

"The grace of our Lord Jesus Christ be with you all. Amen"

CHAPTER 15

EQUIPPING WARRIOR LEADERSHIP IN THE KINGDOM OF GOD

NEEDED: GREAT LEADERS

Greatness in leadership is not an attribute one is born with; it must be earned. All soldiers in the Army of God have the potential to positively impact other people whom they have been called to lead. Greatness is not pursued for the sake of greatness. It is about one's desire to die to himself, his ambitions, and his personal comforts in order to achieve his calling in life. Our Commander in Chief has a predestined mission for each of His people, and those who actively seek for it will find it; and those who find it must then act upon it. Such actions will produce great leaders who can impact many lives for the kingdom of God.

Good leaders can get things done in normal times, and we can generally get by with good leaders. But we no longer live in normal times, and there is a desperate need for great leaders, leaders who lead by example as they continually display great courage and wisdom in the face of life-threatening challenges. Such leaders have a deep passion to see the kingdom of God manifested in glorious strength, not simply in the institutional churches, but in the workplaces, the neighborhoods, the downtown areas, and individual homes, where "real life" occurs.[372]

Great leaders also recognize that they have weaknesses, but the difference is that they are committed to focusing on their strengths. This creates a spirit of excitement when there is no expectation to continue in one's weaker, less gifted areas. They trust their fellow leaders to provide fruit in those areas where they are less gifted. Thus, great leaders have no desire to control everything, for their sole focus is on God and His kingdom people.

We must be cautious, however, for there are numerous bad leaders in today's churches—leaders who are great only in their own eyes. They usually deny the reality of an ongoing spiritual war and teach their followers that they can have power and glory in this life without sacrifice and suffering. They reduce people's dreams and expectations to a much lower level than God intended for them. During periods of hardship, this form of leadership leads people into a life of whining, feeling sorry for themselves, and failing to grow in a true understanding of God's plan for them. These are people who continually focus on their weaknesses. Their spiritual lives are directed and controlled by bad leaders. Wake up, you people who are imprisoned by these leaders! Come out from under them, or you will not hear His calling for your life's true direction.

Finally, true leadership has little to do with rank and everything to do with responsibility. Leaders think, envision, and ask questions. Above all, the great leaders "act." Even when leaders don't think they are capable, when they realize they are weak and fear begins to invade their consciousness, they still step up to the plate and "act" like leaders. Listen to a great leader as he speaks to his followers.

> *Be watchful, stand firm in the faith, <u>act like men</u>, be strong. Let all that you do be done in love. 1 Corinthians 16:13-14*

ARAGORN—AN EXAMPLE OF GREAT LEADERSHIP

In the popular movie *The Lord of the Rings* a warrior brotherhood composed of nine committed men start out on a mission to destroy the power of evil in their world. As their journey progresses, they have confrontations with armed forces of darkness, which appear to be winning each of these battles. Eventually they arrive at a very depressing point, where Boromir has been killed, Gandalf had disappeared, Frodo and Sam are gone, and Merry and Pippin have been captured by a platoon of orcs. Only Aragorn, Legalos, and Gimli remain of the original fellowship of warriors, and so success appears hopeless. As these remaining three gather together Gimli says, "Then all of this has been in vain; the fellowship has failed." Legalos remains silent, but Aragorn suddenly puts his hands on their shoulders and says, "Not if we remain true to each other. We cannot abandon Merry and Pippen to torment and death, not while we have strength left. Let's hunt some orcs!" Suddenly the three look up and smiled with renewed energy and vision and say, "Let's do it!"

DISCIPLINE IN THE ARMY OF GOD

A priority of great soldiers is self-discipline in day-to-day living. Their growing love for the Lord results in their desire for a moment-by-moment walk with Him throughout each day. This certainly requires discipline in Bible study and commitment to continual intercessory prayer; but, even more, soldiers need discipline at those times of the day when they are at their weakest, those times when the spirit of procrastination invariably falls upon them. Great soldiers have learned through growing experiences to deal with such issues and not allow worldly temptations to render them impotent during this time. If we do not conquer such temptations, we become POWs in the camp of the enemy for a short period of time. And at some point it becomes recognizable, for it creates a deep emptiness in our spirit and a sense of depression begins to creep into out soul. Great soldiers have learned that the "fear of the Lord" certainly means "redeeming the time" for Him. Sadly, the vast majority of American Christians spend the bulk of their days in these POW camps.

One further note of caution: Christian soldiers are more suscep-tible to attacks from the enemy immediately following a significant spiritual victory. This is a principle that military leaders learn both in their training and during combat—we are more vulnerable to enemy counterattack immediately after achieving a hard-fought objective. As we begin to internally celebrate our victory, we have a tendency to relax and let down our guard. Be careful here, for this is the most critical time for a counterattack by our enemy.

DEVELOPING OUR MISSION IN THE ARMY OF GOD

Every Christian I have known has a desire to hear our Lord Jesus say, on that day when we enter into His presence,

*Well done, good and faithful servant. You have been faithful over a little; I will set you over much. Enter into the joy of your master. (**Matthew 25:21**)*

Yet, not every Christian who enters into His presence will hear those words. Each of us has a mission assigned that we must pursue; and in order to hear those words, we must move forward in the Lord and His mission for us. This doesn't mean simply being faithful in church attendance and tithing. That is all well and good, but each of us has his or her own mission. Wherever you work, you have a mission—seek for it! Wherever you live, you have a mission—seek for it! We are all called to be partakers of the work God intends to complete, which will usher in the reign of our Lord on this earth. If we don't complete our assigned mission, someone else will, and then that person will reap the reward that was initially set aside for us.[373]

God's leaders of this generation must understand and internalize the following truth if they intend to prevail in their mission: The great warriors of the Bible always went through periods of darkness before they were brought into the purposes of God. Before we reach those places where we receive the promise and the fulfillment of the promise, there will be a wilderness experience that is the exact opposite of what has been promised. The purpose of the wilderness journey is to conform us to the image of Jesus Christ and to bring us to a place of maturity, where He can trust us with more

322

authority. Many Christians will never walk in the promises of God to which they were called because they fall into whining, grumbling, and complaining about their wilderness experiences. Remember, warriors, there is no victory without a battle. We must see every test as a great opportunity. No matter how dark it seems to get, the light will surely dawn, just as the sun comes up in the morning.

However, as we continue to move through the wilderness of life, it is crucial for every soldier in the Army of God to know how far they can go in Christ, where they are at the present time, and the next step along the way. The church is about to enter a very challenging time, which is a necessary prerequisite for entry into its most fruitful times. The darkness is gathering its forces, but so is the light. The Lord has given each of us a specific part to play in His overall plan, and it must be our continual quest to search for our individual mission assignment. Almost everyone has a vision for what they want to accomplish, but it's going to require a difficult and continuous work discipline.[374]

WHAT OUR MISSION IS NOT

Soldiers in the Army of God need to understand that we are not forces of a revolution attempting to establish a righteous government in this present world. This world is not our home. Until it is finally liberated at the end of this age, it belongs to the Enemy. In fact, warriors in God's army are despised by the world. However, the mission of warriors within His army may be characterized as acting as guerillas behind enemy lines with a command to proclaim the true gospel of Christ to those currently in the world. As warriors witnessing for the kingdom, we can expect to be continually ridiculed, scorned, and persecuted. Yet, the greater the persecution, the more powerful the gospel message becomes. The evil of the world becomes more and more visible to the masses when they witness the tremendous hatred toward those who possess a heart of sacrificial love.

OUR MISSIONAL CALLING

As warriors in the Army of God in these last days, we must be totally committed to walk the pathway that our Commander in Chief has laid before each of us. Therefore, it is important for each of us to internalize our personal understanding of the mission to which He has called us. This mission exists in the passion of our hearts, and our direction becomes clearer as it is written down and internalized each day in our hearts. The following is an example of a *general mission statement* that is designed to drive Christian leadership through the wilderness journey of a committed life to the Lord:

> To live out the spirit of the gospel in my life in such a way that it will positively affect others for the strengthening and expanding of the kingdom of God and to stand strong for my Lord Jesus Christ against the forces of darkness in this world.

Specific mission statements are established when His will is revealed to us each day as we follow Him along the narrow road of a godly life.

When I look at the cities of the United States, I see the Christians as a group of bewildered survivors going about their daily business with little sense of a unifying purpose. In time of war, battles are won by the strategic concentration of force. Soldiers don't just attack along a scattered front. They follow a plan designed by a general with a big map and lots of information. In some of our cities, it's been so long since our soldiers received news about the progress of the battle that they have stopped fighting. They are wandering in the rear of the battlefield, preparing food and generally attending to their own comforts.[375]

Now, let's take a look at the frontlines of the battlefield, that place where Christian soldiers are provided opportunities by their Commander in Chief to make a strong impact for the kingdom of God.

THE FRONTLINES OF THE BATTLEFIELD

Over the last several years, many Christians have awakened to the realization that the traditional church is not where the Lord's soldiers are expected to carry on their respective ministerial assignments. The mission of the traditional church is in the rear, with the responsibility of equipping the troops to be sent to the frontlines of the battlefield. The frontlines of the battlefield are where people spend the majority of their time. There is a growing need for Christians to arise and minister to those people who will not be found in Sunday church services. Pastors have influence over a limited number of people for only a couple of hours per week. Television, movies, computer games, casinos, and such things are much more influential in the individual lives of people in today's culture.

Now soldiers may ask, "Where are the frontlines of our respective battlefields?" Well, ask yourself the following questions: Where is that place, outside of our homes and churches, where Christian soldiers can have a tremendous impact for the kingdom of God? Where is that place that requires so much of our time and efforts in life, and yet most of us approach it grudgingly? Where is that place where the Lord brings so many people into our lives over the years, and yet most of us do not envision it as ministry opportunity?

MINISTERING IN THE WORKPLACE

Early Christians made the workplace their ministerial focus because their occupations regularly took them there. As a result, the workplace played a vital role in establishing and expanding the early church. In fact, most early followers of Jesus remained in full-time business while simultaneously conducting full-time ministry. Christian soldiers need to realize that today millions of God's people are similarly called to full-time ministry in their respective business occupations. Whether one is a business owner, banker, electrician, insurance agent, plumber, landscaper, factory foreman, ditch digger, doctor, lawyer, or government worker, it makes no difference; all can have great influence in their respective areas of employment, for that is where they encounter the world and that is where their lives have been positioned by the Lord.

Unfortunately, many Christians feel like they have a second-class ministerial calling compared to people who serve full-time in a church. This should not be the case, for contrary to what many traditional churches imply, there is no hierarchical distinction between pastors and ordinary people in the eyes of our Lord. The calling to pastoral ministry is not necessarily higher than the blue-collar workers driving daily through rush-hour traffic to get to work on time in order to provide a living for their families. Christians who work in jobs outside the confines of the church need to understand that they are not perpetual privates in God's army just because they have not gone to seminary. They need to discover that they have the potential to become full-fledged "generals" whose ministry influence can grow far beyond the bounds of the workplace and the walls of their local church and into the very heart of the city. Unfortunately, many of these marketplace ministers fail to fulfill their divine destiny because they are often derided by others as untrained or uneducated. This is not a new accusation. Both Peter and John, who were fishermen by profession, certainly experienced this ridiculing. Additionally, Jesus, who was a carpenter, recruited His disciples from the workplace rather than from those trained by the synagogues.[376]

The church fails to understand that there are significant pastoral communication problems with men. Many workingmen refuse to identify with the pastoral culture and therefore will not seek help from the perceived church. Yet, deep within themselves, many of these folks, who may be your fellow employees, or customers, or simply third-party contacts, unknowingly hunger for strong Christian leaders with whom they can relate, namely, peers who engage on the same battleground and who understand their world and their ongoing temptations and struggles. Those with grievances and those who have lost loved ones through death, divorce, or adultery are unknowingly searching to speak with someone who may be able to restore some degree of comfort to their lives. Additionally, there are many people on this battlefield who hopelessly see themselves in dead-end jobs: young men paying fifty percent of their paycheck for child support; blue-collar workers hanging out in casinos, hoping to change their status in life; and business owners struggling to stay afloat. This sense of hopelessness among a majority of the workforce continues on and on and on. Yet this provides a tremendous opportunity for Christ's warriors to move toward the front of this battlefield to fight for the souls of their fellow workers.

Christian warriors must free themselves of the American workers' mindset that Monday morning is the lowest point of the week and TGIF is something to embrace. Great missional opportunities present themselves in the workplace on a daily basis, yet a warrior for Christ must take the initiative, or opportunities will be lost. Soldiers become warrior leaders when they commit to making personal sacrifices in order to show a true, loving concern for those people encountered daily in the workplace. One example: As one ministering in his business world, I have written a letter that I send annually to several hundred of my clients. Friendships and trust were built with my client base over several years, and this letter, which communicates a loving concern for them, continues to open several doors for ministry opportunities. A copy of the letter is found in appendix B. Perhaps it will help you draft a letter communicating your burden for family members, fellow employees, neighbors, or others.

Warriors, this is a critical time to sound the alarm. Many of our fellow workers, though not Christians, are very concerned about events that are taking place in our country. Taking advantage of opportunities to speak with them concerning today's economic concerns, potential terrorist activity, and increased violence throughout the country definitely will open up most people to serious conversation. Once they realize your concern for them, communication becomes more frequent and open, and then it is only a small step to speak of the warnings given in Scripture and the call of Jesus Christ on their lives.

NETWORKING WITH FRUSTRATED CHRISTIANS IN THE WORKPLACE

Most Christians know many fellow Christians in the workplace who have a deep passion for Christ but have left the traditional Sunday church out of frustration and boredom. Men who possess a warrior spirit deep within themselves, but traditional American churches have left them feeling empty and spiritually directionless. These are potential warriors who are searching for their calling and have reached a dead end — yet they too have numerous relationships within the workplace environment. Making contact with them on a one-to-one basis and discussing the opportunities that present themselves in the workplace could result in a revitalizing of their spirit and the establishment of a working network that could make a tremendous impact in a great number of lives. Such networks could result in the planting of home churches, which may eventually evolve into a network of underground churches in America.

THE UNDERGROUND CHURCH MAY BE NEXT

The Western world is rapidly progressing toward the establishment of a unified society under the authority of a worldly government that will outlaw the proclamation of Jesus Christ and His atoning sacrifice for sinful mankind. Man sees himself, not God, as the absolute sovereign within this kingdom. Moreover, the people of this worldly kingdom will speak of righteousness and brotherly love and strive to realize the universal brotherhood of man. They want to abolish the effects of sin with their own efforts and usher in a universal, blissful state. All religions will be acceptable, including those compromising churches that call themselves Christian, as long as they rally around the government programs and do not proclaim the gospel message of Jesus Christ or the sinful nature of mankind.

As warriors for Christ, we must be aware that the time is rapidly approaching when it will be illegal for the church in America to proclaim the gospel message that Jesus Christ is the true Son of God and it is only through Him that one can enter into eternal life. At that time, many compromising churches will side with this worldly government and betray those Christians who continue to stand for the glorious name of Jesus Christ. Ancient and modern history reveals that when governments come against these Christian warriors who continue to stand for Him and have escaped capture—they form together as a body known as the underground church. These are places that will not compromise their faith in the Son of God and will rise up in the midst of these times and reach out to broken hearts that feel directionless within both the world and its churches.

However, it is essential that these small, underground churches do not operate independently but that they are networked with one another in order that they might each grow greater in strength within the corporate body of Christ. These churches should remain small, perhaps no greater than seven or eight families, but they should each receive ongoing training from an established group of leaders who have formed a partnership to network with and minister to these small groups.

Let us now examine a proposal designed to assist Christian warriors in the fulfillment of their missional calling within a nation committed to criminalizing the public proclamation of the biblical gospel message. The following is a breakdown of proposals that may assist in developing a mission objective and encouraging soldiers to engage in warfare.

ESTABLISH TEAMS FOR "EQUIPPING SMALL GROUPS"

Consider establishing partnership teams composed of men with leadership experience who share a passionate burden for the growth and strengthening of the kingdom of God within a network of small groups. The direction is to train, disciple, and evangelize with a gospel message that focuses upon dying to self and glorifying Jesus Christ in our day-to-day living.

The composition of these teams could include businessmen who teach and mentor other businessmen, workers who teach fellow workers, military who teach military, elderly who teach elderly, and so on. This will open up real issues that never surface in the traditional church environment and create a close bond among those with similar callings in life. These teams would be designed to establish small groups within neighborhoods and/or in workplaces where they can gather together.

Here are some key teaching suggestions:

- Develop a biblical presentation such as "Through the Bible in 24 hours" in order to provide foundational teachings to people who will certainly flock to these groups in the challenging days that are shortly before us.
- Prepare and teach key biblical doctrinal training.
- Prepare and teach eschatological issues that will bring clarity to the times.
- Teach and supervise spiritual preparations.
- Teach and supervise physical preparations.

All these small group teachings should be uniformly prepared and/or supervised by an experienced partnership team. It is recommended that this partnership team would teach only a gathering of group leaders, who would then take the materials to their respective groups.

Besides preparing and presenting teachings, additional proposed objectives of this partnership are as follows:

- Cultivate potential leaders from the neighborhoods who have a passion for the souls of their fellow neighbors. These may be people who are struggling to make sense of their lives and long to discover their destiny. They need to be taught how to listen to, and engage with people experiencing tremendous stress and confusion within their lives. They need to learn to step out without regard for their reputation or concern for being ridiculed.
- Cultivate leaders from the workplace arenas. This includes developing an awareness of what God is doing among His people. Many people are struggling to make sense of their lives. They long to understand how to form alternative ways of living as God's people, yet they are unclear as to how to

proceed. Training of these leaders must be effective in over-coming the "image and cultural barriers" that distance the unreached workers from the church. Many have an "image" of the church as boring, intolerant, untrustworthy, and irrelevant to their lives. A "cultural barrier" exists among those who cannot identify with or feel comfortable around their perception of the Christian culture. The worship, the dress, the Christian jargon, and the silent arrogance portrayed by the churchy culture have created an invisible but huge division among people in our country.

- Plant house churches throughout the respective communities as the evangelistic outreach grows. This will impact believers who are unchurched, as well as unbelievers. Now a house church is different from the home groups, which are part of a larger church. As the house churches grow, they will multiply, not enlarge a single church organization. The house church may be a venue that can best overcome those "image and cultural" barriers that keep many people from coming to the Lord. House churches provide face-to-face communications within a small group that are much more relational and provide a comfortable environment for effective discipleship.

- Training these churches in the "storying" concept of learning the Bible would be extremely valuable. People listen to stories with full attention and then are invited to participate. Obviously this was the method of teaching utilized by the church before the widespread printing of Bibles. It also will prove a valuable technique when Bibles become illegal.[377]

- Organize and connect these small groups with one another, and train potential leadership to lead and oversee their respective networks. Develop networks with other churches and para-church organizations that share a similar passion for workplace outreach and the approaching need for under-ground churches. The idea is to share resources in order to assist one another in fulfilling their respective missional plans.

- Develop a strategic prayer network among those who have the same deep burden for the needs addressed in the workplace and underground church. This should encompass building a "wall of prayer" and establishing "watchmen" to organize and connect these prayer groups with one another. A watchman is one who teaches intercession, provides ongoing encouragement, tracks accountability, and communicates the reports of its prayer warriors to the partnership team. Information concerning the military formation of a "wall of prayer" can be found on the Watchman Ministries website hosted by Tim Taylor, a naval war veteran with high-level intelligence experience.[378]

In order to prepare strategic plans for equipping leaders and soldiers in the Army of God, members of this partnership must be on the same page concerning coming developments within our country and the response we will be facing within the traditional American church system. The leaders comprising this partnership should all possess discernment and understanding of the troubling times that will soon confront the world and the church. Also, they must be passionate about joining forces with their peers as they step out on the battlefield to face a horrific enemy. The cost may be their lives in this world, but the reward will be eternally glorious.

A SECOND PARTNERSHIP PROPOSAL — "A TEAM OF WATCHMEN"

A partnership team that potentially could make a huge impact within their respective areas is one composed of a few men (e.g., seven or eight) with leadership experience, biblical training, and a similar vision. They would be peers with equal input into team direction but would elect a facilitator to administer the meetings. This "watchman partnership" would develop a team presentation that "sounds the alarm" of the Lord's call to "be ready" for the Day of the Lord, which is rapidly approaching.

*For you yourselves are fully aware that the day of **the Lord will come like a thief in the night.** While people are saying, "There is peace and security," then sudden destruction will come upon them as labor pains come upon a pregnant woman, and they will not escape. **1 Thessalonians 5:2-3***

There are many nervous people in our country who sense that "hard times" are just around the corner, but they lack understanding concerning the nature and intensity of these future "events." These are concerned people within the traditional church system, as well as in the secular world, who are searching for leaders who will provide them with insight concerning the immediate future. Those with insight are being called to respond to them.

The following proposed presentations could take place in a modular session of a seminary, or in receptive churches, or, more likely, in workplace or small community venues that express a desire to hear the message. Each of these "team presentations" will need to be followed up with additional in-depth teaching concerning the "gospel message" and an understanding of the "last days." Therefore, designated members of the team probably would need to maintain a presence for a few days.

PROPOSALS FOR "WATCHMEN TEAM" PRESENTATIONS

The target audience for these presentations would be existing leaders and potential leaders who will "act" to establish additional teams. I would suggest that seminar presentations prepared by this team focus upon two main subject areas.

1. A direct and strong gospel message designed to bring out the truth of Christ's teachings concerning the kingdom of God.

   - The person of Jesus Christ as the eternal Son of God
   - His strong teachings, which have become the "forgotten gospel" within the church system

- His mission objectives among mankind during His first coming—not peace, but war[379]
- The nature of man and the need for redemption
- His covenants with mankind
- Importance of understanding the inerrancy of the Bible
- The narrow road that leads through the wilderness of life—what does it look like?
- The certainty of His second coming

All of the above should be presented in a way that will *expose the false teachings* that permeate the Western church and are leading many down the broad road to destruction.

2. A direct and strong message focusing on the events that precede Christ's second coming.

- Overview of the truth and purpose of the spiritual war between our Lord and Satan
- Prophetic teachings on the approaching "Day of the Lord"
- A scenario of the catastrophic events that are soon coming
- Exposing false teachings in eschatology that are causing deafness in the church
- The opportunity for Christian warriors in the midst of tribulation
- Our Lord's perspective on persecution and suffering
- How warriors prepare for and handle suffering
- Our evangelistic mission within the midst of tribulation
- The eternal glory that awaits His committed soldiers of war

Obviously many questions will arise out of these presentations concerning how to prepare for these events. In other words, "What do we do now?"

PHYSICAL PREPARATIONS FOR THE BATTLEFIELD

Those who understand the message of these days should be communicating with their family and friends. It is likely that they are not as committed to preparing as His warrior leaders, but they need an understanding of the situation. The first step is to meet with them individually, family by family, and lay out a scenario of a sudden shutdown of banks, stores, and gas stations, along with gang violence and chaos throughout our country. Then, one by one, discuss in detail how each family would require the following material preparations.

- Food supplies for a minimum of six months to a year: How long would their supplies last that they currently have in their homes? What type of purchases should be made for long-term storage? Are they financially able to acquire the required food supplies?
- Drinking water for an indefinite period of time: Discuss methods of storing and purifying water.
- Medical supplies, batteries, toilet paper, gasoline, propane, tools, flashlights, radios, etc.: Discuss what may be needed for an indefinite period of time.
- Items to survive a six-month "nuclear winter," such as clothing and sleeping bags. Perhaps folks also would need a plan to handle nuclear "fallout" if they are in the vicinity of a nuclear blast. Those who wish to build a "fallout shelter" will discover that it's easier than most people realize, and they only need to stay in it for a few days—just long enough for the fallout to lose its radioactivity.
- Discuss the relationship that each individual member of the family has with the Lord, and develop a plan on how to proceed with the deepening of each relationship.

There are plenty of Web sites that provide information, as well as sell products, to those who intend to make such preparations; so it is recommended that each family do some researching. Remember, leaders, you cannot micromanage the situation; you need to assign responsibility to each individual within the unit.

Finally, set a date when all will again meet together with five to six other families in order to present recommendations and finalize plans. At this meeting, it is very important that the leader who initiated this movement act as the facilitator to help the group see and think about things that they would normally never consider. Facilitators must assist in helping individual families see where they fit in the bigger picture, as well as monitor the progress of the meeting with periodic summarization, group encouragement, and affirmation of each member's input, yet not allow the meeting to lose focus on its intended mission. Lastly, leaders should get individual commitments from each family and set a date for completion, whereupon another meeting is scheduled to affirm completion.

Go to the ant, O sluggard; consider her ways, and be wise. Without having any chief, officer, or ruler, she prepares her bread in summer and gathers her food in harvest. How long will you lie there, O sluggard? When will you arise from your sleep? A little sleep, a little slumber, a little folding of the hands to rest, and poverty will come upon you like a robber, and want like an armed man.
(Proverbs 6:6-11)

An additional scenario that needs to be discussed at these meetings is gang violence that may occur in various cities and neighborhoods, for each individual family certainly could be exposed to this tremendous danger. One recommendation to deal with this possibility is to plan for each family to gather together on a predetermined property and live in community. They should have their "supplies" inventoried and ready to move to the selected property on a moment's notice. Telephone communications may not be possible, so the timing of this gathering together must be well planned in advance. A community of friends and families that have gathered together are much more capable of fending off gang-related assaults.

You may hear some Christians argue from Scripture that God will provide "manna" for His people, and so we don't need to be concerned about food to eat or clothes to wear.[380] It is true that the Lord provides, but the context of this verse is one in which Jesus was teaching His followers how to live day to day in their hearts. The Lord did provide manna in the wilderness for His people but only after a significant period of time had elapsed and their prepared supplies had been depleted. It is also true that He calls us to "be prepared" for the coming times, and the meaning here should wisely be applied to physical preparations as well as spiritual. Consider the story of Joseph, who stockpiled food for a famine that was coming in seven years. Likewise, God is certainly calling us to use wisdom in our preparations. Finally, we also should consider that our prepared supplies might be a great blessing to many of the unprepared families who will be suffering from shock and hunger.

*Therefore you also must be ready, for the Son of Man is coming at an hour you do not expect. Who then is the faithful and wise servant, whom his master has set over his household, to give them their food at the proper time? Blessed is that servant whom his master will find so doing when he comes. Truly, I say to you, he will set him over all his possessions. (**Matthew 24:44-47**)*

There is another reality that warriors must prepare for. We must understand that the brighter the light of those in the kingdom of God becomes, the more threatened those living and loving the darkness will become, and the more they will attack the light. Christians who are not prepared for persecution are not prepared. Like it or not, the brighter our light becomes, the stronger we become, and the more we will have to fight. Even so, there can be no victory without a battle and the bigger the battle, the bigger the victory will be. Stay encouraged. We are on the side that cannot lose, and we will one day rejoice in the victory if we remain faithful![381]

Share in suffering as a good soldier of Christ Jesus. No soldier gets entangled in civilian pursuits, since his aim is to please the one who enlisted him.
(2 Timothy 2:3-4)

HANDLING SUFFERING IN THE ARMY OF GOD

The Lord's Word tells us that suffering is a necessary experience that His warriors must experience in order to receive His glory. This truth will be severely tested when the trumpets continue to blast forth devastation upon the earth, for then we will be expected to confront our personal sufferings so that we are not derailed from our calling during that critical time.

The Spirit himself bears witness with our spirit that we are children of God, and if children, then heirs—heirs of God and fellow heirs with Christ, provided we suffer with him in order that we may also be glorified with him. (Romans 8:16-17)

Suffering is a means by which God breaks the vessel so that His glory might be revealed, but it will be revealed only if we respond in the proper way. One might ask, "What actually is suffering?" Suffering may be physical, or it may be mental or emotional, but suffering really is anything that we don't like, anything that is uncomfortable or painful for us. It is present in every life, but leaders need to understand how to deal with it if they are to manifest the glorious leadership that will strengthen ourselves and others in the kingdom of God.[382]

It is through suffering in life that leaders develop the characteristics of holiness that are inherent in God's glory and allow them to become more and more conformed to the image of His Son. Characteristics such as a strong compassion for people, a spirit that is slow to anger, a passionate desire for truth and justice, and the ability to forgive our enemies all develop within as the leader experiences personal suffering. The warrior's passion is all about reflecting the character of God in day-to-day living. It is true that the glory already has been given to believers by Christ through the Holy Spirit, but we often fail to manifest that glory in our "earthen vessels." However, as we continue to live moment by moment for Him, the light will gradually shine brighter and brighter and ultimately produce a great harvest of fruit in the midst of the last-days tribulation period. Sufferings in life should no longer be a surprise, yet leaders must learn to handle them today so they will be prepared tomorrow, when the trumpets begin to blast.

> *Beloved, do not be surprised at the fiery trial when it comes upon you to test you, as though something strange were happening to you. But rejoice insofar as you <u>share Christ's sufferings</u>, that you may also rejoice and be glad when his glory is revealed. If you are insulted for the name of Christ, you are blessed, because the Spirit of glory and of God rests upon you.* (**1 Peter 4:12-14**)

OUR PRAYER CLOSET—WHERE UNDERSTANDING GROWS

Historically, when God moves upon the earth in judgment and deliverance, He first reveals His plans to His faithful warriors, who are continually praying as He seeks to receive them into cooperative agreement with His coming mission. Remember that God shared His plans concerning the destruction of Sodom and Gomorrah with His friend Abraham. Likewise, He will seek to share His plans with his prophetic people who are praying with discernment of the times about events forthcoming on America and this world. The closer we walk with our Lord in obedient friendship and fellowship, the more He will include us in His counsel of operations.[383]

> *For the Lord God does nothing without revealing his secret to his servants the prophets.* (**Amos 3:7**)

God moves upon the hearts of His people and they, in turn, begin to pray. These prayers will affect circumstances and events upon the earth. There are certain events that are due to take place; they are prescheduled by prophetic Scriptures. However, these events don't just arbitrarily take place. They happen as God moves upon the hearts of His prophetic people, and those people begin to pour out intercessory prayer. These events already have been prophesied to take place, but we put them in gear by our obedient commitment to intercessory prayer.

Since all these things are thus to be dissolved, what sort of people ought you to be in lives of holiness and godliness, waiting for and hastening the coming of the day of God, because of which the heavens will be set on fire and dissolved, and the heavenly bodies will melt as they burn! (2 Peter 3:11-12)

Today our focus should not simply be on observing the times and discussing them with our friends. We need to apply ourselves through discerning the times, with intercession, and with involvement. We should not be interested in end-time events for themselves; but through them we need to seek awareness of the strategies of spiritual warfare and of our mission engagement both prior to and in the midst of the tribulation events.[384]

A FINAL PRAYER

Our Father in heaven, hallowed be your name. Your kingdom come, your will be done, on earth as it is in heaven. (Matthew 6:9-10)

Our Father, we thank You for quickening our hearts once more with this message. We await this day with great expectation. Come, Lord Jesus, even today in the person of the Holy Spirit, and prepare us for the work that You have chosen for each one of us to do.

As a watchman waits for the dawn, so we also wait and long for You. Move as You have in the days of old. Summon Your power, and show us Your strength as You have done before.

Be exalted once more in the midst of the nations. Raise up the standard of Your people. Pour out Your favor upon us so that people around us will know that Your presence is with us and will be able to distinguish Your soldiers from the people of the world. May the labors of Your army of warriors glorify Your name and be a bright light and a strong salt that will bring a mighty increase of people into the kingdom of almighty God.

Thank You for revealing Your plans and Your heart to us for the coming days. We wait for them with great expectation and with thanksgiving in our hearts. Now, unto You and You alone, be all glory and power for all that You have done, are doing, and will do in our lives.

In Jesus Christ's name, we say, Amen!

APPENDIX A

HISTORICAL EMPIRES OF THE BEAST

FIRST HEAD OF THE BEAST = EGYPT

A Brief Background

God's chosen people, the family of Jacob, migrated to Egypt sometime between 1900 and 1800 BC. They numbered less than one hundred persons at that time, but the Lord blessed the wombs of the mothers, and their numbers rapidly increased. Some two hundred years later, the spirit of the Beast began its work in the Egyptian rulers; this resulted in a brutal enslavement of these descendants of Jacob.

Satan's Objective

- The tactics of Satan included the enslavement of these people of God so that they might be used to build up the world's kingdom.
- To control the growth of the sons of Abraham by slaughtering newly born babies and to take pleasure in the suffering of their families.
- Thus, he undoubtedly rejoiced, believing that he openly humiliated and defeated the purposes of God for His people.

Our Lord's Objective

- However, it was Satan who was unknowingly being controlled. Because of slavery, the Israelites did not marry among the heathen Egyptians, and so the experience of enslavement allowed them to grow in numbers and bond together as one people. This is like men in the military who go through difficult and traumatic times together; they bond for a lifetime.
- Thus, this long period of enslavement of God's people created a national identity for Israel. So 430 years after the family of Jacob migrated from the Promised Land into Egypt, they now numbered more than two million, and the time had come for almighty God to raise up a champion warrior who would confront Satan's champion.

Certainly our Israelite brothers and sisters in the Lord suffered tremendous affliction during this period of brutal enslavement, but it was a sacrifice that resulted in the Lord establishing a large and mighty nation in the midst of the world. Through this nation He would reveal His almighty power and glory to the world and make this spiritual war visible to those with eyes to see and a heart to understand. And through this nation He would eventually bring forth the Messiah, who would lead a numberless multitude into the glory of the eternal kingdom.[385]

SECOND HEAD OF THE BEAST = ASSYRIA

A Brief Background

Approximately 900 BC, following the death of King Solomon, the nation of Israel split into nine northern and three southern tribes. Thus, two nations were formed. The northern tribes immediately turned from God and followed the idolatrous practices of the Beast. Our Lord continually sent prophets into the land of the northern tribes, calling them to repent and return to the Lord who led them out of Egypt. However, every northern king ignored the prophets and continued to lead their people along the path of darkness. Finally, after 280 years of warning, in the year 722 BC, the Lord withdrew His hand of protection from the ten northern tribes and allowed a mighty Assyrian army to conquer the land of the north.

Satan's Objective

- This Assyrian invasion led to a brutal massacre including thousands of women, children, and babies. Military leaders of the northern army were tortured, stripped naked, and lifted up alive on the heads of spears in a horrendous display before their families and friends. Thus, Satan visibly manifested his merciless hatred for these sons of Abraham.
- Rejoicing in his supposed victory, Satan subsequently directed the Assyrian army to launch an invasion into the southern kingdom, but during this siege the Angel of the Lord went out at night and struck down 185,000 Assyrians, resulting in a tremendous defeat that would severely weaken their empire.

Our Lord's Objective

- Our Lord's divine judgment over sin is visibly manifested to the remainder of His people in the southern tribes.
- The northern survivors were carried off to foreign lands, but the Lord has not forgotten them, and many of their descendants who now reside in countries throughout the world will once again be reunited with the southern tribes to form one holy kingdom under the reign of the Lord Jesus Christ. Certainly, many contemporary Christians are among these descendants of Ephraim, the former northern kingdom.

THIRD HEAD OF THE BEAST = BABYLON

A Brief Background

God's remaining nation in the south, consisting primarily or the tribe of Judah, also fell into idolatry. Under evil leadership, the nation established cultic worship and developed contempt for God, whom they blamed for the catastrophe that decimated the northern kingdom. They did this in the face of continuing warnings from all the messengers God sent. It is said that their abominations even exceeded those of the northern tribes and even those of ancient Sodom.[386] But like their northern brethren, the tribes of the south would not escape judgment. God would allow another army to invade Jerusalem and the southern territories. However, it would not be the Assyrians this time, for the third head of the Beast had recently defeated the Assyrian army and established itself as the great empire in the Middle Eastern world. So in 605 BC, the Babylonian army, under the command of King Nebuchadnezzar, captured Jerusalem and removed the great riches of silver and gold from Solomon's temple. Over the next eighteen years, prophets from God (Jeremiah and Ezekiel) continually proclaimed that this was a judgment allowed by God and that the Judean nation should humble themselves and submit to the Babylonian kingship. However, many false prophets arose and convinced the godless Judean leadership that God was on their side and they should not serve the Babylonians. Subsequently, the glory of God departed from the temple, and the protecting shield of heaven was lifted. Then in 587 BC, King Nebuchadnezzar came again to Jerusalem and brutally seized the city. Only this time he showed no mercy to the inhabitants; the temple was completely destroyed, the walls surrounding Jerusalem were leveled, and all those who escaped the sword were carried captive back to Babylon.

Satan's Objectives

- To weaken the power of God upon the earth by destroying a nation through whom God could manifest Himself.

- To assimilate the Judeans into the Babylonian culture, believing this would effectively wipe out the sons of Abraham from the earth.
- To annihilate Solomon's temple, which had housed the glory of God upon the earth, and thus wipe out all worship of the Lord.
- To eliminate the people through whom the promised Messiah would come and thus prevent the crushing of the serpent's head.

There was no more nation of Israel. The testimony of the Lord who worked on behalf of His people was visibly wiped out as the country became desolate and its survivors taken captive. It would appear as if the spirit of the Beast had won the war. The nation that was to bring forth the Messiah was no more, and its people were being assimilated into the Babylonian culture.

Our Lord's Objective

- To righteously judge His people for their disobedience to the Mosaic covenant and for ignoring the warnings of His true messengers.
- To raise up a faithful remnant that would have a tremendous influence over the government of the Babylonian Empire and provide tremendous prophetic insights to future generations of believers.
- To expose the idolatry of the Babylonian system and manifest Himself as the one true God by working through this faithful remnant.
- To purify the Holy Land and its people by rebuilding a nation from a faithful remnant out of a seemingly impossible situation.

The Lord previously had decreed some 150 years earlier that this captivity would not be permanent and that they would be delivered after seventy years by a man named Cyrus.[387] Thus, in 536

BC, Cyrus, the commander of the Persian army, invaded the city of Babylon and assumed control over the Mediterranean world.

THE FOURTH HEAD OF THE BEAST = PERSIA

A Brief Background

Under the leadership of Cyrus, the Jews were allowed to return to their homeland. However, only a faithful remnant of approximately 50,000 actually chose to leave Babylon and rebuild the city of Jerusalem and their nation. The vast majority decided to stay, for they had assimilated the culture of Babylon and chose to no longer be Jews.

Satan's Objectives

- To annihilate the entire Jewish race using a high-ranking Persian authority by the name of Haman to deceive the king and turn him against the Jews. However, God overturned this deceitful attempt by raising up His champions, Esther and Mordecai, who exposed the lies of Haman before the king, resulting in Haman's execution.

Our Lord's Objective

- To rebuild a nation using a small remnant of loyal Jews who were willing to leave the comforts of Babylon in order to settle a land that had been desolate for seventy years.
- To rebuild the temple for the Lord in Jerusalem; construction began around 520 BC.
- To rebuild the walls of Jerusalem; construction began around 440 BC.

Thus, the "Jewish nation" was established in the land of Israel, even though it remained under the authority of the Persian government.

THE FIFTH HEAD OF THE BEAST = GREECE

A Brief Background

As time progressed, the Persian government had more and more trouble keeping its wide empire in submission. Meanwhile, the Greeks had been building a powerful kingdom for some decades, and in 333 BC, under the leadership of Alexander the Great, they defeated the Persian armies. With the swiftness of a leopard, they extended their borders all the way to India and became the largest empire up to that time. Alexander died ten years later, and the Greek Empire was then divided into four geographical provinces. During this time, Israel was made subject to the Hellenistic culture because of its geographic location between two of these provinces: the Seleucid province of the north, comprised of Syria and much of the Middle East, and the Ptolemaic province of the south, comprised of Egypt and Palestine. While initially under Ptolemaic rule, conflicts also brought the Jews under Seleucid rule. Descendants of both Seleucus and Ptolemy were intent upon infusing the Greek way of life (Hellenism) over their respective domains.

Hellenism constituted a lifestyle of "eat, drink, and be merry for tomorrow we die." Merchants could amass great wealth; public eating halls serving rich foods and wines were very popular; music filled the cities from end to end; and gymnasiums were very popular among the youth, and many of the young Jewish men who were ashamed of their heritage had operations to undo their circumcisions.

Satan's Objectives

- To create the mentality, "Take pleasure today; don't worry about tomorrow."
- To move 100,000 Jews to Alexandria in 312 BC in an attempt to train them in Greek practices and destroy Jewish traditions.
- To raise up a new king out of the northern province in 175 BC with a passionate dedication to enforce Greek Hellenism over the entire nation of Israel. This was Antiochus IV

Epiphanes, who launched one of the darkest periods in Israel's history. He is widely considered to be a "type" of the latter-day Antichrist.

- Under the reign of Antiochus, Jews were forbidden under the penalty of death to (1) practice circumcision, (2) observe the Sabbath, (3) observe Jewish feasts, and (4) destroy all copies of the Hebrew Scriptures. This created a greater apostasy among the Jews, but at the same time the resistance toward Hellenism grew stronger.

- In 168 BC, Antiochus rode into Jerusalem and ordered a pagan deity (perhaps Jupiter) to be erected in the Holy of Holies. This event has been called the "abomination of desolation" by the Jews and is believed by many to refer to the prophecy in Daniel 11:31.

- Additionally, pigs and not lambs, were to be sacrificed on the temple altar, a drunken orgy was made compulsory with the temple sacrifices, and a pagan priest was appointed to oversee this new form of worship.

- All Israelites were required to pay homage to this form of worship or they were killed. Many died, including women who continued to have their children circumcised.

Our Lord's Objectives

- To raise up a resistance force to oppose the cultural impact of Hellenism and to stand fast to their Jewish heritage.

- To use the 100,000 Jews who were shipped to Alexandria to influence the other cultures. This was accomplished when they translated the Hebrew Bible into Greek (Septuagint), which allowed it to be read in the Gentile provinces.

- To initiate a rebellion under the leadership of the Maccabees, which eventually forced the Syrian Greeks to withdraw from Jerusalem. This began as a small group of guerilla fighters who had continuing success, and with each victory, their army grew until forty-two months later, they threw off the Hellenistic yoke. On December 25, 165 BC, the Levite priesthood began cleansing the temple and reinstating the worship of their Lord. This event is still celebrated as Hanukkah. The power of Antiochus had waned, and he was no longer involved in Israel's affairs.

SIXTH HEAD OF THE BEAST = ROME

A Brief Background of the Roman Empire and Israel

In 63 BC, the Roman Empire under General Pompey threw off the Greek yoke in the Middle East. This officially exchanged Grecian influence for Roman power over Israel. Rome was the Beast empire that established Herod as king over Israel. He was reigning at the birth of Jesus Christ and failed in his attempt to locate and murder Him. Thirty years later, this sixth Beast kingdom allowed the crucifixion of Jesus Christ. Subsequently, in AD 70, Rome completely sacked Jerusalem, which had rebelled against its authority. A great slaughter took place as the wrath of the Beast was directed against the Jewish populace. It was during this time that the Jews began to lose their national identity, as many were forced to flee to other countries. Yet a remnant of the Jewish populace still remained. Later, in AD 135, following a second Jewish revolt, Rome banned all the Jews from Jerusalem. They would not gather again as a nation until 1948.

A Brief Background of the Roman Empire and Christianity

Rome saw the early Christians as an unauthorized, separate religion that they couldn't control. In those days, the Roman Empire mandated "emperor worship," and those who refused to recognize the emperor as a god were viewed as traitors to Rome. Christians were accused of cannibalism and incest because of their talk of "eating flesh, drinking blood, and loving one another." Thus, Christianity became a capital offense, and many suffered martyrdom. This murderous persecution was extremely brutal, yet Christianity continued to experience rapid growth throughout the Roman Empire.

In the third century, Constantine became the Roman emperor and embraced Christianity. Under his reign, Christianity became the "official religion" of Rome. Constantine was actively involved in key church decisions, and as a result the church became very politically oriented. Additionally, in order to appease the angry pagan religious sects within the empire, many of their pagan traditions were allowed into the Christian environment and remain today. Thus, Christianity became identified with the Roman Catholic Church, which was a tremendously powerful force in the religious and political worlds. This power continued to grow over the centuries, for it was ruled that the Catholic priesthood held the power of "eternal life or damnation." This allowed people to live any lifestyle they chose because they could always be forgiven by a priest. Throughout the Dark Ages, the Catholic Church persecuted millions of Christians who refused to embrace Catholicism. They also were committed to killing the Jewish population. Thus, the intent of the sixth head of the Beast was to annihilate all aspects of Christianity not under the control of Catholicism. This slowed down greatly when Christians migrated to America to avoid persecution. Later, their descendants established a Christian government that has been a powerful factor in the expansion of the kingdom of God throughout the world. Yet the spiritual and political arm of the ancient Roman Empire continues into the twenty-first century and remains a force within the world today. That is why many Christian teachers believe that the seventh head of the Beast is a "revived Roman Empire." An empire that judged and persecuted the Lord at His first coming would then be judged and destroyed by the Lord at His second coming.

APPENDIX B

CLIENT-FRIENDS LETTER

A MESSAGE FOR TRULY VALUED
FRIENDS—"GET READY"
(Please set aside some quiet time for this reading)

Dear Valued Friend,

I have a number of close friends, but over my years in business, I have developed a deep, caring heart for my clients, whom I see less often. It has developed into something much more than just a business relationship; it is truly a friendship that is very close to my heart. As a former Marine, I understand the value of a friendship. It's more than simply kind words, for a true friend is one who will sacrifice himself to stand alongside those who are experiencing difficulties in life; and we all know that life can definitely be a battlefield.

You know that I am certainly available to assist with tax and financial issues, but you probably don't know that I am also available as your friend to support you during times of challenges that we all face in life. Everyone faces difficult challenges in life, and our level of joy, prosperity, and maturity all depends on how we handle those events that periodically confront each of us. None of us can handle these things alone. We all need true friendship.

As a concerned friend, I truly believe that it is time that I share some things with you about God, our Father and Creator, and about

His Son, Jesus Christ. First of all, I want to assure you that I have no motive for writing to you except out of a loving concern for my friends and my passion for the Lord. This isn't about religion or about choosing a particular church; it's about you and your eternal destiny, which hinges on your relationship with the Lord during this lifetime. This is something that the Lord Himself has put into my heart, for the times we are facing in today's world are visibly becoming more and more troubling; and I believe that the future for ourselves and our families will present some very challenging circumstances.

By now you are probably surprised and wondering why your CPA would be writing to you about such matters, and perhaps you may not have known about this aspect of my life. Therefore, I will start by attaching a short biography, which might provide insight into my life both past and future.

From a friend who truly cares for you,

A SHORT BIOGRAPHY

I am not a pastor by profession, but I am a professional businessman with a deep, deep passion to see our Lord's kingdom visibly manifested in our country during this present generation.

I have been self-employed for the past twenty-five years, but prior to that, I served our country for twenty years in the Marine Corps. Part of that time I spent in a combat environment, fighting for the rights of our country. I certainly wasn't a God-fearing man back in those Marine Corps days. In fact, I lived a wilder life than most. But there came a day when I was changed forever. It was November 6, 1979, and I attended a church service with my wife, and I remember the sermon had to do with the sacrifice of Christ on the cross. Surprisingly, it touched me quite deeply when the pastor emphasized that it wasn't just about dying and going to heaven but that Jesus deeply desired a relationship with us in this life. Then as I was talking with some men about this after the service, one suggested that I go home and read the gospel of John. Well, I left church that morning without any real expectation that the Bible would do much for me, but I was wrong. When I got home and had brunch with my wife and young son, I jumped into our backyard hottub and opened the Bible the guys gave me. I found the first chapter of John's gospel, which begins,

> *In the beginning was the Word, and the Word was with God, and the Word was God. He was in the beginning with God. All things were made through him, and without him was not any thing made that was made. In him was life, and the life was the light of men. . . . And the Word became flesh and dwelt among us, and we have seen his glory, glory as of the only Son from the Father, full of grace and truth.*

That hot tub suddenly got much hotter. During my younger years, I had hardened my heart against God, but as I read this, I broke, and I wept for the first time since I was a young boy. My years on the front lines of the Vietnam conflict never broke me down. I thought I was too tough for "wimpy" things like the Bible. I kept reading and weeping and reading and weeping, constantly crying out, "My God, my God, I didn't know these things. Please forgive me." I could not stop. The Spirit of God continued to pass through me like an electric current over and over and over until I was completely overwhelmed; and this continued until 1:00 AM the following morning. This was the first of many other experiences that have occurred during my years of having that personal relationship with the Lord.

Before this occurred the Bible was just another book in Grandma's bookcase, but it was at this point that I came to understand deep in my spirit that it was truly God's Word for us. Yes, I know it was physically written by men, but it was written by those men upon whom God's Spirit "breathed His words" into their spirit for the purpose of speaking to His people, including you (2 Tim.3:16).

I've traveled the tough, sinful road of the unbeliever, and I do understand that until this happens to a person, the Bible will have little credibility. But after this "born-again" experience happens, just as sure as a light will come on when you flip the switch, you truly know that the words in Scripture come to us from a loving Father who calls us unto Himself.

My client friends, it is not coincidental that we have been brought into each other's lives. I cannot ignore the fact that our Lord desires us to teach and encourage others in the truth. He brought us together. Read on, and perhaps you can get a deeper understanding as to why.

A BUSINESSMAN BUT ALSO A DISCIPLE OF THE LORD

As my relationship with the Lord grew over the years, I started attending seminary part-time, as well as working the business. I share this with you because I want you to know that I have the same educational background of most pastors. I say this not because I want you to think more highly of me but so that my message to you might be received with more credibility. Actually, this past summer I received a Doctorate in Ministry from Tacoma's Faith Seminary in the area of "Strategic Leadership."

A CALL TO PREPARE

We really need to prepare ourselves and our families for the fallout from economic and/or terrorist events that will suddenly confront us. I've attached a short section to this letter having to do with physical preparations. I pray that you will take it seriously and begin preparations for the challenges that are before each of us. Think about it: a nationwide terrorist strike and/or sudden economic meltdown hits our nation, and before ordinary folks like us can adjust, the grocery stores, banks, and gas stations will be locked down. I am not trying to be pessimistic; this is a reality that lies before us, and I want to alert my friends to "prepare now."

When this time of tremendous challenge comes, we will need to stand "shoulder to shoulder" with one another and work together in developing our personal missions, focusing upon how we will move forward from here.

BRIEF FINANCIAL SUGGESTION

Start living like a steward, not a consumer. Consumers focus on satisfying themselves—their pleasures, appetites, toys, etc. Stewards focus on the Lord, asking how He wants us to use the talents and resources He has provided for us at this time of our life. Every person has three basic resources to steward—time, talent, and money. God has created you for a purpose—continually seek for it. You will never find peace and joy in life until you seek, discover, and fulfill God's will for your individual life. Ask God to reveal His vision for you. Perhaps it will mean a reduction in your standard of living, but if you follow His lead, you will find tremendous fulfillment in this life and, even more, in the eternal life that lies ahead.

AN EVEN STRONGER MESSAGE

Again, I want to assure you that I have no other motive for writing this letter than my sincere love and concern for my "client friends" whom the Lord has brought to me over the years of my business life. I begin with telling you a basic biblical truth that so many religions and worldly philosophers do not want to hear.

*Jesus said . . . "I am the way, and the truth, and the life. No one comes to the Father except through me." **John 14:6***

My friends, we cannot be looking in another direction for eternal life; those who try to enter the heavenly kingdom another way, Jesus calls *"thieves and robbers,"* and they will not be allowed to enter. Jesus is the only "doorway" into the eternal kingdom! Do not buy into the worldly gospel that there are many ways to eternal life. There is only one, and I do pray that each of you and your loved ones find it. So, my friends, how do you enter into the family of our Lord? It is very simple.

If you confess with your mouth that Jesus is Lord and believe in your heart that God raised him from the dead, you will be saved. Romans 10:9

It sounds simple, right? Yet so few find the way.

Jesus said "Enter by the narrow gate. For the gate is wide and the way is easy that leads to destruction, and those who enter by it are many. For the gate is narrow and the way is hard that leads to life, and those who find it are few." Matthew 7:13-14

My friends, I strongly and lovingly exhort you to not shrug off these words. Do not think that all things will work out in time and continue to live out your life as if tomorrow will be no different than today. A time is coming for all of us when there will be no tomorrow.

I have numerous client friends who range in age from teenagers to the elderly in their nineties. To each of you, I say that it makes no difference where you are in your stage of life or how great you think your sins have been; if you call out to Him for forgiveness with all your heart, He promises to remove all of your transgressions as far from Him as the east is from the west (Psalm 103:11-12). I can personally vouch for that, for when it happened to me it was like ten thousand pounds was removed from my back that I never even realized was there until it was gone and a tremendous love for the Lord began to fill my heart. The rewards and forgiveness are the same for those who are elderly as they are for those who are young. So don't let your age or deep feelings of guilt keep you from opening your heart and asking for forgiveness for a lifetime of sins in the name of Jesus Christ, the Son of God, who at the cross on Calvary hill atoned for the sins of all who will confess and believe. We are all youngsters in the light of eternity.

Over my years in the CPA business, I have had thousands of interviews with people and have witnessed people involved in divorce, adultery, loss of jobs, fighting over parents' estates, and much more. All of this creates anger and hurt among family and former friends, and I've learned that we all tend to hold onto our anger in our hearts forever. This is such a deep hindrance to our desire to live a life of joy. I would exhort each of you to rid yourselves of this heavy weight in your inner being by "forgiving those" who have hurt you. It's not a question of who is right or wrong; it doesn't matter, just forgive and release the weight from your spirit and allow the Lord to handle matters. Forgive others, even if they refuse to forgive you; the important thing is that you forgive. Then stand back and watch the weight come off of your back that you didn't realize was there.

IS THIS MESSAGE OFFENSIVE TO SOME?

This message is going out to every single client who has engaged me to help him or her in business and tax issues. Yes, I know it will be offensive to some, perhaps many. Obviously, writing a message that is offensive to some is not my concern; my concern is for you and your eternal, as well as your current, well-being. I am reminded of a preacher by the name of George Whitefield, who lived during the 1700s. He said, "I would crawl across England on my hands and knees if it would result in a single person finding eternal life with God." Perhaps I wouldn't attempt such an endeavor, but I certainly identify with his heart. If I offended hundreds of people but a single soul came to find the Lord and eternal life, then I would certainly believe this to be a worthy endeavor. The chance of offending people cannot stop us from proclaiming a truth that can save others. This is a belief that more church pastors should embrace in their twenty-first-century messages.

FINAL RECOMMENDATION FOR THOSE WHO WISH TO SEEK THE LORD

If you've read to this point and want to know how to proceed, I would suggest that you get a Bible, if you don't already have one, and open to the gospel of John, found in the New Testament section. Then ask God to open your heart to His truth, and begin to read. Read with an open heart, believing that Jesus is right alongside you, and your direction will be made plain. See what happens when you ask if Jesus is truly the Lord. Eventually, you will feel a deep desire to cry out for forgiveness, and that will be the time when He removes the weight of sin from your soul, and He will remember those sins no more; they are completely gone from your life and from His remembrance. There is no way of finding the Lord except to seek Him. He stands at the door of your heart, but you must open up.

That's it! Hopefully, some seed has been sown, but it is the Lord who will bring the growth.

Finally, I have attached a prayer that has been very important in my day-to-day spiritual walk. It is a prayer honoring the Son of God, and I prepared it to provide a brief understanding of who Jesus is, what He did, and why He did it. There are numerous false religions in the world, as well as in this country, that call themselves Christian, and their differing views of Christ can be very misleading to those who are truthfully seeking Him. If you have never truly sought the Lord for forgiveness in your life, try opening your heart up to Him, and call out for forgiveness. The following prayer is a suggestion for those who wish to open up to Him for the first time.

Pray the following prayer from a seeking heart:

It is hard for me to believe in You, Jesus. Yet I do believe what is written. It has the ring of truth. You are the one I have run from. You are what I have longed for all of these years. Maybe I never believed even when I thought I did. You're the King, not me. I'm tired of trying to run my life. I'm not qualified. I've messed up everything. I do believe now that You, Jesus, are the Christ, the Son of God. I ask for the life You promised. I ask for Your Holy Spirit to live inside me. Please wash me from my sins. Please fill the hole in my heart, Jesus. Please be to me what I've always longed for. I can't make it on my own. I need You.

FINAL RECOMMENDATION FOR THOSE WHO WANT TO TRASH THIS LETTER

Don't throw it away; put it away, for a challenging and troubling time is coming when many will be seeking for answers. Perhaps that will be your time to open your heart, and if so, you may find this letter and the accompanying prayer helpful and enlightening.

PHYSICAL PREPARATIONS AND STRATEGIC FAMILY PLANNING

Those who understand the message of these days should be communicating with their family and friends. The first step is to meet with them individually, family by family, and lay out a scenario of a sudden shutdown of banks, stores, and gas stations, along with gang violence and chaos throughout our country. Then, one by one, discuss in detail how each family would require the following material preparations.

Food supplies for a minimum of six months: How long would their supplies last that they currently have in their homes? What type of purchases should be made for long-term storage? Are they financially able to acquire the required food supplies?

- Drinking water for an indefinite period of time: Discuss methods of storing and purifying water.
- Medical supplies, batteries, toilet paper, gasoline, propane, tools, flashlights, radios, etc.: Discuss what may be needed for an indefinite period of time.
- Items to survive a six-month "nuclear winter," such as clothing and sleeping bags.
- Discuss the relationship that each individual member of the family has with the Lord, and develop a plan on how to proceed with the deepening of each relationship.

There are plenty of Web sites that provide information, as well as sell products, to those who intend to make preparations, so it is recommended that each family do some researching. Remember, leaders, you cannot micromanage the situation; you need to assign responsibility to each individual within the family unit.

Finally, set a date when all will again meet together with five to six other families in order to present recommendations and finalize plans. At this meeting, it is very important that the leader who initiated this movement act as the facilitator to help the group see and think about things that they would normally never consider. Facilitators must assist in helping individual families see where they fit in the bigger picture, as well as monitor the progress of the meeting with periodic summarization, group encouragement, and affirmation of each member's input, yet not allow the meeting to lose focus on its intended mission. Lastly, get individual commitments from each family and set a date for completion, whereupon another meeting is scheduled to affirm completion.

> *Go to the ant, O sluggard; consider her ways, and be wise. Without having any chief, officer, or ruler, she prepares her bread in summer and gathers her food in harvest. How long will you lie there, O sluggard? When will you arise from your sleep? A little sleep, a little slumber, a little folding of the hands to rest, and poverty will come upon you like a robber, and want like an armed man.* **Proverbs 6:6-11**

An additional scenario that needs to be discussed at these meetings is gang violence that may occur in various cities and neighborhoods, for each individual family certainly could be exposed to this tremendous danger. One recommendation to deal with this possibility is to plan for each family to gather together on a predetermined property and live in community. They should have their "supplies" inventoried and ready to move to the selected property on a moment's notice. Telephone communications may not be possible, so the timing of this gathering together must be well planned in advance. A community of friends and families that have gathered together are much more capable of fending off gang-related assaults.

You may hear some Christians argue from Scripture that God will provide "manna" for His people, and so we don't need to be concerned about food to eat or clothes to wear. It is true that the Lord provides, but the context of this verse is one in which Jesus was teaching His followers how to live day to day in their hearts. The Lord did provide manna in the wilderness for His people but only after a significant period of time had elapsed and their prepared supplies had been depleted. It is also true that He calls us to "be prepared" for the coming times, and the meaning here should wisely be applied to physical preparations as well as spiritual. Consider the story of Joseph, who stockpiled food for a famine that was coming in seven years. Likewise, God is certainly calling us to use wisdom in our preparations. Finally, we also should consider that our prepared supplies might be a great blessing to many of the unprepared families that will be suffering from shock and hunger.

Therefore you also must be ready, for the Son of Man is coming at an hour you do not expect. "Who then is the faithful and wise servant, whom his master has set over his household, to give them their food at the proper time? Blessed is that servant whom his master will find so doing when he comes. Truly, I say to you, he will set him over all his possessions.
Matthew 24:44-47

FOR ALL OF YOU, NO MATTER YOUR BELIEF

If you are currently facing grievous circumstances, no matter what it is, I will make myself available to listen and intercede for you, or with you, before the Lord. I can also share your petition(s) with others who will also faithfully pray for you.

Perhaps you have a deep hunger inside (a sense of emptiness) for something more in life (I call it an unfulfilled warrior spirit). Let me know!

If you would like to know more, the best way to contact me is via E-mail.

NOTES

Introduction

[1] Matthew 25:1-13
[2] David Murrow, *Why Men Hate Going To Church* (Nashville: Thomas Nelson, 2005), 53.
[3] Ibid., 72.
[4] Luke 12:40-48; Joel 2 and 3.
[5] 1 Chronicles 12:32
[6] Matthew 24:21
[7] Isaiah 60:1-2
[8] Psalm 23:4
[9] Ezekiel 9:4-6
[10] 1 Peter 4:17
[11] Luke 21:28-31; Daniel 12:10

Chapter 1
WARRIOR LEADERSHIP IN THE ARMY OF GOD

[12] Reggie McNeal, *Practicing Greatness* (San Francisco: Jossey-Bass, 2006), 7.
[13] This point is made by Greg Austin, pastor of Gardiner Community Church, Gardiner, Washington.
[14] Genesis 3:15
[15] Job 1:1-5
[16] Meredith G. Kline, "Trial by Ordeal" in *Through Christ's Word: A Festschrift for Dr. Philip E. Hughes*, (Phillipsburg, NJ: Presbyterian and Reformed, 1985),.6.
[17] Job 1:12
[18] Matthew 22:37; Mark 12:30; Luke 10:27
[19] Revelation 12:11
[20] 1 Peter 1:19-21; Revelation 13:8
[21] Arthur W. Pink, *The Divine Covenants* (Grand Rapids: Baker, 1973), 31.

[22] Arthur W. Pink, *The Sovereignty of God* (Grand Rapids: Baker, 1973), 247-52.

[23] Kline, "Trial by Ordeal," 6.

[24] Andrew Murray, *The Believer's Prayer Life* (Minneapolis: Bethany House, 1983), 20-21.

[25] Ryan Wyatt, "The Kingdom Time Is Now," *Visionary Advancement Newsletter,* n.d.

[26] Reggie McNeal, *Practicing Greatness* (San Francisco: Jossey-Bass, 2006), 8.

Chapter 2
ONE WORLD – TWO KINGDOMS

[27] Mark 4:11-12

[28] Ephesians 1:9

[29] John 3:3

[30] George Eldon Ladd, *The Presence of the Future* (Grand Rapids: Eerdmans, 1974), 225.

[31] Dan Juster and Keith Intrater, *Israel, the Church and the Last Days* (Shippensburg, PA: Destiny Image, 1990), 40-45.

[32] Matthew 13:24-30

[33] D. A. Carson, *How Long, O Lord?* (Grand Rapids: Baker, 1990), 8.

[34] Romans 8:19-21

[35] Tal Brooke, *When the World Will Be As One* (Eugene: Harvest House, 1989).

Chapter 3
WARNINGS FOR THE CHURCH IN AMERICA

[36] Matthew 24:9-11

[37] Charles Stanley, *A Touch of His Freedom* (Grand Rapids: Zondervan, 1991).

[38] Matthew 5:20

[39] Herman Hoeksema, *Behold He Cometh: An Exposition of the Book of Revelation* (Grand Rapids: Reformed Free Publishing Association, 1969), 61.

[40] Paul Marshall, *Their Blood Cries Out* (Dallas: Word, 1997), 4.

[41] Matthew 25:1-13

[42] Matthew 24:9; Mark 13:13; Luke 21:17

[43] David Ravenhill, *The Jesus Letters* (Shippensburg, PA: Destiny Image, 2003), 80-81.

[44] Ibid, 86.

[45] Psalm 23:4; 1 Corinthians 2:9

[46] Gregory R. Reid, *The Gospel of Vague* (Enemies of the Cross – Prosperity Movement: www.etpv.org/2008).

[47] Ibid

[48] Ravenhill, *The Jesus Letters,* 115-16, 120-21.

[49] Hoeksema, *Behold He Cometh,* 132-33.

[50] Ravenhill, *The Jesus Letters,*139.

[51] Ibid, 142-44.

[52] Al Houghton, *"Word at Work* Newsletter, Volume XXI, Ch. 7.

[53] Ravenhill, *The Jesus Letters,* 151.

[54] Rick Joyner, "The Army of God Mobilizes," Part 9, www.morningstarministries.org

[55] Jack Deere, *Surprised by the Power of the Spirit* (Grand Rapids: Zondervan, 1993).

[56] Matthew 24:11

[57] Isaiah 26:9

[58] Quoted in David Pawson, *When Jesus Returns* (London: Hodder & Stoughton; 1995), 199-200.

[59] Keith Intrater, *From Iraq to Armageddon* (Shippensburg, PA: Destiny Image, 2003), 141-42.

[60] Revelation 2:10; 12:10; 2 Timothy 3:12; John 17:15; Acts 14:22

[61] Tim Taylor of Watchman Ministries, e-mail to the author.

[62] Andrew Walker, *Enemy Territory* (Wilmore, KY: Bristol Books, 1990), 15-16.

[63] Al Houghton, *Word at Work* Newsletter, Volume XXI, Number IX, Chapter 10.

Chapter 4
HORSEMEN, MARTYRDOM, AND A GREAT WAR

[64] Philip Mauro, *Things Which Soon Must Come to Pass* (Swengel, PA: Reiner Publications, 1974), 182.

[65] 2 Kings 19:35; Isaiah 37:36

[66] Revelation 1:12-18; Daniel 10:5-12

[67] 1 Corinthians 2:9-10

[68] Mark 12:28-30

[69] Mauro, *Things Which Soon Must Come to Pass,* 180.

[70] David Pawson, *When Jesus Returns* (London: Hodder & Stoughton, 1995), 133.

[71] Mauro, *Things Which Soon Must Come to Pass,* 187-89.

[72] Matthew 13:24-30 (The Parable of the Weeds)

[73] Herman Hoeksema, *Behold, He Cometh: An Exposition of the Book of Revelation* (Grand Rapids: Reformed Free Publishing Association, 1969), 216.

[74] 2 Timothy 3:12; Romans 5:3-4

[75] James 1:2-4; Romans 8:16-18

[76] Ephesians 6:12

[77] Romans 8:28; 1 Corinthians 2:9

[78] John 14:2-3

[79] Matthew 5:14-16

[80] Roderick Graciano, "The True Spirit of Martyrdom," Timothy Ministries, www.tmin.org.

[81] Ibid.

[82] Ibid.

[83] Genesis 3:15

[84] Hoeksema, *Behold, He Cometh,* 230-31.

[85] Revelation 6:15

[86] Hoeksema, *Behold, He Cometh,* 244.

[87] Revelation 6:16

[88] Ezekiel 3:17-20

[89] Joel C. Rosenberg, *Epicenter: Why the Current Rumblings in the Middle East Will Change Your Future* (Tyndale House, 2006), 68-69.

[90] Ezekiel 38:4

[91] Rosenberg, *Epicenter,* 132.

[92] Isaiah 17

[93] Rosenberg, *Epicenter,* 114–19.

[94] Ayatollah Ibrahim Amini, *Al-Imam, al-Mahdi, The Just Leader of Humanity,* trans. Dr.Abdulaziz Sachedina (Qum, Iran: Ahul Bayt Digital Islamic Library Project, al-islam.org/Mahdi/nontl/Toc htm (accessed April 15, 2006, emphasis mine).

[95] Ibid.

[96] Rosenberg, *Epicenter,* 249-50.

[97] Ibid.

[98] Ezekiel 38:13

[99] Reuters, "U.S. Envoy: Anti-Semitism in Europe Nearly as Bad as in 1930s," February 13, 2004.

[100] Robin Shepherd, "In Europe, an Unhealthy Fixation on Israel," *Washington Post,* January 30, 2005.

[101] Revelation 20:7-10

[102] Rosenberg, *Epicenter,* 254.

[103] John Mintz, "U.S. Called Unprepared for Nuclear Terrorism," *Washington Post,* May 3, 2005.

[104] Rosenberg, *Epicenter,* 120-23.

[105] Charles W. Miller, *Today's Technology in Bible Prophecy* (Lansing, MI: TIP, 1990), 135.

[106] Rosenberg, *Epicenter,* 250.

Chapter 5
TRUMPETS, NUKES, AND A LITTLE BOOK

[107] Joel 2; Jeremiah 46:10; 2 Peter 3:10; 1 Thessalonians 5:2; Isaiah 13:6-9; Acts 2:19-21; Amos 5:18

[108] Acts 2:20-21

[109] Ezekiel 39:6

[110] Charles W. Miller, *Today's Technology in Bible Prophecy* (Lansing, MI: TIP, 1990), 142.

[111] Ibid.

[112] Herman Hoeksema. *Behold, He Cometh: An Exposition of the Book of Revelation* (Grand Rapids: Reformed Free Publishing Association, 1969), 296-97.

[113] Revelation 6:12; 8:5; Ezekiel 38:19

[114] Miller, *Today's Technology in Bible Prophecy,* 161-65.

[115] Exodus 9:23-26

[116] Exodus 7:20-21

[117] Jeremiah 9:15

[118] Miller, *Today's Technology in Bible Prophecy,* 176.

[119] Ibid., 178-82

[120] Exodus 10:20-23

[121] Judges 6:3-5

[122] Miller, *Today's Technology in Bible Prophecy,* 196-213.

[123] Joel 2:1-11 and Isaiah 24:1-15

[124] Revelation 9:20-21

[125] Psalm 23; Job 1:21

[126] Revelation 1:10-16; Daniel 10:5-6

[127] Revelation 10:4

[128] Jeremiah 6:14

[129] Ezekiel 2:8—3:3

[130] Hoeksema. *Behold, He Cometh,* 23.

Chapter 6
GOD'S WARRIORS IN THE END TIMES = 144,000

[131] Romans 1:1; Galatians 1:10; James 1:1; 2 Peter 1:1; Acts 4:29; 16:17

[132] Revelation 1:1; 10:7; 11:18; Jeremiah 7:25; 25:4

[133] Joshua 1:1; Revelation 15:3

[134] Acts 10:36; Ephesians 6:6

[135] 1 Corinthians 7:23

[136] Matthew 24:44; Luke 12:40

[137] Romans 11:25-29

[138] Micah 5:7-8; Hosea 1:10

[139] Galatians 3:29; Philippians 3:3; Romans 2:28-29; 9:6

[140] 1 Kings 12:24

[141] Hosea 11:8-9; Zechariah 10:6; Ezekiel 37: 16-22; Micah 5:7-8

[142] Genesis 48:19

[143] Ellis H. Skolfield, *Hidden Beast 2* (Fort Myers, FL: Fish House, 1990), 130-31.

[144] Hosea 1:10

[145] Hosea 7:8, 8:8, 9:17; Micah 5:7-8

[146] Hosea 11:8-9

[147] Hosea 2:14-23; Zechariah 10:6

[148] Larry Simmons, *42 Months to Glory* (Oklahoma City: Ephraim House, 1994), 86.
[149] Ezekiel 37:19-21; Romans 10:26; Hosea 1:10
[150] Skolfield, *Hidden Beast 2,* 140.
[151] Hosea 11:10; Douglas S. Winnail, *Early Christianity and Europe's Western Isles,* www.tomorrowsworld.org.
[152] Zechariah 9:13-14
[153] Skolfield, *Hidden Beast 2,* 135-36.
[154] Romans 11:25-27
[155] Simmons, *42 Months to Glory,* 91-92.
[156] Revelation 21:9-26
[157] Revelation 14:1-5
[158] Revelation 7:9-17
[159] Joel C. Graves, *Gathering Over Jerusalem,* (Xulon, 2003), 6.
[160] John 14:12-14
[161] Numbers 13 and 14
[162] Luke 9:23
[163] John 15:20-21; Genesis 22; Matthew 10:37
[164] James 1:2-4
[165] Isaiah 21:6; Ezekiel 3:17
[166] Ezekiel 9:4
[167] Revelation 14:1-5
[168] Ephesians 4:15

Chapter 7
THE "SEVENTY WEEKS" OF DANIEL

[169] Jeremiah 25:11-12; 29:10
[170] Isaiah 45:13
[171] Daniel 9:1-23
[172] Exodus 32:12-13
[173] Ezekiel 40-46
[174] Ezra 7:12-26; 9:9
[175] Nehemiah 2:5-8
[176] Isaac Newton, *Observations upon the Prophecies of Daniel and the Apocalypse of St. John* (London, 1733), 135.
[177] Revelation 14:4-5
[178] Revelation 14:1-5
[179] Benjamin Baruch, *The Day of the Lord Is at Hand* (Baruch Publishing, 2004), 21.
[180] Ibid, 28-29.

Chapter 8
WARRIORS FOR CHRIST IN THE MIDST OF
THE GREAT TRIBULATION

[181] Rick Joyner, "The Church will Begin to Take On More of a Military Mentality in the Coming Times," *MorningStar Newsletter*, April, 2008.

[182] Matthew 24:14

[183] Revelation 11:15-19

[184] 1 Corinthians 3:16-17; Ephesians 2:19-22

[185] Isaiah 60:14

[186] Gleason L. Archer, "Isaiah" in *The Wycliffe Bible Commentary*, ed. Charles F. Pfeiffer and Everett F. Harrison (Chicago: Moody, 1962), 642-43.

[187] Zephaniah 3:1-2

[188] Matthew 21:12-13

[189] Herman Hoeksema, *Behold, He Cometh: An Exposition of the Book of Revelation* (Grand Rapids: Reformed Free Publishing Assn, 1969), 369-70.

[190] Benjamin Baruch, *The Day of the Lord Is at Hand* (Baruch Publishing, 2004), 27.

[191] Revelation 12:6

[192] Revelation 13:5-7

[193] Zechariah 4

[194] Revelation 1:20

[195] Revelation 14:1-5

[196] Like 1:17; Matthew 11:14

[197] Matthew 3:3

[198] Baruch, *The Day of the Lord Is at Hand*, 48

[199] A.W. Tozer, "'Prophetic Preaching,' This Is the Need of Our Day and It will Come," quoted in "A New Breed of Modern Preachers," sermon by Greg Gordon, www.sermonindex.net

[200] Baruch, *The Day of the Lord Is at Hand*, 76-77.

[201] Rosha Judah, *Prophets Still Speak* (The Sound of a Trumpet, 1991).

[202] Matthew 24:14

[203] John 14:12

[204] Hoeksema, *Behold, He Cometh*, 390-92.

[205] John 15:20; Matthew 24:10

[206] Matthew 5:11-12

[207] Daniel 9:24

[208] Revelation 11:5

[209] Revelation 11:8

[210] Daniel 3:8-12

Chapter 9
CONFRONTATION BETWEEN THE WOMAN
& THE DRAGOM

[211] Jeremiah 4:31; Micah 4:8-9

[212] Genesis 6:1-4

[213] Matthew 2:1-18

[214] Matthew 4:1-11

[215] Job 1:6; 2:1; Zechariah 3:1

[216] John 14:30; Ephesians 2:1-3

[217] Jude 9; Matthew 24:31; Luke 4: 10-11; Daniel 12:1

[218] Herman Hoeksema, *Behold, He Cometh: An Exposition of the Book of Revelation* (Grand Rapids: Reformed Free Publishing Assn, 1969), 431-35.

[219] John 15:19; 17:16

[220] Dave Hunt, *A Woman Rides the Beast* (Harvest House, 1994), 70-79.

[221] Philip Mauro, *Things Which Soon Must Come to Pass* (Swengel, PA: Reiner Publications, 1974), 384-389

[222] Hoeksema, *Behold, He Cometh*, 448-49.

[223] Isaiah 14:12-14 (emphasis mine)

Chapter 10
THREE BEASTS – AN UNHOLY TRINITY

[224] Revelation 12:12

[225] Isaiah 57:20; Revelation 17:15

[226] Daniel 7-8

[227] Revelation 12:3

[228] Matthew 4:8-10

[229] Revelation 17:9-10

[230] Revelation 17:13; 17

[231] Revelation 17:11; Daniel 7:8

[232] Herman Hoeksema, *Behold, He Cometh: An Exposition of the Book of Revelation* (Grand Rapids: Reformed Free Publishing Association, 1969), 576.

[233] Isaiah 14:13-14

[234] Daniel 11:39

[235] Daniel 7:8

[236] Daniel 11:32

[237] Daniel 7:7-8

[238] Revelation 13:4

[239] Daniel 3:1-7

[240] Benjamin Baruch offers the example of *"Prince Charles of Wales,"* which equals 666 when calculated using the Hebrew alphabet. Prince Charles seems an unlikely candidate in today's political arena. However, this is an example of

how one's name can be translated into a number (*The Day of the Lord Is at Hand* [Baruch Publishing, 2004], 178).

[241] Matthew 11:19

[242] Daniel 9:24

[243] Daniel 9:27; 11:22-24; Isaiah 28:15-22

[244] Matthew 24:15-22

[245] Hebrews 10:8-10

[246] Baruch, *The Day of the Lord Is at Hand*, 26-29.

[247] Daniel 11:33;

[248] Baruch, *The Day of the Lord Is at Hand*, 44-46.

[249] Dan Juster and Keith Intrater, *Israel, the Church and the Last Days* (Destiny Image, 1991), 137-47.

[250] Ellis H. Skolfield, *Hidden Beast 2* (Fort Myers, FL: Fish House, 1990), 175.

[251] Randy Alcorn, *Safely Home* (Carol Stream, IL: Tyndale House, 2001), 288-89.

Chapter 11
MYSTERY BABYLON THE GREAT:
CAPITOL OF WEALTH, PLEASURE, & HARLOTRY

[252] Daniel 2

[253] Benjamin Baruch, *The Day of the Lord Is at Hand* (Baruch Publishing, 2004), 52-56.

[254] Ibid., 124-27.

[255] Jeremiah 51:25; Daniel 2:35; Zechariah 4:7

[256] Dave Hunt, *A Woman Rides the Beast* (Eugene: Harvest House, 1994), 70-71.

[257] 1 Timothy 5:8

[258] Roderick Graciano, "Battling Babylons," Timothy Ministries, www.tmin.org, 49.

[259] Matthew 6:24

[260] Revelation 13 and Revelation 11

[261] Daniel 7:8; 20-22; 24-25

[262] Ezekiel 16:8-22

[263] Ibid. p.96

[264] Charles Pretlow, *Revelation Six, Get Ready* (Westcliffe, CO: Get Ready Publishing, 2004), 282-83.

[265] Larry Simmons, *42 Months to Glory* (Oklahoma City: Ephraim House, 1994), 215-18.

[266] Randy Alcorn, *Safely Home* (Carol Stream, IL: Tyndale House, 2001), 309.

[267] Ibid., 277-85

[268] Isaiah 48:20; 52:11; Jeremiah 50:8-9; 51:6-8; Zechariah 2:6-7; 2 Corinthians 6:17-18; Revelation 18:4-8

[269] Philip Mauro, *Things Which Must Soon Come to Pass* (Swengel, PA: Reiner Publications, 1974), 494.

[270] Arthur W. Pink, *Elijah* (Edinburgh: The Banner of Truth Trust, 1956), 129-33.

Chapter 12
THE LAST HARVEST FOLLOWED BY DESTRUCTION

[271] Philip Mauro, *Things Which Must Soon Come to Pass* (Swengel, PA: Reiner Publications, 1974), 432-34.

[272] Luke 19:17-19

[273] Herman Hoeksema, *Behold, He Cometh: An Exposition of the Book of Revelation* (Grand Rapids: Reformed Free Publishing Assn, 1969), 494.

[274] 1 Kings 19 (modified for this scenario)

[275] Psalm 23:4

[276] Hoeksema, *Behold, He Cometh*, 501.

[277] Matthew 13:24-30

[278] Matthew 13:36-43

[279] 1 Thessalonians 4:15-17

[280] Daniel 3:8-30

[281] Exodus 15:1-18

[282] Hoeksema, *Behold, He Cometh*, 521-23.

[283] Job 2:7-8

Chapter 13
THE RETURN OF THE KING

[284] Psalm 23:5

[285] Herman Hoeksema, *Behold, He Cometh: An Exposition of the Book of Revelation* (Grand Rapids: Reformed Free Publishing Assn, 1969), 546.

[286] Joel 3:1-3; 12

[287] Isaiah 14:12-21; Ezekiel 28:13-19

[288] Zechariah 14:16; Isaiah 52:10; 66:20; Psalm 86:9

[289] Ephesians 2:2; 6:12

[290] Joshua 10:11; Ezekiel 38:18-22)

[291] John 19:30

[292] George Eldon Ladd, *A Commentary on the Revelation of John* (Grand Rapids: Eerdmans, 1972), 214.

[293] Judges 7:20-22

[294] Zechariah 12:6

[295] Luke 19:10; John 3:17

[296] David Pawson, *When Jesus Returns* (London: Hodder & Stoughton, 1995), 166.

[297] Amos 9:1-4

[298] Revelation 2:17

[299] Ladd, *A Commentary on the Revelation of John*, 256.

[300] Revelation 15:2-3; Mark 8:38; Luke 9:26; 1 Thessalonians 3:13; 2 Thessalonians 1:7-8

[301] 1 Thessalonians 4:17

[302] Revelation 6:11

[303] 2 Thessalonians 1:10

[304] Revelation 14:20

[305] John 1:1-2; 14

[306] Hoeksema, *Behold, He Cometh*, 634.

[307] Psalm 79:1-2

[308] 1 Samuel 17:44-47

[309] Genesis 19:24

[310] Keith Intrater, *From Iraq to Armageddon* (Shippensburg, PA: Destiny Image, 2003), 216.

Chapter 14
THE KINGDOM OF GOD REIGNING UPON THE EARTH

[311] David Pawson, *When Jesus Returns* (London: Hodder & Stoughton, 1995), 260.

[312] Alan F. Johnson, "Revelation" in *The Expositor's Bible Commentary*, ed. Frank E Gaebelein (Grand Rapids: Zondervan, 1981), 12:578.

[313] Pawson, *When Jesus Returns*, 259.

[314] Dan Juster and Keith Intrater, *Israel, the Church and the Last Days* (Shippensburg, PA: Destiny Image, 1990), 193.

[315] 2 Peter 3:4-8

[316] Juster and Intrater, *Israel, the Church and the Last Days*, 195.

[317] Keith Intrater, *From Iraq to Armageddon*, (Shippensburg, PA: Destiny Image, 2003), 154-55.

[318] William R. Villanueva, *Signs of the End of the Age: Revelation Unravelled*, (Ramseur, NC: Solid Rock Publishing, 1996), 176-77.

[319] Ezekiel 47:1-9

[320] Isaiah 11:6-7

[321] Amos 9:13

[322] Isaiah 11:8-9 (NIV)

[323] Isaiah 65:20 (NIV)

[324] Isaiah 65:22

[325] Pawson, *When Jesus Returns*, 228.

[326] Luke 24; John 20

[327] Matthew 27:53

[328] Matthew 25:21; Luke 19:17

[329] Pawson, *When Jesus Returns*, 222.

[330] George Eldon Ladd, *A Commentary on the Revelation of John* (Grand Rapids: Eerdmans, 1972), 269.

[331] Pawson, *When Jesus Returns*, 226-27.

[332] Luke 16:19-31

[333] Matthew 27:52-53; Ephesians 4:8-9; 2 Corinthians 12:1-4

[335] Anthony A. Hoekema, *The Bible and the Future* (Grand Rapids: Eerdmans, 1979), 273.

[336] David Reagan, "The Reality of Hell," *Lamplighter*, Mar-Apr 2006, 3-6.

[337] Ibid., 12.

[338] Revelation 6:8

[339] Hoekema, *The Bible and the Future*, 253-54.

[340] Herman Hoeksema, *Behold, He Cometh: An Exposition of the Book of Revelation* (Grand Rapids: Reformed Free Publishing Assn, 1969), 659.

[341] Hebrews 1:13; 8:1; 12:2; 1 Peter 3:22

[342] 1 Corinthians 6:3

[343] Hoeksema, *Behold, He Cometh*, 665.

[344] Matthew 11;20-24

[345] Romans 1;18-21

[346] Hoekema, *The Bible and the Future*, 260-61; James 2:26.

[347] Psalm 103:12

[348] Hoekema, *The Bible and the Future*, 265-67.

[349] Luke 19:12-19; 1 Corinthians 3:10-15

[350] Matthew 6:20; 20:21-23

[351] Intrater, *From Iraq to Armageddon*, 210-11.

[352] Ibid., 212.

[353] Hoekema, *The Bible and the Future*, 264.

[354] Genesis 1:28; 3:17

[355] Hoekema, *The Bible and the Future*, 280-81.

[356] Romans 8:20-23

[357] Isaiah 50:2

[358] Randy Alcorn, *Heaven* (Carol Stream, IL: Tyndale House, 2004), 245-48.

[359] Randy Alcorn, *50 Days of Heaven*, (Carol Stream, IL: Tyndale House, 2006), xii.

[360] 1 Corinthians 1:10

[361] Alcorn, *50 Days of Heaven*, Day 44.

[362] Ibid., 92.

[363] Ibid., 114-15.

[364] Alcorn, *Heaven*, Table of Contents.

[365] Alcorn, *50 Days of Heaven*, Day 14.

[366] Hoeksema, *Behold, He Cometh*, 718.

[367] 1 Thessalonians 5:1-5

[368] 1 Chronicles 12:32

[369] Matthew 25:1-13

[370] Hoeksema, *Behold, He Cometh,* 722.

[371] Ibid., 723.

Chapter 15
EQUIPPING WARRIOR LEADERSHIP IN THE KINGDOM OF GOD

[372] Reggie McNeal, *Practicing Greatness* (San Francisco: Jossey-Bass, 2006), 5.

[373] Matthew 25:14-30 (parable of the talents)

[374] Rick Joyner, *50 Days for a Soaring Vision* (Shippensberg, PA: Destiny Image, 2003).

[375] John Dawson, *Taking Our Cities for God; How to Break Spiritual Strongholds* (Lake Mary, FL: Creation House, 1989), 136.

[376] Ed Silvoso, "Ministry in the Marketplace," *Visionary Advancement Strategies Newsletter,* August, 2006.

[377] See Michael Novelli and Caesar Kalinowski, "Bible Storying" workshop, Soma Community Church, Tacoma, 2003-2004.

[378] Tim Taylor of *Watchman Ministries,* personal conversation with the author.

[379] Luke 12:51

[380] Matthew 6:25

[381] Rick Joyner, "The Church Will Begin to Take on More of a Military Mentality in the Coming Times," *MorningStar Newsletter,* April, 2008.

[382] Don Walker, "Suffering and the Glory of God," *Visionary Advancement Strategies Newsletter,* February 16, 2008.

[383] Dan Juster and Keith Intrater, *Israel, the Church and the Last Days* (Shippensburg, PA: Destiny Image, 1990), 107

[384] Ibid., 110.

Appendix A
HISTORICAL EMPIRES OF THE BEAST

[385] Deuteronomy 29:4

[386] Ezekiel 16

[387] Isaiah 44:48; 45:1-13; Jeremiah 25:11-12

SELECTED BIBLIOGRAPHY

Alcorn, Randy. *50 Days of Heaven*. Carol Stream, IL: Tyndale House, 2006.

———. *Heaven*. Carol Stream, IL: Tyndale House, 2004.

———. *Safely Home*. Carol Stream, IL: Tyndale House, 2001.

Barna, George. *Revolution*. Wheaton, IL: Tyndale House, 2005.

Baruch, Benjamin. *The Day of the Lord is at Hand*. Baruch Publishing, 2004.

Bass, Clarence B. *Backgrounds to Dispensationalism*. Grand Rapids: Baker, 1960.

Brooke, Tal. *One World*. Berkeley: End Run Publishing, 2000.

———. *When the World Will Be As One*. Eugene: Harvest House, 1989.

Butler, Phill. *Well Connected*. Colorado Springs: Authentic, 2005.

Carson, D. A. *How Long, O Lord?* Grand Rapids: Baker, 1990.

Clinton, J. Robert. *The Making of a Leader*. Colorado Springs: NavPress, 1988.

Frost, Michael, and Alan, Hirsch. *The Shaping of Things to Come.* Peabody, MA: Hendrickson, 2003.

Gaebelein, Frank E., ed. *The Expositor's Bible Commentary,* vols.7 and 12. Grand Rapids: Zondervan, 1981.

Graciano, Roderick. *Battling Babylons.* Tacoma: Timothy Ministries (www.tmin.org), n.d.

— — —. *The True Spirit of Martyrdom.* Tacoma: Timothy Ministries (www.tmin.org), n.d.

Graves, Joel C. *Gathering Over Jerusalem.* Xulon, 2003.

Hitchcock, Mark. *Iran, the Coming Crisis* (Sisters, OR: Multnomah, 2006.

Hoekema, Anthony A. *The Bible and the Future.* Grand Rapids: Eerdmans, 1979.

Hoeksema, Herman. *Behold, He Cometh.* Grand Rapids: Reformed Free Publishing Assn, 1969.

Hunt, Dave. *A Woman Rides the Beast.* Eugene: Harvest House, 1994.

Intrater, Keith. *From Iraq to Armageddon.* Shippensburg, PA: Destiny Image, 2003.

Jensen, Richard A. *Thinking in Story.* Lima, OH: CSS Publishing, 1993.

Joyner, Rick. *Epic Battles of the Last Days.* New Kensington, PA: Whitaker House, 1995.

— — —. *Overcoming Evil in the Last Days.* Shippensburg, PA: Destiny Image, 2003.

Juster, Dan, and Keith Intrater. *Israel, the Church and the Last Days.* Shippensburg, PA: Destiny Image, 1990.

Kah, Gary H. *En Route to Global Occupation.* Lafayette, LA: Huntington House, 1991.

Kern, Lynn R. *Jesus Is Coming! But When?* Proctor, MN: Know the Truth Publications, 1999.

Kline, Meredith G. *"Trial by Ordeal" in Through Christ's Word: A Festschrift for Dr. Philip E. Hughes.* Phillipsburg, NJ: Presbyterian and Reformed, 1985.

Ladd, George Eldon. *A Commentary on the Revelation of John.* Grand Rapids: Eerdmans, 1972.

———. *The Presence of the Future.* Grand Rapids: Eerdmans, 1974.

MacPherson, Dave. *The Unbelievable Pre-Trib Origin.* Kansas City: Heart of America Bible Society, 1973.

Mathews, R. Arthur. *Born For Battle.* Wheaton, IL: Harold Shaw Publishers, 1978

McNeal, Reggie. *Practicing Greatness.* San Francisco: Jossey-Bass, 2006.

Mauro, Philip. *Things Which Must Soon Come to Pass.* Swengel, PA: Reiner Publications, 1974.

Miller, Charles W. *Today's Technology in Bible Prophecy.* Lansing, MI: TIP, 1990.

Morris, Henry M. *The Revelation Record.* Wheaton, IL: Tyndale House, 1983.

Mounce, Robert H. *The Book of Revelation*. Grand Rapids: Eerdmans, 1977.

Murrow, David. *Why Men Hate Going to Church*. Nashville: Nelson, 2005.

Newell, William R. *The Book of Revelation*. Chicago: Moody, 1935.

Pawson, David. *When Jesus Returns*. London: Hodder & Stoughton, 1995.

Pink, Arthur W. *Elijah*. Edinburgh: The Banner of Truth Trust, 1956.

— — —. *The Sovereignty of God* Grand Rapids: Baker, 1973.

Poythress, Vern S. *Understanding Dispensationalists*. Grand Rapids: Zondervan, 1987.

Pretlow, Charles. *Revelation Six, Get Ready*. Westcliffe, CO: Get Ready Publishing, 2004.

Ravenhill, David. *The Jesus Letters*. Shippensburg, PA: Destiny Image, 2003.

Reagan, David. *Living for Christ in the End Times*. Green Forest, AR: New Leaf, 2000.

— — —. "The Reality of Hell," Lamplighter, Mar-Apr 2006.

— — —. *Wrath and Glory*. Green Forest, AR: New Leaf, 2001.

Richardson, Joel. *Antichrist, Islam's Awaited Messiah*. Enumclaw, WA: Pleasant Word, 2006.

Roberts, Vaughn. *God's Big Picture.* Downers Grove, IL: InterVarsity, 2002.

Rosenberg, Joel C. *Epicenter.* Carol Stream, IL: Tyndale House, 2006.

Rosenthal, Marvin. *The Pre-Wrath Rapture of the Church.* Nashville: Thomas Nelson, 1990.

Roxburgh, Alan J., and Fred Romanuk. *The Missional Leader.* San Francisco: Jossey-Bass, 2006.

Simmons, Larry. *42 Months to Glory.* Oklahoma City: Ephraim House, 1994.

Skolfield, Ellis H. *Hidden Beast 2.* Fort Myers, FL: Fish House, 1990.

Stetzer, Ed. *Planting Missional Churches.* Nashville: Broadman and Holman, 2006.

Stetzer, Ed, and David Putman. *Breaking the Missional Code.* Nashville: Broadman and Holman, 2006.

Vandergriff, Henry. *Mystery Babylon.* Raleigh: Lamb Publishing, 2000.

Van Kampen, Robert. *The Sign.* Wheaton, IL: Crossway, 1992.

Villanueva, William R. *Signs of the End of the Age: Revelation Unravelled.* Ramseur, NC: Solid Rock Publishing, 1996.

Wagner, C. Peter. *The Church in the Workplace.* Ventura, CA: Regal, 2006.

Walker, Andrew. *Enemy Territory: The Christian Struggle in the Modern World.* Wilmore, KY: Bristol Books, 1990.

ABOUT THE AUTHOR

A BRIEF BIOGRAPHY AND TESTIMONY

I am not a pastor by profession, but I am a professional businessman with a deep, deep passion to see our Lord's kingdom visibly manifested in our country during this present generation.

I have been self-employed for the past twenty-five years, but prior to that I served our country for twenty years in the Marine Corps. During that time, I spent two tours in the combat environment of the Vietnam War. Now I really wasn't a God-fearing man back in those Marine Corps days. In fact, I lived a pretty wild life. But there came a day when I was changed forever. It was November 6, 1979, and I attended a church service with my wife. I remember the sermon had to do with the sacrifice of Christ on the cross and His desire to have an ongoing relationship with each of us. Surprisingly, it touched me quite deeply, and as I was talking with some men after the service, one suggested that I go home and read the gospel of John. Well, I left church that morning without any real expectation that the Bible would do much for me, but I was wrong. Early that same afternoon, I sat down in a hot tub, expecting to read a couple of Bible verses and then switch to a more interesting detective novel. So I opened to the first chapter of John's gospel, which begins,

In the beginning was the Word, and the Word was with God, and the Word was God. He was in the beginning with God. All things were made through him, and without him was not any thing made that was made. In him was life, and the life

was the light of men. . . . And the Word became flesh and dwelt among us, and we have seen his glory, glory as of the only Son from the Father, full of grace and truth.

Suddenly the reality of those words struck me like lightning, and the Spirit of God dropped upon me like a strong wind flowing through my body over and over. Up to this point in my life I had hardened myself toward God but as I read these words, my heart was broken and I wept for the first time since I was a young boy. My years on the front lines of the Vietnam conflict never broke me down like this; I thought I was too tough for "wimpy" things like the Bible. I kept reading and weeping and reading and weeping, constantly crying out, "My God, my God, I didn't know these things. Please forgive me." I could not stop. The Spirit of God continued to pass through me like an electric current over and over, and I was completely overwhelmed. This continued on for twelve hours, until 1:00 AM the following morning. By then I had read through the books of John, Acts, Romans, and part of 1 Corinthians. Even though I had been in a hot tub for much of the time, I was probably quite dehydrated due to the amount of tears that had been shed. I was completely broken, yet overwhelmed with joy and a deep, deep love for my Lord.

Before this occurred, the Bible was just another book in Grandma's bookcase, but it was at this point that I came to understand deep in my spirit that it was truly God's Word for us. I've traveled the tough, sinful road of the unbeliever, and I do understand that until this happens to a person, the Bible will have little credibility. Yet, that all changes for those who have been truly "born again." Those who arrive at that point in life truly understand that the words in Scripture come to us from a loving Father who calls us to Himself.

AN EVENT THAT CHANGED MY LIFE'S DIRECTION

In July, 1980, the Lord woke me at 3:30 AM and spoke these exact words:

The Spirit of the gospel will come out of you, and joy will be spread among the land.

I was a very young believer at this time, and as I prayed and contemplated these words, I began to think that this was a call to the church pastoral ministry. A few years later, I sold a growing accounting practice and enrolled in seminary, where I pursued a Master of Divinity degree. Five years later I graduated, but during my time in seminary, I discovered that I had neither the gifting nor the passion for church pastoral ministry. So I started up a new accounting practice in order to assist small businesses to achieve success in life. Yet I continued to search for my calling in ministry; for I knew that those words spoken from the Lord had not yet been manifested in my life. In 2005, at the urging of a close friend, I determined to return to my studies in seminary and subsequently graduated with a Doctor of Ministry in strategic leadership. It was during my doctoral studies when I felt the calling to write this book.

BRIEF OVERVIEW OF A VISION RECEIVED
SEVERAL YEARS AGO

During a period of early morning intercessory prayer, suddenly a trancelike vision appeared which showed the church in the form of a huge, gloriously white, round boulder full of beautiful light. I immediately fell in love with it. But as I began to walk toward it, I suddenly saw that it was being progressively consumed by a "black octopus-like demon" that continued to swallow the "light of the church" until there remained only a small remnant of the church (approximately 10 percent) that was not consumed by this "darkness." In the final scene, this "demonic octopus" was continuing to go after this remaining remnant, and I knew that it would not be satisfied until it had consumed the entire church. When I came out of the trance, I was weeping deeply, knowing that I was feeling the loving emotions of the heart of Jesus Christ for His church.

This vision definitely has contributed to my cautious perception of the visible church. The church of this present generation is under attack from the worldly kingdom, whose influence is rapidly creeping in and consuming much of the traditional church community. It appears that only a small, holy remnant will respond to God's call to the spiritual battlefield during the catastrophic times that lie shortly before us.

WHAT CONTINUES TO DRIVE ME

The twenty-first-century American church is not preparing for those challenging events that the Lord Jesus Christ warned us will precede His second coming to physically establish the kingdom of God on this earth. The contemporary evangelical church acknowledges the truth of the future return of the Son of God, but it completely ignores the multiple biblical warnings concerning the tremendous warfare the church will face in both the natural and spiritual arenas of combat.

The Lord is calling many among His people to champion His kingdom purposes, on the spiritual battlefields of this world. My teachings are primarily intended for those Christians who possess a warrior spirit deep inside and are searching for their individual position within the Army of God. It is for men and women who truly want to stand strong for our Lord in the face of a world that is becoming increasingly darker year by year. It is for a people who will not shy away from being counted among those soldiers in His army who will embrace this warning from our Commander in Chief:

If the world hates you, know that it has hated me before it hated you. If you were of the world, the world would love you as its own; but because you are not of the world, but I chose you out of the world, therefore the world hates you. Remember the word that I said to you: "A servant is not greater than his master." If they persecuted me, they will also persecute you. If they kept my word, they will also keep yours. (John 15:18-20)

LaVergne, TN USA
07 November 2010
203836LV00005B/2/P